W9-CPO-152

THE
PASTOR'S
BIBLE STUDY®

VOLUME FOUR

A NEW INTERPRETER'S®
BIBLE STUDY

THE
PASTOR'S
BIBLE STUDY®

VOLUME FOUR

A NEW INTERPRETER'S®
BIBLE STUDY

Abingdon Press
Nashville

THE PASTOR'S BIBLE STUDY®
Volume Four
A NEW INTERPRETER'S® BIBLE STUDY

Copyright © 2007 by Abingdon Press

This book is printed on acid-free paper.

Cataloging-in-publication information applied for with the
Library of Congress

ISBN-13: 978-0-687-49340-1

07 08 09 10 11 12 13 14 15 16—10 09 08 07 06 05 04 03 02 01

MANUFACTURED IN THE UNITED STATES OF AMERICA

Contents

Contributors

David Albert Farmer, General Editor, is an ordained American Baptist minister. He earned his M.Div. (1981) and Ph.D. in Homiletics with a minor in New Testament Theology (1984) from Southern Baptist Theological Seminary. He is Visiting Professor of Preaching at Palmer Theological Seminary in Philadelphia and also teaches at Wilmington College in Delaware. He has served seven congregations and is now pastor of Silverside (American Baptist) Church in Wilmington, Delaware. He was editor of *Pulpit Digest* for eighteen years and *The African American Pulpit* for three years. He is author of *Unmerited Favor: Teaching Sermons on the Love and Grace of God, Basic Bible Sermons on Hope, And Blessed is She: Sermons by Women,* and *Pilgrim Prayers for Single Fathers.* He has contributed to several journals and additional books including *The Storyteller's Companion to the Bible.*

Michael Willett Newheart is Associate Professor of New Testament Language and Literature at Howard University School of Divinity, where he has served since 1991. His books include *"My Name is Legion": The Story and Soul of the Gerasene Demoniac, Word and Soul: A Psychological, Literary, and Cultural Reading of the Fourth Gospel,* and *Wisdom Christology in the Fourth Gospel.* Prior to coming to Howard, he taught at a college and four seminaries in Kansas City, and he served as a missionary in Costa Rica. Michael's Ph.D. is from The Southern Baptist Theological Seminary. He is an ordained Baptist minister and a member of the Religious Society of Friends (Quakers).

Frank M. Yamada is Assistant Professor of Old Testament at Seabury Theological Seminary. He earned a B.A. in Religion from Southern California College and his M.Div. and Ph.D. degrees from Princeton Theological Seminary. His dissertation topic was "Configurations of Rape in the Hebrew Bible: A Literary Analysis of Three Rape Narratives." Frank's scholarly interests are in the areas of hermeneutics, ethics of reading, and culturally contextual interpretation, especially Asian American biblical interpretation. His scholarship emphasizes literary and theological interpretations of the Hebrew Scriptures and explores the difference that social and cultural location makes in the interpretative process. His two most recent articles are: "Shibboleth and the Ma(r)king of Culture in Judges 12: Judges 12 and the Monolingualism of the Other," in *Derrida's Bible*; and "Dealing with Rape (in) Narrative (Genesis 34): Ethics of the Other and a Text in Conflict," in *The Meanings We Choose.*

Glenn Hinson retired from his position as Professor of Spirituality and John Loftis Professor of Church History at Baptist Theological Seminary in Richmond, Virginia, in 1999. Educated at Washington University in St. Louis (B.A.), The Southern Baptist Theological Seminary (B.D., Th.D.), and Oxford University (D. Phil.), he taught for more than thirty years at Southern Baptist Theological Seminary in Louisville, Kentucky. Currently, he serves as Visiting Professor of Church History at Candler School of Theology at Emory University. Glenn is the author or editor of twenty-six books and more than a thousand articles and book reviews. His most recent books are *The Early Church, Love at the Heart of Things: A Biography of Douglas V. Steere*, and *Spiritual Preparation for Christian Leadership*. He also wrote a section of *Companions in Christ*. He has served on the board of *Weavings* from its beginning and is a frequent contributor to it. Glenn has been a member of the Faith and Order Commissions of both the National and World Council of Churches. He is a member of the Ecumenical Institute of Spirituality and has been a faculty member for the Academy for Spiritual Formation since its founding in 1983.

Kandy Queen-Sutherland earned the M.Div. and the Ph.D. in Old Testament Studies at Southern Baptist Theological Seminary in Louisville, Kentucky. Her dissertation was on "The Futility Curse in the Old Testament." She teaches Biblical Hebrew and Hebrew Scripture at Stetson University in Deland, Florida. Earlier in her career she taught at the Baptist Theological Seminary in Ruschlikon, Switzerland. Kandy has been the editor of the Old Testament Series, Smyth and Helwys Bible Commentaries (1994-present) and is writing the entries on the Song of Songs, Esther, Lamentations, and Ruth for the commentary. Among her published articles are "Sacrifices and Offerings," *Eerdmans Handbook to the Bible*; "Mining Baptist History and Tradition for Biblical Studies," *Perspectives in Religious Studies, 1998*; "Sticks and Stones = Broken Bones, But Words...?" *Perspectives in Religious Studies*, 1997. She also has contributed entries in the *Mercer Dictionary of the Bible*.

Uwe C. Scharf is an ordained minister of the Christian Church, (Disciples of Christ). He served for over five years as Clinical Pastoral Education Supervisor at Duke Medical Center and Administrative Chaplain for Duke University's Heart Center. In January 2006, he became Director of the Pastoral Care Department at Johns Hopkins Hospital in Baltimore, Maryland. Uwe received the B.D. from The International Baptist Theological Seminary in Rueschlikon, Switzerland (1986), the S.T.M. from Christian Theological Seminary in Indianapolis, Indiana (1987), and the Ph.D. in Philosophical Philosophy from the University Of Virginia (1995). He is the author of *The Paradoxical Breakthrough of Revelation: Interpreting the Divine-Human Interplay in Paul Tillich's Work 1913-1964* and a number of articles in theological journals. Uwe Scharf is a citizen of Germany and a permanent resident of the United States.

Foreword

Welcome to *The Pastor's Bible Study*, volume 4. In volumes 1-3, you found lessons on Synoptic Gospels for a given Lectionary year (A, B, C) and lessons on an Old Testament book used heavily in the Lectionary text selections for those same years.

In this volume, we have not returned to the gospel lectionary for this year (Matthew) but center our textual emphases on the Gospel of John. (Acts of the Apostles, the "part two" of Luke, will follow next year in volume 5.) Our Old Testament focus in this volume is Exodus.

♦ Dr. Michael Newheart, Associate Professor of New Testament at Howard University Divinity School and a widely published Johannine scholar, has prepared this lively and insightful set of lessons on the Gospel of John. The poetry of the Fourth Gospel comes to life in this study. Humor, irony, and necessary ambiguity stand out in this interpretation of the lofty-themed Gospel.

♦ Dr. Frank Yamada, Assistant Professor of Old Testament at Seabury Western Theological Seminary, has offered us a fresh, insightful, and moving run through the pivotal Old Testament book of Exodus. A Japanese American who knows through family stories the reality of loss of liberation, his sensitivity to a diverse readership is evident. As he writes, "An interpreter's race, ethnicity, and gender have an impact on the way that one reads."

♦ One of the deans of the study and practice of spirituality, a New Testament scholar, and a leading historian of the early church is Dr. E. Glenn Hinson. Retired recently from the Baptist Theological Seminary in Richmond where he was Professor of Church History and Spirituality, Glenn offers us a study on great texts of spirituality and devotion filled with enrichment materials from secular literature and the great classics of Christian devotion.

♦ Dr. Uwe Scharf is Director of Pastoral Services at the Johns Hopkins Hospital in Baltimore. He brings his theological and pastoral perspectives to bear on a study of Peter. Each study has been refined in the classroom, in counseling rooms, and at hospital bedsides. Uwe explores the questions: How could Peter be so devoted to Jesus one minute and deny their very acquaintance the next? How is it that we can do exactly the same thing?

♦ Dr. Kandy Queen-Sutherland is Professor of Religious Studies at Stetson University. Popular among her students and as a pastors' conference leader, Kandy has us join her for an overview study of five Old Testament books that deal in a focused way with feasts and festivals in the ancient Hebrew world. The result is a delightful and unique grouping of books and pivotal Hebrew Scripture stories that invite us both to pray and to party.

♦ I hope the five lessons that I'm calling collectively "A Time to Laugh" provide a suitable follow-up to Kandy's eye-opening studies. Recognizing that there are many different kinds of humor, especially across cultures, I have prepared these lessons because I believe that the Bible is filled with instance after instance of laughter that we typically overlook; we need to see it. I have also prepared this unit because I am convinced that laughter is a great contribution to our spiritual and physical health.

♦ I thank you for supporting this Bible study project. Best wishes as you join me in new learning and in the highest of all privileges: making known God's good news.

Faithfully,
David Albert Farmer

Introduction

The Pastor's Bible Study is part of Abingdon Press' *New Interpreter's Bible®* publications that provide the best in scholarship for the service of the church. Designed to help pastors lead Bible studies for their congregations, this series is intended to enhance the study, teaching, and preaching of the Scriptures.

Each volume includes fifty lessons written by recognized biblical scholars, professors of preaching and pastoral care, and outstanding pastors and church educators. The fifty sessions include:

♦ Fifteen lessons from the New Testament

♦ Ten lessons from the Old Testament

♦ Ten lessons on a special topic (e.g., biblical themes, pastoral care)

♦ Four or more lessons on relational themes and the Christian life (e.g., social justice, ethics, diversity, the Kingdom of God)

♦ Four or more lessons on issues of faith (e.g., inspirational themes, prayer, healing, spiritual gifts)

Whether your study group meets for thirty minutes or an hour, for four weeks or the entire year, the flexible structure of *The Pastor's Bible Study* will meet your preparation needs. Its versatile design is also useful whether you choose to follow the lectionary, the canonical order of the Bible, a key biblical theme, or life application.

As you prepare to lead your Bible study, look for the useful sidebars that include teaching aids to facilitate discussion. **Sources** will provide you with resources for further study derived from the lessons. **Study Bible** sidebars will indicate points of integration with *The New Interpreter's Study Bible.** **Teaching Tips** and **Reflections** foster participation, encourage discussion, and prompt interaction with the biblical text.

Supplementing the studies in this volume is a CD-ROM containing valuable data and suggestions for classroom use, such as:

♦ The full text of *The Pastor's Bible Study*: Volume Four, completely searchable by key words.

♦ An outline of each lesson

♦ PowerPoint® slides

♦ Supplementary material that can be customized for handouts and screen viewing.

It is our hope that *The Pastor's Bible Study* will help you lead Bible studies in your congregation, in order to advance and increase the study, teaching, and preaching of the Scriptures.

> *Note: The Pastor's Bible Study* frequently cites material
> from *The New Interpreter's Study Bible*,
> the recommended text for study participants.

THE GOSPEL OF JOHN

A STUDY BY
MICHAEL NEWHEART

*Michael Newheart is Associate Professor of New Testament Language and Literature
at Howard University School of Divinity in Washington, DC.*

THE GOSPEL OF JOHN
Outline

Introduction

The Pastor's Bible Study on John

ot questions?
Whether or not you "got milk" (as the seemingly ubiquitous milk ads say), do you "got questions"? You probably do. I know that I do, and I'm going to use them to structure these lessons in *The Pastor's Bible Study*. In dealing with each session's text I will ask:

A. What is happening in this text?
B. How is what is happening in this text like what is happening in the world today?
C. How is what is happening in this text like what is happening in your life?

I have adapted these questions from the *Bible Workbench*, an interactive, lectionary-based Bible study tool. (For more information on *Bible Workbench*, see www.bibleworkbench.com.) When I "test-drove" these sessions in one of my classes on John at Howard University School of Divinity, the students responded positively to the questions and encouraged me to use them in my lessons. I will occasionally refer to answers that my students gave to the questions. In this introduction, I want to use these questions to introduce John, so that when I refer to "this text," I am referring to the Gospel of John as a whole.

What Is Happening in this Gospel?

Poetry.

That's right, poetry is happening in the Gospel of John. Jesus (as well as John the evangelist) is God's poem and poet whose verses are misunderstood and finally silenced, but the beat goes on! All the elements of poetry are there in John: rhythm, imagery,

Teaching Tips

In preparation for teaching this study, read John all the way through, preferably in one sitting. Skim it, pore over it, and read sections of it aloud. (Remember, this book was written to be read aloud in the context of worship!) However you deal with it, get some sense of the Gospel as a whole. (You might choose to watch the movie *The Gospel of John* [directed by Philip Saville, 2003], which is a word-for-word dramatic presentation of the Gospel. You might also listen to an audio version of the Gospel, such as the NRSV Audio New Testament [published by World Bible Publishing, 1998].) As you read John, keep in mind the question, "What is happening in this Gospel?" After you've read it all the way through, sit and savor your experience. Write (or draw!) your impressions in a journal.

Study Bible

The introductory article to the Gospel of John is found in *NISB*, 1905-07. The Gospel itself follows in *NISB*, 1908-51.

metaphor, symbolism. Can you hear it, feel it…in the beginning? "In the beginning was the Word, and the Word was with God, and the Word was God" (John 1:1). In the middle, "I am the gate" (10:7, 9), "I am the good shepherd" (10:11, 18), "I lay down my life for the sheep" (10:11, 15, 17-18). And in the end, "Peter, do you love me?…Feed my sheep" (21:15-17). This poetry is almost hypnotic, ushering us into a realm different from the one in which we normally live. So the purpose of this poetry is worship, centering the community in a transcendent place. When one is worshiping "in spirit and truth" (4:23-24), then one has a heightened sense of awareness, an altered state of consciousness, so to speak. Such worship leads to ethics; altered states of consciousness nurture an alternative consciousness. One lives as if one is "not of this world," pursuing love, peace, and truth.

John's poetry attempts to ground the community of Jesus-believers in the Jewish tradition, in opposition to the synagogue leaders (referred to as "the Jews"), some of whom have compromised the ancient faith by cooperating with the Romans in the oppression of the people. John's poetry, then, is poetry of resistance. It opposes the religious and political powers of the world in the name of life over against death; love over against hate; peace over against war; and Lord Jesus the Son of God over against Lord Caesar, who claimed to be the Son of God.

Stephen Mitchell writes in his anthology of sacred poetry *The Enlightened Heart*, "Most of what we call religious poetry is the poetry of longing: for God, for the mother's face. But the poems in *The Enlightened Heart* are poems of fulfillment." The Gospel of John also contains "poems of fulfillment." These poems allow readers or listeners to see God the Father's face (for which they have longed) in Jesus the Son's face. Come and see ! (John 1:39)

How Is What Is Happening in this Gospel Like What Is Happening in the World Today?

Who are the individuals or communities that are resisting "the world" through poetry? I think of the group Poets Against the War, which says on its website

Sources

This introduction, as well as the lessons, is dependent on my book *Word and Soul: A Psychological, Literary, and Cultural Reading of the Fourth Gospel* (Collegeville, MN: The Liturgical Press, 2001). For matters brought up in this introduction, see xiii-xxviii.

Reflections

1. In his first words in the Gospel, Jesus says, "What are you looking for?" (John 1:38). What are you looking for in this study?
2. What do you know about the Gospel of John? What impressions do you have of it?
3. Quote some verses you know from it.

Teaching Tips

Plan a movie night in which you watch *The Gospel of John* (directed by Philip Saville, 2003). The DVD contains both a three-hour unabridged version and a two-hour edited version, so you can choose which one to watch. Have popcorn available.

Sources

Mitchell, Stephen, ed. *The Enlightened Heart: An Anthology of Sacred Poetry* (New York: HarperPerennial, 1989), xv.

that it "continues the tradition of socially engaged poetry by creating venues for poetry as a voice against war, tyranny and oppression" (http://poetsagainstthewar.org). Its Web page, "Poetry Matters," tells of an event on Veterans' Day 2004 in Port Townsend, Washington, called "Heart to Heart: Vietnam Vets in Community." Inspired by the reading of the poem "Address to the Lord" in a worship service, a veteran organized a dialogue that brought together twenty-five vets and fifty community members where poetry reading had a central place. Other such dialogues have followed.

How Is What Is Happening in this Gospel Like What Is Happening in Your Life?

In many ways, this question is the toughest, for it requires introspection and vulnerability. But here it goes: I too seek transcendence from my world of self-condemnation. I often have the troubled heart and the fear that the Gospel of John speaks about (14:1; 20:19). I long for that other world. And sometimes I find it—in corporate worship, in personal prayer, in poetry.

Teaching Tips

For this introductory session, you might show some artwork depicting scenes from John (see the Johannine Literature website http://catholic-resources.org/John/Art.html) and read passages that will be covered in the study.

Reflections

1. Complete the sentence: "For me, poetry is like…"
2. Quote a line or two from a poem that has been meaningful to you.
3. What do you think about treating the Gospel of John as poetry? What do you gain by thinking of it in this way? What do you lose?

Teaching Tips

Ask the second question. Have people make a collage from magazines and newspapers, showing where they see the Gospel of John happening in the world today.

Teaching Tips

Ask each participant to write a prayer-poem that expresses his or her desire for this study. Then ask for volunteers to share with the group.

Beginning with a Hymn!

Think back upon the last Sunday morning worship service in your church. How did it begin? More than likely, it began with the singing of a hymn, maybe even a processional hymn. If it was not the first thing, it was probably very close behind. It seems that Christian worship services almost always place a hymn at or near the start. An opening hymn gathers us together as a body. At the outset of the service, it engages us—as singing almost always does—physically, emotionally, and intellectually. It enables all worshipers (not just the leaders) to participate.

It has often been suggested that John 1:1-18, called the Johannine Prologue, was originally a hymn sung in the worship of first-century believers that the evangelist has adapted as the opening section of his Gospel. (Indeed, the editor of this series, David Albert Farmer, and I used to sing this passage in Greek when we were in seminary together almost thirty years ago!) Whether or not this passage actually began as a hymn, it is certainly "hymnic."

What Is Happening in the Johannine Prologue?

When people describe the Gospel of John as "poetic," they usually have the Prologue in mind. You can hear the rhythm right from the beginning, as John uses what is often called "stairstep parallelism," in which a term that appears at or near the end of one line is repeated at or near the beginning of the next line. I have translated the first two verses literally in order to emphasize the parallelism: "In the beginning was **the Word**, //and **the Word** was with *God*, // and what *God* was, **the Word** was. // He [**the Word**] was in the

Lectionary Loop
Second Sunday after Christmas, Year A, John 1:(1-9), 10-18

Study Bible
Read the notes for this passage in the *NISB*, 1908-09.

Sources
For a poetic commentary on this text, see my *Word and Soul: A Psychological, Literary, and Cultural Reading of the Fourth Gospel* (Collegeville, MN: The Liturgical Press, 2001), 1-20.

beginning with God." (Look also at 1:3-5.) The Roman writer Pliny wrote in the early second century that Christians sing a hymn "to Christ as to a god." That description certainly fits John 1:1-18 but also Col 1:15-20 and Phil 2:6-11. It is exciting to think that first-century Jesus-followers were not only hearing and speaking their poetry of resistance but also singing it! What better way to an altered state of consciousness than through worship in song!

We sing the Lord's song—first of creation. Beginning, Word, God, life, light, humanity (1:1-5). Yes, we remember: Creation! Genesis. In the beginning, God spoke the world into existence, beginning with light, continuing to living creatures, and culminating with humanity (Gen 1:1-27). John gives the creation story a "Jesus-spin." That which God spun in Jesus was already spinning at the beginning. Word! God brought us into this world (and God can take us out) through the Word!

Not only do we sing a song of creation but also a song of witness, which is John's job. John, the one we refer to as John the Baptist, is the witness in the beginning (John 1:6-8), just as the Beloved Disciple (BD) is the witness in the end (21:24). John (the Baptist) witnesses to the light, which was coming into the world, but that wicked world, though Word-created, was not Word-knowing or Word-accepting. But some were accepting, believing in his name and becoming the powerful God-begotten God-children! Yippee! This song of creation and witness becomes a song of community (1:9-13).

And the song of community intensifies: The Word spins into flesh and lives among "us," the in-his-name-believing-God-children with whom we sing. And "we" see his glory (i.e. God-presence as was seen in the sea-parting, manna-giving, fire-burning, and cloud-appearing; see Exod 14:17-18; 16:7, 10; 24:16-17), and that's glory like the Father's only son, grace-full and truth-full. As a community in the Word, we're all fully grace-graced! Law through Moses, gracious truth through Jesus Christ. Nobody has seen God (not even Moses; see Exod 33:17-23), but the Son opens up the Father's heart (lit. "bosom") to make him known (lit.

Teaching Tip

It is important that you begin each session by reading and hearing that session's text. Try to do that imaginatively by using drama (e.g. skits, readers' theatre), cinema (e.g. using clips from *The Gospel of John* movie mentioned in the introduction to this section), or movement (e.g. the suggestion that follows). Have everyone stand up. Tell them that in a few moments you are going to ask them to close their eyes while you read aloud John 1:1-18. As you read they are to move their bodies, eyes closed, as they feel led. Ask them to be conscious of what movements they make to particular words. Remind them that everyone will have their eyes closed so no one can see them. Then ask them to close their eyes and pray for openness to the Word. After some silence, read the passage meditatively, yet dramatically. After you've read the passage and allowed for some more silence, tell participants to return to the standing positions in which they began this exercise. Ask: What word or words did you find particularly "moving"? Exactly how did your bodies move?

Sources

Bettenson, Henry, ed. *Documents of the Christian Church*. 2nd ed. (Oxford: Oxford University Press, 1963), 4.

"exegetes" him). Jesus is God's poem and poet, exegete and exegesis. Just as the first stanza of the hymn (1:1-5) picks up language from Genesis, this last stanza (1:14-18) picks up language from Exodus. The hymn of creation ends as a hymn of liberation! As we hear and sing, we are created and liberated anew. God has created us and taken us out of this world! The world ain't got nothing on us! Now that's something to sing about!

How Is What Is Happening in the Prologue Like What Is Happening in the World Today?

My students reminded me of the function of the spirituals for African-Americans during slavery. For example, a slave can "Steal Away to Jesus" in many ways: death, attendance at a secret worship service, and escaping to freedom. See also "Swing Low, Sweet Chariot" and "Go Down, Moses," the latter of which is overtly political. Students talked about the function of worship for people in oppression: Worship relieves oppression for a time. One student said, "The alienation is gone, and we experience that oneness we sing about—that paradise, that 'there,' here."

How Is What Is Happening in the Prologue Like What Is Happening in Your Life?

What word from the Prologue is welling up inside me, calling to be released in order to sing, perhaps even to dance? It is "grace" (1:14, 16-17), a word that appears four times here but nowhere else in the Gospel. Perhaps it is swallowed up in life or truth, both of which appear frequently. How about a grace-full poem?

> grace in my flesh
>> which is sometimes wordy
>>> but sometimes
>>>> in a word
>>>>> it relaxes and breathes easier
> grace in others' flesh
>> who hug and handshake my flesh
>>> and speak gracious words to me
> grace, grace
>> God's…

Reflections

Put into your own words the following statements from the Prologue: "In the beginning was the Word," and, "The Word was God"? What does it mean to say, "The Word became flesh and lived among us"?

Sources

"Steal Away to Jesus," (*United Methodist Hymnal*, hymn #704); "Swing Low, Sweet Chariot" (*United Methodist Hymnal*, hymn #703; "Go Down, Moses" (*United Methodist Hymnal*, hymn #448).

Teaching Tip

1. Distribute hymnals and sing some of the spirituals.
2. Listen to a hip-hop version of John 1:1-14 at http://www.gettheepic.com/john_1_14.html. Ask participants to share their reaction to it. What did you like? What did you not like? To what extent do hip-hop music and poetry in general represent *When Words Become Flesh*, to use the title of a recent collection of poetry from the hip-hop generation?

Teaching Tip

Have participants write a poem in response to the Prologue, using as much as possible the vocabulary of John 1:1-18. After people are finished, ask for volunteers to read their work aloud to the group.

Watery Wedding Wine

I teach an elective course at Howard Divinity School entitled "Miracles in the New Testament." Usually, I spend about one week on each Gospel, discussing the miracle stories therein. I sometimes ask the class what the first miracle story is in a particular Gospel. No matter what Gospel we are talking about, students always say, "Changing water into wine." If we're discussing the Synoptics, I respond, "But that's only in John!" Perhaps it is indelibly stamped on our minds because John notes that this miracle is "the first of [Jesus'] signs." And it is a captivating story, almost like a magical tale. John alerts us early that something out of the ordinary is going on in this Gospel. Let us go deeper into the mystery and be amazed!

What Is Happening in this Miracle Story?

What is happening depends on what has happened, and Jesus has been out gathering disciples, including Andrew and another disciple (1:35-40); Simon, whom Jesus has renamed Peter (1:41-42); Philip (1:43-44); and Nathaniel (1:45-51), to whom Jesus has promised that he "will see greater things" (1:50). The first of those "greater things" takes place at a wedding (a good place to begin since God's relationship with Israel is often imaged as a husband and wife; see Isa 54.5; Jer 2.2; Hos 1:2-9). It happens at Cana in Galilee (see NISB, Map 18). And Jesus' mother (unnamed) is there. Oh yes, Jesus and his disciples were there too, but why mention his mother first? As we move through the story, we will encounter a number of things that are a bit strange. Why does Jesus' mother approach him about the lack of wine? Why does Jesus respond the

Lectionary Loop
Second Sunday After Epiphany, Year C, John 2:1-11

Study Bible
See *NISB*, 1910-11.

Teaching Tips
Mime this passage. Ask for volunteers for the following roles: narrator, mother of Jesus, Jesus, disciples, servants, steward, bridegroom. Have the volunteers come up to the front. (Only the narrator will need a Bible.) Tell them (and the group) that the narrator will read while the others silently act out their parts. (Tell the narrator to read slowly and loudly so that the actors can hear and have time to act out their parts.) Ask the actors and narrator: What stood out for you as you presented this passage? Ask the rest of the class: What stood out for you?

way he does? Why does his mother tell the servants to do what he says, even though he hasn't agreed to do anything? Has she already drunk the good wine? This story is intoxicating; when we take it in, it produces an altered state of consciousness. We enter into another world, where Jesus and his Father dwell.

But not everyone knows about that other world. The chief steward doesn't know where the wine came from (though the servants do); he thinks that the bridegroom has been keeping it until now. We laugh at him (Hee-hee-hee!); he misunderstands. He doesn't understand how good this wine kept-until-now is! The Hebrew prophets often speak of the coming of the new age as a time of abundant wine (Isa 25:6; Joel 2:24; Amos 9:13-14). It's coming and now is, in Jesus.

The chief steward doesn't know, but the disciples do; and they believe. The water changes to wine, and the disciples change into believers! Although a wedding happens in this text, we see nothing of the bride, and the only glimpse offered of the groom is so the steward can tell him that he has "kept the good wine until now." The real wedding is between Jesus and his disciples, who see this act as a "sign" (John's word for *miracle*; see 2:23; 3:2; 6:26; 20:30) that Jesus reveals God's glory, that is, God's liberating presence for slaves in the wilderness. (He can't let this Exodus thing go, can he?) So the disciples are married to Jesus, and so are we. We too see his glory, glory as of the only son of the Father, full of grace and truth, and we believe in his name and become children of God (1:12, 14). Drink up!

How Is What Is Happening in this Miracle Story Like What Is Happening in the World?

I write this on June 26, 2006, the first day of a conference in Washington, D.C. entitled "Pentecost 2006: A Covenant for a New America," sponsored by the Call to Renewal, a faith-based movement to overcome poverty. The conference brings together religious and political leaders to forge an anti-poverty agenda. (See http://www.calltorenewal.org.) Last month, also here in Washington, the Network of Spiritual Progressives held a "Conference on Spiritual Activism," which

---

Reflections

1. Look up the passages that deal with the abundance of wine as a symbol of joy: Isa 25:6; Joel 2:24; Amos 9:13-14.
2. Look up the passages that describe Israel as God's wife: Isa 54:5; Jer 2.2; Hos 1:2-9.
3. What significance is there that Jesus' first miracle took place at a wedding and resulted in an abundance of wine?

Teaching Tips

Sing the hymn "As Man and Woman We Were Made" (*The United Methodist Hymnal* 642). Note that in verse 2 explicit reference is made to this passage. How has the passage been interpreted in this hymn? How do you respond to this interpretation?

attempted to bring together people of faith around issues of peace, social justice, and the environment. (See http://www.spiritualprogressives.org) It is exciting, joyful, even intoxicating that people are "wedding" together faith and action, Jesus and justice.

How Is What Is Happening in this Miracle Story Like What Is Happening in Your Life?

At my wedding (in which my wife Joy and I both took the name Newheart, from Ezek. 36:26), we pledged that we would join together in "healing the wounded hearts of the world." Thirteen years after making that pledge, I'm not always sure how to carry it out. Does the Bible have anything to say to that? Does my beloved Gospel of John? Lately, I have been drinking from the "good wine" of engaged biblical scholarship, which sees the spiritual and the political, if not as one, at least as integrally related to one another. During the time in which this Gospel was written, saying, "Jesus is Lord" declared that Caesar was not Lord. In other words, the Gospel stood as a threat to the empire. Does it today? If so, then I must bring all of my energies—intellectual, physical, emotional, and spiritual—to bear on the spiritual/political issues of our day.

Teaching Tips

Distribute a sheet of paper to each participant. Instruct everyone to choose from this story a character who doesn't speak. Ask participants to give these "voiceless" characters a voice by writing down the story from their point of view. After some time, ask for volunteers to share.

Session 3

Just in the Nick of Time

Here comes Nicodemus, or "Nick," as I like to call him. He has seen Jesus do various signs in Jerusalem. Maybe he has even seen Jesus clearing house at the Temple. He now comes by night to talk with Jesus, and they talk about being born again. An evangelical Christian might ask someone, "Are you born again?" The phrase "born again," which has become quite popular recently, appears in the Bible only in this passage. So, our discussion comes "just in the Nick of time."

What Is Happening in this Discourse?

Jesus leaves Galilee, where he has turned water into wine, and goes to Jerusalem to celebrate the Passover (2:13). While there, he does some Father's-house-cleaning (2:14-22) and some signs (2:23-25). Nicodemus, one of the religious and political elite, comes to Jesus by night (Nick at Nite!) and says that "we know" Jesus is from God because of his signs (3:1-2). (But what does Nick really know?) Jesus, beginning as he often does with "Very truly I say to you," says that it is necessary to be born *anōthen* (Greek), in order to see the kingdom of God. *Anōthen* can mean "again" or "from above." (See the text note *n* in *NISB*, 1912.) In John's poetry, words often have double meanings. Nicodemus understands Jesus' words in terms of "born over again," but Jesus means "born from above." He later says, "I am from above" (*ek tōn anō*, related to *anōthen*, 8:23). Jesus charges Nicodemus (and you all, 3:7) to be born from above, to undergo a radical reorientation of life from this world to the world in which God dwells. Jesus repeats

Lectionary Loop
Second Sunday of Lent, Year A, John 3:1-17
Pentecost Sunday, Year B, John 16:4b-15

Study Bible
See *NISB*, 1912-13.

Sources
See my *Word and Soul: A Psychological, Literary, and Cultural Reading of the Fourth Gospel* (Collegeville, MN: The Liturgical Press, 2001), 21-29.

what he has just said, substituting "of water and Spirit" for "from above." Does he have baptism in mind? Dunno, because he then starts talking about the Spirit and the wind, both of which are translations for the Greek *pneuma*. Oh God! More double meaning! Nick asks his third and final question, "How can these things be?" Through the Spirit, man, which you obviously don't understand, you Israelite teacher! We roll our eyes and shake our heads.

Jesus continues to "very truly tell him" that "we" (in-his-name-believers and glory-seers, 1:12, 14) speak what we know, and that folks like Nicodemus don't receive it, because they are of the world. Jesus continues to testify, this time about the Son of Man's descent from heaven and ascent into heaven, the latter of which comes through being "lifted up," or "exalted"—another double meaning. Believing in the lifted-up/exalted Son of Man, who is God-given for the God-loved world, results in eternal life, which is salvation and not condemnation. And that's not in the sweet (or sour) by-and-by, but it's now! In fancy language, this is realized (as opposed to futuristic) eschatology. Eternal life, salvation, condemnation happens now in relationship with Jesus. Believe in Jesus' name: eternal life; don't believe: condemnation! Judgment happens because the light has come into the world, that is, the true light that enlightens everyone (1:9), but people are darkness-lovers and evil-doers. Truth-doers come to the light. Let's use another fancy term: Johannine dualism. It finds its best expression in the dualism of light and darkness, which we first met in the Prologue (1:5). Jesus later says, "I am the light" (8:12; 9:5). Faith in Jesus is life and light, as one imaginatively ascends with the Son to heaven, where one finds one's source of being, in the God of love.

Nicodemus apparently couldn't keep up with all the double meanings, Johannine dualisms, and realized eschatology. He couldn't keep the beat! So he beat it! He was in the dark, which is where he came from. We, however, are in the light; we know; we understand, and we experience life even in the midst of death.

Teaching Tips

1. Sing "Wash, O God, Our Sons and Daughters," (*United Methodist Hymnal*, hymn #605) where John 3:3-8 is cited as inspiration for the words.
2. Divide the class into two groups and have the groups stand and face each other. Tell one group that together they will read aloud Jesus' part, and tell the other group that they will read Nicodemus' part. Encourage them to read expressively, using not only their voices but their bodies as well. You read the narration. After you've completed the reading, have folks return to their original seats. Ask each group what it was like to read their part.

Reflections

1. Based on what you read here, what would you say is happening in this discourse?
2. Read Nicodemus' two other appearances: 7:50-51; 19:39. Do you think that he believes?

Teaching Tips

Explain "realized eschatology," the fancy language used to describe the Gospel of John's sense that eternal life, salvation, and condemnation happen now (as opposed to on a future day of judgment). This term will keep reappearing in our study.

How Is What Is Happening in this Discourse Like What Is Happening in the World Today?

The language of this passage is rife in contemporary American culture. Politicians and performers proclaim that they are "born again," and people unfurl banners screaming "JOHN 3:16" at televised football games. Indeed, entering the phrase "born again" as a search query in Google returns over nine million results! What's going on? Some might see this as evidence of a revival sweeping the nation; others might consider it the trivialization of religion. Unfortunately, born-again, evangelical Christians have become known mostly for what they are against: abortion, homosexuality, feminism. Yet some who claim to be born again are attempting to change that image. Concerned about such stereotypes, Ron Sider began Evangelicals for Social Action (http://esa-online.org) over thirty years ago. According to its website, it is "an association of Christians seeking to promote Christian engagement, analysis and understanding of major social, cultural and public policy issues." It has created organizations such as Evangelical Environmental Network (best known for its "What Would Jesus Drive?" campaign of a few years back), PRISM ("America's Alternative Evangelical Voice"), and Crossroads (on faith and public policy). These efforts offer hope in bringing evangelical fervor to contemporary cultural issues. It allows "born again" to show itself as also "born from above."

How Is What Is Happening in this Discourse Like What Is Happening in Your Life?

My wife's Episcopalian uncle and aunt have a bumper sticker on their car that says, "Born OK the First Time." One of my students interviewed a major biblical scholar some years ago and asked him if he were born again. He said that he was born again every day of his life. I understand both sentiments, as well as that of the evangelical Christian. Yes, I was born OK, and I'm still OK, though it is difficult for me to accept that. And I was born again at a Billy Graham crusade in 1967, when I was eleven years old, having grown up in the church. And I was born again early this morning

---

Reflections

1. If a person asks you if you are "born again," what do you say? Why?
2. What are your impressions of people who say that they are "born again"? What do they mean by the phrase?
3. How does their use of the term compare to what Jesus says in his conversation with Nicodemus?

at the lake as I saw purple martins fly against the pink sky. But am I born from above, where love is, where peace is, where…Where? Where? Where? Be where? Beware…of the Spirit, because it blows where it will.

Teaching Tips

Write an account of what Nicodemus might have said to his wife when he returned home from his meeting with Jesus.

Session 4   John 4:1-42

Wooing the Watery Woman

Thirsty? Yeah, me too. How about a big glass of ice cold water? Maybe that woman over there can get us some. Ma'am, could you get us something to drink? What? Did you hear what she said? She said to read the text first. What does that mean? What text? Man, I sure am thirsty.

What is Happening in this Discourse?

We find Jesus once again waxing poetically with someone who misunderstands. We have a number of differences between this story and the story we studied in our last session together. First, the conversation is with an unnamed Samaritan woman rather than a Jewish ruler and teacher named Nicodemus—that is, a non-elite as opposed to an elite. Furthermore, the conversation is much longer and more involved, principally because his partner keeps up with him. And at the end she does not fade away; rather, she goes away—and talks about Jesus to the Samaritan people, who come out to the city and believe in him. This story is long, as is characteristic of John. It is tempting to take snippets of this passage, but I encourage you to consider the whole passage in order to feel its flow...and thus experience the living water.

After talking with Nick in Jerusalem, Jesus heads back up to Galilee, going through Samaria, which sits between Judea and Galilee. He really doesn't have to go through Samaria—he could have gone around through Perea. Samaritans and Jews did not trust each other. Jesus stopped at a city called Sychar and sat by Jacob's well. (Well, well, Jacob met his future wife Rachel by a well, Gen 29:1-20, as did Isaac, Gen

Lectionary Loop
Third Sunday of Lent, Year A, John 4:5-32

Study Bible
See *NISB*, 1914-15, esp. Excursus: "I am" Sayings.

Sources
See *Word and Soul: A Psychological, Literary, and Cultural Reading of the Fourth Gospel* (Collegeville, MN: The Liturgical Press, 2001), 29-41.

24:10-33, and Moses, Exod 2:11-22. Will Jesus meet his wife here? He has already wedded his disciples at Cana and let the Nicodemus fish get away. What now?) A Samaritan woman comes to draw water from the well, and Jesus begins the dialogue by asking her for a drink, thus beginning a conversation about living water (4:7-15). Here we have more wordplay, as in the discourse with Nicodemus. The contrast here is not between water and wine, but between well water and living water. The water of life, yes, life—present in the beginning from the Word (1:4), given by God to those who believe in the Son (3:15-16). The woman asks if he is greater than Jacob, a statement at which we giggle because we know that Jesus is greater than Jacob! Jesus contrasts drinking well water, after which folks will be thirsty again, and drinking the water that he gives, after which people will never ever be thirsty! The woman wants the water so that she will not be thirsty and will not have to come to the well again. Whoops! We thought she had it, but, nope, she doesn't. She still misunderstands.

Jesus then initiates a new line of conversation by asking her to call her husband. (Apparently he has gotten his drink from his own spring of living water.) She says that she doesn't have one, which Jesus confirms, saying that she has had five husbands and now has a non-husband, a comment that has led interpreters over the centuries to condemn the woman as a "five-time loser" and a "tramp." Hmm, it seems like people are projecting their own sexual hang-ups on the woman. Jesus doesn't comment. He has bigger fish to fry!

The woman senses that this Jew, who is perhaps greater than Jacob, is a prophet, so she asks him a theological question: Where should we worship? On this mountain, Mount Gerizim, where Samaritans worship, or Jerusalem, where Jews worship? In other words, where do folks gather together to drink this living water? But the question for Jesus is not where but when, how, and who: When? Now. (More "realized eschatology"!) How? In spirit (which engenders birth from above, 3:5, 8) and truth (which Jesus is graciously full of, 1:14, 17). Who? God the Father, and the coming Messiah, whom the woman asks about. Jesus says,

Teaching Tips

1. Try this meditation exercise to begin the session. Distribute paper cups and fill each cup with water. Instruct the group to sit in silence for a moment and then drink the water mindfully. Ask: What did it taste like, feel like, smell like, look like, and sound like? What words come to mind?

2. Have the class perform this story as a readers' theatre. Ask for volunteers for the following roles: narrator, Samaritan woman, Jesus, disciples, Samaritan townspeople. Have them come up front with their Bibles. Instruct them where to stand, and have them read the story aloud as dramatically as possible. After the reading, ask each reader what words of the text and actions of their own stood out for them?

3. Sing "Fill My Cup, Lord" (*United Methodist Hymnal*, hymn #641), in which John 4:5-15 (as well as 6:35) is noted as the inspiration for the words. What words and phrases from John 4 are picked up in these words?

Study Bible

See *NISB* Map 18, in the back of the Bible. Locate Galilee in the north, then trace Jesus' route south through Samaria to Judea. Note that he could have skirted around Samaria by going through Perea.

"I am" (Greek, *egō eimi*), echoing the "I am" of the burning-bush God (Exod 3:14) and the choosing, creating God (Isa 43:10; 45:18). The "I am" makes possible the living water and the spiritually true worship.

The astonished disciples come, and the woman goes—to tell the Samaritans to "come and see" (like Philip, 1:46) someone who might be, could be (maybe not?) the Messiah. And the Samaritans come! But the disciples first try to come to some understanding about Jesus' food, and they fail miserably. We shake our heads at them too. We understand about Jesus' food and drink, because we partake it through truly spiritual worship.

And the Samaritans apparently do too, first because of the woman's watery, worshipful witness, but then after Jesus stays two days, lots more believe because of his word (which has now become flesh for them). They tell the woman that they believe now because they've heard for themselves and we know what we worship and that is the Savior of the World, not Caesar, who was referred to by that title, but Jesus, the I am, the Messiah. The Samaritans find their husband at the well. And the woman? After such spirited sparring with Jesus, has she too gotten away?

How Is What is Happening in this Discourse Like What Is Happening in the World Today?

Women, water, and worship. All of these topics are brought up by this passage. So what about women in worship? How about marginalized women in worship (though one might argue that all women are marginalized)? I remember in 1984 Leontine T. C. Kelly, an African American, as the first woman of color to be elected a United Methodist bishop. And in 1988 Barbara Harris, also an African American, was consecrated as the first female bishop of the Episcopal Church. And in 2004 Minerva Carcanŏ became the first Latina bishop of the United Methodist Church.

What are some worshiping communities, in which people are experiencing living water, where leadership is shared among men and women? I like to think that the Religious Society of Friends (Quakers) does pretty well in that regard. The Friends have allowed both men

Sources

Koester, Craig R. "'The Savior of the Lord' (John 4:42)," *Journal of Biblical Literature* 109/4 (Winter 1990) 665-680.

A provocative novel about the Samaritan woman is Obery Hendricks *Living Water* (San Francisco: HarperSanFrancisco, 2003).

and women to lead almost from the beginning. As I think of recent Quaker worship services (which are silent until anyone who feels led of the Spirit gives a message), women and men have spoken.

How Is What Is Happening in this Discourse Like What Is Happening in Your Life?

Who is the watery, worshiping woman in me? How does she need to be engaged, to be wooed? She is that one who is always thirsty, who longs for the living water. She lets down my bucket into a deep well, the well of the world, my own wellspring. I thirst for peace, for relationship, for meaning. In what ways does my spiritual practice quench my thirst? In what ways does it not?

What is that in your bucket, ma'am? What? What? Oh, you say, Come and see.

Sources

See Samuel, Bill. "Friends (Quakers) and Women," at Quakerinfo.com. http://www.quakerinfo.com/quak womn. shtml.

Reflections

1. What role does worship have in the ongoing life of your congregation?
2. What style is used? Who leads? What is the ratio of men to women in worship leadership?
3. To what extent are texts and stories about women integrated into the service?

Teaching Tips

Have the group members write an imaginary dialogue with the Samaritan woman. Without thinking very much, write "Me" to the left of the margin and write what you would like to say to her. When you've written all that you need to say, skip a line and write "SW" (for "Samaritan woman") to the left of the margin and write what she would like to say to you. After everyone is finished, ask who would like to share.

Fathering the Son

We go now farther, to the Father (not a bother). He and the son are close. Indeed, the glory of the Word-became-flesh is that of an only son from a father (1:14). Jesus Christ is the only son, who has made known the Father from his privileged position close to the Father's heart, "into the bosom of the father" (1:18 my trans.). So this boy keeps talking about his daddy!

The feminine energy of the previous passage (and the Cana miracle) has now disappeared. It is now a "guy thing." But can we enter into this text, into the relationship of the Father and the Son, in a way that includes all of us? Can we?

What Is Happening in this Discourse?

After staying with the Samaritans a couple of days (4:40), Jesus returned to Galilee, where he is welcomed. He goes back to Cana—the water-to-wine place—where a royal official begs him to heal his sick son (2:1-11; 4:46-54). Jesus does so without going to the official's house, which results in the whole household believing. And John tells us this was Jesus' second sign (4:46-54). The next one follows quickly. Jesus goes back to Jerusalem for an unnamed festival. There he heals a thirty-eight-year-long paralytic on the Sabbath (5:2-9a). The Jewish leaders get all bent out of shape at this man getting put back into shape because it was a Sabbath, when no work should be done. Jesus says that he is working because his Father is still working, thus setting the theme for our text. The Jewish leaders then start looking for an opportunity to kill Jesus because he was a Jewish Sabbath-breaker and a

Study Bible

See *NISB*, 1916-18, also the "Special Note" on 1911.

Sources

See *Word and Soul: A Psychological, Literary, and Cultural Reading of the Fourth Gospel* (Collegeville, MN: The Liturgical Press, 2001), 44-52.

Teaching Tips

Ask for three volunteers, one to read the text slowly and expressively and two others to mime the story during its reading. Encourage them to be as dramatic as possible. After the reading, ask all three what stood out for them, what word and gesture was particularly meaningful.

"blasphemer," someone who claimed to be equal to God. (5:9b-18). Violence raises its ugly head for the first time in John, over Jesus' speech and action.

Jesus defends his Sabbath healing through a long poetic discourse. Here, Jesus talks not with an individual as in the two previous texts but with a group. And this group is rendered mute by Jesus (and John). No response at all, unlike Nicodemus or the Samaritan. And this discourse follows a "sign." We will see this pattern several times over the next few sessions: sign and discourse, deed and word. In this discourse Jesus emphasizes first his relationship to God as Son to Father (5:19-29) and then presents as witnesses on his behalf John the Baptist, Jesus' works, God the Father, and Moses (5:30-47).

Jesus begins this discourse in the same way that he did with Nicodemus: "Very truly, I tell you" (or "Amen amen I say to you," as I translate it). He says that line three times in this discourse (5:19, 24, 25), just as he did with Nicodemus (3:3, 5, 11). This is obviously important stuff, so we had better listen up, in order that we might know the "I am" and worship in spirit and truth (4:23-26). Jesus grounds his actions in his intimate relationship with God, which he expresses by calling himself "the Son" and God "the Father." In eight verses he uses this language "the Father/the Son" eight times (5:19-26). There is a certain austerity about this kind of speech. Ordinary people do not speak this way. This is the voice of "The Other," someone not of this world but from above (8:23), where believers are born in the Spirit (3:7-8) and drink of living water (4:13-14). The intimacy of the Father and the Son is an intimacy of operation. Out of love, the Father shows the Son what he is doing: raising the dead and giving life to believers, who honor both Father and Son. "Very truly" this dead-raising happens now (realized eschatology again!) just as the spiritually true Father-worshiping happens now (4:23). The grave-dwellers will hear the Son of Man's (sometimes translated "Human One's") voice and come out (like Lazarus is gonna do, 11:43-44).

Jesus further says that he seeks (What do you seek, Jesus? [1:38] "the will of him who sent me" [5:30]).

Reflections

1. How do you respond to Jesus' exclusive use of male imagery in speaking about his relationship with God?
2. What language do you use in speaking about your relationship with God?
3. How has your relationship with your father (and with your mother) shaped your view of God?

Indeed, that's the food that he is always munching on (4:34). For Jesus, God is not only Father but also the one who sent him (see 5:23, 36-38). It is as if he is saying, "Hey, your argument is not with me but rather with the Father who sent me."

Jesus' focus then turns to "testify" and "testimony" in this second and final section of his discourse (5:31-47). Jesus is bringing witnesses in his defense. His speech reads like a defense in a trial. His witnesses include John the Baptist, a burning and shining light (5:35) but not the true light (1:8), who has decreased as Jesus has increased (3:30); Jesus' works (5:36); the unseen-and-unheard, sending-Jesus Father (5:37-38); and the searched Scriptures (5:39). The Jewish leaders don't have a lock on the Father's word (incarnate in Jesus, 1:14) and do not manifest God's love in them (5:38, 42); they do not appear to seek God's glory (revealed in Jesus' signs, 2:11). As a result, Moses, who gave the law (1:17), lifted up the serpent in the wilderness (3:14) and will accuse the Jews. He is not going to be their advocate anymore (see Exod 17:1-7; 32:30; Ps 106:23)! Echoing what he said to Nicodemus (3:12), Jesus concludes, "But if you do not believe what he [Moses] wrote, how will you believe what I say?" (5:47). They did not! But we want to believe Jesus' words and works! The love of God is in us!

How Is What Is Happening in this Discourse Like What Is Happening in the World Today?

I stumbled onto the Web edition of the June 2006 issue of fathermag.com, which has a Web page on fathers and sons (http://www.fathermag.com/Father-Son.shtml). I was struck with how fatherhood (and sonhood) has evolved over the two millennia since the Gospel of John was written. Articles included fathering poetry to bedwetting boys, an interview with a single father who has raised his son without a mother present in the boy's life, and two news items about the high incarceration rates of fatherless boys.

From the human to the divine. Feminist theology has brought some new metaphors to understand God. Some of this language involves recovering feminine imagery of the divine from the Bible (such as Wisdom

---

Reflections

In the synoptic Gospels (Matthew, Mark, and Luke), Jesus uses parables to speak of the kingdom of God. But in John he speaks about himself, using "Father/Son" and "I am" sayings. What do you make of this difference?

in Prov 1:20-33; 8:1-9:6). I am aware of the Women's Alliance for Theology, Ethics, and Ritual (WATER), with offices in suburban Washington, D.C. It describes itself as "an international community of justice-seeking people who promote the use of feminist values to make religious and social change" (See http://www.his.com/~mhunt/index.htm).

How Is What Is Happening in this Discourse Like What Is Happening in Your Life?

I am a fatherless son. And a sonless father. So it goes. My father died when I was 16. So this passage presents particular poignancy to me. I have written about it to some extent in my book *Word and Soul* (see xxii-xxiv, 51-52). What more do I have to say now? I have no more to say because it is time for me to pick up my daughters, along with some of the boys that are involved in the cooperative summer day camp that my wife organized. See ya!

But before I go, I realize that I must be my own father. In some ways Jesus' father was absent. He was present only in Jesus' word. My father? Present in my word? My word, my word. I remember a line from Ralph Ellison's *Invisible Man*: "Be your own father." I am.

Reflections

1. What recent trends do you see in the way fathers and sons relate?
2. What new images of the divine-human relationship do you see emerging?

Sources

Ellison, Ralph. *Invisible Man* (New York: The New American Library, 1952), 139.

Teaching Tips

Give the following instructions to the group: Using the language of the discourse here, write a prayer-poem that speaks about how you relate to God.

Session 6

John 6:22-59

Breading Life

Food and drink are significant in the Gospel of John. Jesus turns water into wine at Cana, he talks about living water to the Samaritan woman, and in this text he offers himself as the bread of life to the religious authorities in Galilee. Water, wine, and bread are all vehicles of revelation for Jesus. Ingesting them is an important metaphor for believing in him.

What Is Happening in this Text?

Jesus was in Jerusalem at the end of chapter 5, but he is suddenly back in Galilee at the beginning of chapter 6. Here by the Sea of Galilee at Passover (the second one mentioned in John, see 2:13) he feeds a hungry crowd of five thousand with a boy's five loaves and two fishes. (This miracle is the only one narrated in all four Gospels, see Mark 6:30-44; Matt 14:13-21; Luke 9:10-17. Only John, however, says that the loaves and fishes came from the boy rather than the disciples, John 6:9.) The people, after eating, say that Jesus is the coming prophet and want to make him king, but Jesus goes back to the mountain. That evening the disciples begin their trek across the sea to Capernaum, and Jesus follows, walking on the sea. He says, "I am" to the disciples and gets into the boat.

The crowd chases Jesus, and when they find him, they ask when he is coming there. Again, Jesus begins a discourse following a sign with, "Very truly I tell you" (6:26, the first of four times, see also 6:32, 47, 53). Jesus says that they are looking for him because they filled up on bread, but he tells them to work for "food that endures for eternal life" (6:27), which the

Lectionary Loop
**Ninth Sunday after Pentecost, Year B, John 6:35, 41-51
Tenth Sunday after Pentecost, Year B, John 6:51-58
Eleventh Sunday after Pentecost, Year B, John 6:56-59**

Study Bible
See *NISB*, 1919-21, also "Excursus: 'I am' Sayings," 1915, and "Excursus: The Eucharist in John," 1920.

Sources
See *Word and Soul: A Psychological, Literary, and Cultural Reading of the Fourth Gospel* (Collegeville, MN: The Liturgical Press, 2001), 52-64

descending/ascending, judging Son of Man (3:14; 5:27) gives. But the people are now interested in God's work, not God's food—in doing, not eating. Jesus says that God's work is to believe in the one whom God has sent, that is, the Son, that is, Jesus. The people then ask for a sign like the manna in the wilderness. But hey, didn't Jesus give you that sign? Anyway, Jesus says that the law-giving, lifting-up, accusing Moses (1:17; 3:14; 5:45) didn't give the heavenly bread, but that God gave (gracious and spirited? 1:14, 17; 4:23-24) true bread. The people say, like the Samaritan woman concerning living water (4:15), "Give us this bread always" (6:34). Yes, give it to us too, Jesus, though we know that we already have it because we have believed in God's sent one (6:29).

Jesus says, "You got it! I AM the bread of life." This is the first "I am" saying with a predicate, which is usually a significant image from Jewish Scripture, such as here. With these "I am" sayings, we enter into the heart of John's poetry. Jesus brings together the divine name and the divine gifts. We are taken out of our normal lives, the world below, and brought into another realm, the world above, which gives our lives new meaning and purpose in this world so bedeviled with death. "Whoever comes to me will never be hungry, and whoever believes in me will never be thirsty" (6:35b). We hunger...for life beyond death. We thirst...for meaning in this precarious existence. Lady Wisdom, the feminine face of God, also calls people to participate in her feast: "Come, eat of my bread and drink of the wine I have mixed" (Prov 9:5; see also Sir 24:21). We sit at the table, filled with the outreaching love of the spheres. As bread, Jesus has come down from heaven to do the sending-one's will, which is to give believers eternal life and raise them up on the last day (6:39, 40, 44, 54). The hour is coming, and is now; the last day is today!

The people are now called "Jews" (6:41), and they begin to complain, just like the Israelites in the wilderness (see Exod 16). They don't get this I-am-coming-down-from-heaven-bread poetry. Jesus tells them not to complain, not to be wilderness whiners! He quotes from Isa 54:13, a vision of life when the Israelites are

Teaching Tips

1. As people are gathering, play John Michael Talbot's "I am the Bread of Life" from *The John Michael Talbot Collection: A Library of 35 Favorite Songs* (Sparrow/Emd, 1995), disc 1, track 17.

2. Sing "Eat This Bread" (*United Methodist Hymnal*, hymn #628), in which John 6:35 is noted as the inspiration for the words.

3. Have one volunteer read the narrator's part, another read Jesus' part, and then everyone else read the Judeans/Jews' part. Have the narrator and Jesus come up front. Tell everyone to be particularly aware of how their part strikes them, especially in terms of volume, pitch, speed, etc. After they have read the text, ask those who read each part about their experience of reading. Where did you find your voice changing? At what words? What gestures did you use? For what words?

free from oppression and are God-taught. The Father's hearing and learned ones come to Jesus, who, as the close-to-the-Father's-heart Son (1:18) and ascending-descending Son of Man (3:14), has seen the Father. Jesus very truly tells them that believers have eternal life, and he repeats, "I am the bread of life" (6:48), contrasting the dead manna-eaters and the never-dying heavenly bread-eaters. Again, "I am the living bread that comes down from heaven" (6:51). Then Jesus really throws them a curveball and says that the bread is his flesh, which sends the Judeans into orbit: How can this guy give us his flesh to eat!? (Sound like Nick, don't they? 3:9. They don't understand because they're not born from above, from the Spirit, 3:7-8). Jesus then pushes his point by saying that "very truly, I told you" you've gotta eat the Son of Man's flesh and drink his blood. Yuck! What's worse, Jesus uses two different words for eating in 6:53-58; one is the regular word for eating, and the other is the word for munching or gnawing. Gnawing on Jesus' flesh?! Ugh! The poetry extends almost to the breaking point. Even some of Jesus' disciples are offended and turn back (6:60-61, 66). They can't stomach it. Can we? Yes, because we understand and have eaten the poetic living bread.

How Is What Is Happening in this Text Like What Is Happening in the World Today?

Where are people hungering for today, both metaphorically and literally? Who is attempting to alleviate that hunger? How are these hungry folks grumbling? As we read the newspaper, we see that people are hungering in Africa, in Asia, and in the U.S.A. The Hunger Site (www.thehungersite.com), run by Mercy Corps, allows one to "Give Food for Free to Hungry People in the World" simply by clicking. There is plenty of information on hunger in Africa (esp. Darfur, Sudan), in Asia (esp. Indonesia), and in the U.S.A. (For more information about the genocide in Darfur, see http://savedarfur.org.) Also, Bread for the World (www.bread.org) is a grassroots organization of Christians lobbying against hunger.

> ### Reflections
> Read Exod 16. How is Jesus interpreting it? Why do you think Jesus uses such coarse language in 6:53-58?

> ### Reflections
> What is your congregation and/or denomination doing concerning hunger-related issues? In articulating the need for action in response to hunger, to what scriptural passages do people refer?

How Is What Is Happening in this Text Like What Is Happening in Your Life?

The placemat at one of our favorite Chinese restaurants has a Chinese zodiac that says I was born in the year of the goat. (I prefer another one that says I was born in the year of the ram.) The description says in part: "You are elegant and artistic but the first to complain about things." My wife often reminds me of this description. I complain, and my stomach grumbles. I am hungry. For what? Peace, relationship, creative expression, community, meaning, God. In what ways do I grumble? I grumble at the current political situation in this country, but I also grumble at how elusive are those things for which I hunger. Therefore, I feel anger, anxiety, and judgment. All are a part of the hunger, all are a part of the same grumblings, physical and spiritual. May the "I am" give me such meaning-full food. Eat up!

Teaching Tips

Lead people in a guided meditation exercise. Have people get in a comfortable position in their chairs, with feet flat on the floor and backs up against the backs of the chairs. Have them close their eyes. Tell them to take a deep breath and with the exhalation, release any tension that they might be aware of. Say the following: "What do you hunger for? Allow the answer to come from the depths of your soul. Maybe you will have to answer that question a number of times. If you had that for which you hunger, what would it feel, look, sound, smell, and taste like? Be with that for a while. After a time of silence, open your eyes and be with your experience. You might want to write or draw something, so there are materials available." Have anyone share who wants to do so.

I Am / You Are

O nce again, we come to a text in which Jesus says, "I am": "I am the light of the world" (8:12), and "Before Abraham was, I am" (8:58). But now he says to the Judeans, "You are from below" (8:23), and, "You are from your father the devil" (8:44). This is not a pleasant exchange, but neither is some of the history of Jewish-Christian relations. Let us explore these issues as we look at what is happening in the text.

What Is Happening in this Text?

After his "bread of life" discourse (6:22-59), Jesus goes up to Jerusalem for the Feast of Booths (also called "Tabernacles"). He continues to debate with the Jews, echoing many of the themes introduced previously (7:14-24, 37-39). People are divided over him (7:25-31, 40-44). Then, in a story that may not have originally appeared in John, Jesus non-condemns the woman caught in adultery.

Jesus then speaks to them again. To the Pharisees, again his dialogue partners, he says another "I am" saying, followed by a statement of benefits for the believer: "I am the light of the world. Whoever follows me will never walk in darkness but will have the light of life" (8:12). As in the previous text, Jesus delivers a poetic discourse with the Judeans involving "I am" sayings, at a feast, in conjunction with a sign. As O'Day notes on 8:12, light was an important image used in the celebration of the Feast of Tabernacles (NISB, 1924). Golden candlesticks were set up in the Temple, and, according to the Mishnah, "There was not a courtyard in Jerusalem that did not reflect the

Study Bible
See *NISB*, 1924-26, see especially "Excursus: John and Judaism."

Sources
See *Word and Soul: A Psychological, Literary, and Cultural Reading of the Fourth Gospel* (Collegeville, MN: The Liturgical Press, 2001), 64-72.

Teaching Tips
Read this passage in the same way that you read the previous one. Ask for volunteers to read the parts of the narrator and of Jesus. (Make sure they are different people from the ones who read last time.) Everyone else can read the parts of the Jews/Pharisees. Instruct them to read dramatically. After the reading is finished, ask people what stood out for them.

Study Bible
See O'Day's *NISB* annotations on 7:2, p. 1921, and 7:53-8:11, p. 1923.

light." Light was a common image for God's presence, especially in the coming age (see Isa 9:2; 42:6-7; Zech 14:7). Jesus was proclaiming, however, that the coming liberation was now.

The Pharisees charge that Jesus is testifying on his own account (8:13). He needs two witnesses (8:17; see Deut 19:15). So this discourse takes on much the same character as the second section of the discourse following the healing of the paralytic (5:31-47). This time Jesus offers himself and his Father as witnesses (8:18), but the Pharisees misunderstand, demanding to know where his Father is. Jesus says: Know me, know my father (8:19). This was a temple treasury teaching moment but not an arresting moment because Jesus' hour hadn't come yet, which Jesus and John have told us before (2:4; 7:30).

Jesus "again" (see 8:14) says he is going away to where they can't go. The Pharisees, now called Jews, misunderstand and think he is going to commit suicide; Jesus attributes the misunderstanding to a problem of origin: They're from below, of this world, and he is from above, not of this world. They haven't been born from above (3:3, 7). They're going to die in their sins unless they believe that Jesus is I AM, which will be revealed when the Son of Man is exalted/lifted up, like Moses' wilderness serpent (3:14). That happens in death (12:32-33)! That does the trick for some, for many believed in Jesus (8:30).

One wonders, though, how strong their faith is, because when Jesus says that the truth will free them, these Jews say they're never-been-enslaved-Abraham-children (8:32-33). Never been enslaved?! What about in Egypt? What about now, in Roman Palestine? Yet the Son promises freedom, even though these Abrahamites are trying to kill Jesus (8:37-40). Though they protest that God is their Father, Jesus says they don't understand (8:43, also 8:27) because they don't accept his word and are from their father the devil who's been a murderer and liar from the beginning (8:43-44). Ooh! This is tough stuff!

Well, right back at you, because the Jews say Jesus is a Samaritan demoniac. (After all, Jews have no dealings with Samaritans, 4:9.) Jesus refutes this charge,

Sources

Culpepper, R. Alan. *The Gospel and Letters of John*. Interpreting Biblical Texts (Nashville: Abingdon, 1999). See p. 171 for the quotation from the Mishnah.

saying that he honors the Father. Very truly, Jesus tells them that the word-keepers are never-die-ers (8:51). This confirms for the Jews that Jesus is demonized, for Abraham and the prophets died. Jesus isn't greater than Abraham (or Jacob, 4:12), is he? Jesus says that Abraham rejoiced to see Jesus' day (as did Isaiah, 12:41). What?! The Jews don't get this. He is not yet fifty years old, so he can't have seen Abraham. But Jesus very-truly-tells them, "Before Abraham was, I am" (8:58). He was the word in the beginning. The Jews have had enough, even if they have believed in him (8:31). They're going to stone him for blasphemy (Lev 24:13-16), but Jesus is going to play hide and seek with them and get out of the Temple (8:59).

How Is What Is Happening in this Text Like What Is Happening in the World Today?

The inflammatory words "Christ-killers!" have fueled anti-Semitism throughout Christian history, resulting in discrimination and death. I am sorry to say that the Gospel of John has played a role in this. We have in John, however, the voice of a minority Jewish community speaking out against the majority Jewish community. Yet the church, when it became the majority institution, used John to oppress a minority. Witness the pogroms and the Holocaust. Anti-Semitism is still with us. A Jewish friend of mine said that several years ago when he bought his bayside home, the deed said the property could not be sold to blacks or Jews, a proviso that fortunately was ignored. And it is not uncommon still in Christian circles to hear Judaism referred to as a religion of works-righteousness. But also common in our day are dialogues between Jews and Christians, such as the International Council of Christians and Jews. (See their website, http://www.jcrelations.net.)

The kind of heated rhetoric that appears in John 8 is still present in our day, not so much between Jews and Christians, but between political, social, or religious conservatives and liberals. Just turn on talk radio. I remember the two books not long ago: Al Franken's *Rush Limbaugh Is a Big Fat Idiot*, and the rejoinder by J. P. Mauro, *Al Franken Is a Buck-Toothed Moron*. And

Reflections

1. How do you respond to this discourse between Jesus and the Jews? What words are particularly memorable for you? (You may want to stand and dramatically read them aloud.)
2. Read the "Special Note" in *NISB*, 1925 and "the Excursus: John and Judaism" in *NISB*, 1926. What statements there are helpful? (You may want to read them aloud.)
3. What still troubles you about this passage? Where in your body do you physically feel that?

Teaching Tips

Consider some of these suggestions to contribute to Jewish-Christian understanding: Attend a Sabbath service at a local synagogue. Begin a dialogue with people from a local synagogue. Have a rabbi come to your class to discuss this picture of "the Jews" in John.

with the Iraq War, the rhetoric of Al-Qaeda and the U.S.A. seems to mirror each other; one speaker's religious perspective was totally good, and the other's was evil. The Johannine dualism is still with us, as "our side" stands in the light, and "they" are in the dark. Such rhetoric expresses anger and allows us to indulge in self-righteousness, but it certainly does not lead to mutual understanding.

How Is What Is Happening in this Text Like What Is Happening in Your Life?

I am aware of ways in which I have rhetorically consigned people to the outer darkness. For me, certain political leaders are often a target for my anger. I have published poems criticizing them and read this poetry in public gatherings and on the radio. I published a poem a few years back entitled, "shok & awe, shuk & jive," in which I referred to the commander-in-chief as a "chip off the old blockhead." I said that he was brain-dead and added, "THIS JUST IN: EMPTY WAR-HEAD FOUND IN WHITE HOUSE." I must confess that it was cathartic to read this poem in public, as I did many times, even over the radio, and it was always quite well-received. But I wonder, does such an attitude contribute to peace? Or does it simply make me a prisoner of hate rather than hope? "You will know the truth, and the truth will make you…"

Sources

See my poem "shok & awe, shuk & jive" in *DC Poets Against the War: An Anthology*. 2nd ed. Edited by Sarah Browning, Michelle Elliot, and Danny Rose (Washington, D.C.: R.D. Baker and Argonne House Press, 2004) 85-86.

Teaching Tips

Have the group do this exercise: Write an angry paragraph about someone who holds a position different from you on a particular issue. Be nasty! Then rewrite the paragraph in a way that might open up some dialogue. Share.

Blinded by the Light

Two songs come to mind with this text. The first is the famous hymn "Amazing Grace," in which the singer says, "Was blind but now I see," an almost verbatim quotation of the man born blind (see 9:25). But I also think of the title of a '70s song, "Blinded by the Light," because the religious authorities are blind to the light of the world. They, therefore, are the sinners! Let us look at this captivating story!

What Is Happening in this Miracle Story and Controversy?

Jesus hides himself (8:59), and then he walks along, seeing a non-seeing-from-birth man (9:1). Jesus heals plenty of blind folks in the Synoptics, but here the man is "born blind," so that the miracle is new creation! We can read stories in antiquity of gods, heroes, and even emperors healing people of blindness. We can also read instructions given for applying salves, such as "fasting saliva," to ailing eyes. One story tells of someone with only an eye socket growing an eye.

The disciples want to make a case study out of this: "Rabbi, who sinned, this man or his parents, that he was born blind?" (9:2). The disciples raise the story's key question: Who sinned? This man or his parents? Jesus or someone else? Jesus says it wasn't this man or his parents (though that may change as the story unfolds), but that blindness happened so that God's works might be worked while it is still day. Jesus then repeats the "I am" saying from the beginning of the last discourse: "I am the light of the world" (9:5; see 8:12). So Jesus spits, makes mud, puts it on the man's eyes, and tells him to go wash in the Sent pool. (This

Lectionary Loop
Fourth Sunday of Lent, Year A,
John 9:1-41

Study Bible
See *NISB*, 1926-28.

Sources
See *Word and Soul: A Psychological, Literary, and Cultural Reading of the Fourth Gospel* (Collegeville, MN: The Liturgical Press, 2001), 73-83.

is the work of the one who sent him, 9:4). He comes back seeing. His neighbors don't believe it's him, but he says, "I am!" (9:9). When asked how it happened, the man simply says that "a man called Jesus" made mud, etc., repeating what the narrator has already told us.

These "good neighbors" bring the man to the Pharisees on this Sabbath day (see 5:9). They too ask how, and he tells them. The Pharisees are divided about Jesus, and they ask the man what he thinks about Jesus. The once-blind man says that this "man called Jesus" is a prophet (9:17; see the Samaritan woman, 4:19). The Pharisees don't believe that this is the same guy who formerly could not see, so they call his parents, who say they don't know how he gained his sight or who did the miracle. John explains that they responded this way because they were afraid of the Jews, as folks are wont to be in John (see 7:13; 19:38: 20:19). The Jews had determined that Jesus-is-Messiah-confessors would be tossed out of the synagogue (9:22). Until fairly recently, many thought this situation was indicative of the believers who in the late first century were being cast out of the synagogue. But there really is no evidence that that was happening. Perhaps believers felt so alienated from the synagogue leadership that it seemed as though they had been (or soon would be) cast out. Anyway, in refusing to confess Jesus as Messiah, the man's parents indicate that they are, in fact, sinners (see 9:2).

The Jews, however, say they know that "this man," Jesus, is the sinner. The healed man says he doesn't know that; all he knows is that he was formerly sightless but is now sighted! Again they ask him how his eyes were opened. The man responds, saying that he already told them and asking why they want to hear it again. "Do you also want to become his disciples?" (9:27) Ooh, he zinged 'em! And they revile him for it, saying that they are disciples of Moses (who really accuses them for not believing in Jesus, 5:45-47), but that they don't know where Jesus comes from (or where he is going, 8:22). The man knows where Jesus comes from: God. And the proof is that Jesus performed a never-before-heard-of event. The Jews say the man is a sinner, and they toss him out.

Teaching Tips

This text simply must be acted out. You will need people for seven parts: narrator, disciples, Jesus, neighbors, man born blind, Pharisees/Judeans, the man's parents. If you don't have seven people, some folks can double up. For example, the same person can play the disciples, neighbors, and parents. If you have more than seven people, multiple people can play some of the collective characters such as the disciples, neighbors, or Pharisees/Judeans. You will probably need to direct, shuffling people onstage and off. Encourage the actors to read their parts as dramatically as possible, exaggerating their voices and their gestures. After the text is acted out, ask each actor, "What particularly moved you as you acted out this part?"

Study Bible

See the *NISB* annotation on 9:1-12.

Sources

See Cotter, Wendy. *Miracles in Greco-Roman Antiquity* (London: Routledge, 1999), 17-18, 40-41, 214.

Jesus finds him and asks him if he believes in the ascending-descending, lifted-up, judging Son of Man. Jesus says, "That's me," and the man worships (in spirit and truth, 4:23-24). This man is not a sinner! He has faith-journeyed from calling Jesus simply by his name (9:11), to saying he is a prophet (17), to contending that he is from God (33), and finally to worshiping him as Lord and Son of Man (35-38). The Pharisees, though, are judged by the Son of Man as blind sinners (9:39-41).

How Is What Is Happening in this Miracle Story and Controversy Like What Is Happening in the World Today?

Are you ready for some controversy? I would like to suggest that this passage lives on in church trials in which openly gay ministers are removed from their churches or their clergy credentials are removed. Perhaps the most visible case has been that of Beth Stroud, who in December 2004 was stripped of her ministerial credentials by a clergy trial after she announced that she was a lesbian in a committed relationship with another woman. (See the story at the United Methodist website: http://www.umc.org/site/c.gjJTJbMUIuE/b.1145011/k.F51E/Judicial_Council_reverses_lower_court_rules_against_Beth_Stroud.htm.) The beginning of her journey became one of the threads in the PBS documentary *The Congregation*, which focused on First United Methodist Church of Germantown in Philadelphia, where Stroud was serving and continues to serve as associate pastor. (See the church's website at www.fumcog.org, and the documentary's website at http://www.pbs.org/thecongregation.)

How Is What Is Happening in this Miracle Story and Controversy Like What Is Happening in Your Life?

I am certainly no stranger to ecclesiastical controversy. While serving as a Southern Baptist missionary in Costa Rica in 1988, I was fired for "doctrinal ambiguity." I went through a series of interrogations by administrators, which reminds me of the experience of

Teaching Tips

Have group members write a conversation between the man and his parents after he has been expelled from the synagogue. Invite them to share.

Reflections

1. What is your opinion of the Beth Stroud case? What similarities does it have to John 9? What differences?

2. What biblical arguments do you use in your position on homosexuality?

the man born blind. Read more about it in my book *Word and Soul*, xxvii, 82.

I can also take this story inside, so to speak. How do I cast out aspects of myself? In what ways do I suppress anger, depression, anxiety, and sexuality? Usually I stuff my anger. "That student made me angry, but I can't show it because folks would think ill of me." I cast it out. But can I allow Light to come to it and expose the darkness of my own thought processes that lead me to "cast out" my humanity? I do believe in the Son of Man.

Reflections

1. What experiences have you had in which you have felt cast out?
2. What experiences have you had in which you have cast someone out?
3. What parts of yourself do you cast out of yourself? In what way can you reclaim that part of yourself?

Teaching Tips

Following the discussion above, instruct the group to draw those parts of themselves that they have rejected, placing them in the light of God's love.

Resurrecting the Life

"What's that pin you're wearing?" Lazarus asks Martha as she takes his temperature, checks for bedsores, and adjusts the volume on the TV.

"It says, 'Jesus Loves You,'" Martha says.

"Yes, he does," Lazarus responds. "This I know, for the Bible (specifically the Gospel of John) tells me so. Does Jesus know that I'm sick?"

"I don't know," Martha replies, "but Mary and I will send word to him." So they do.

What Is Happening in this Miracle Story?

After upbraiding the Pharisees for the blindness, Jesus then gives the "Good Shepherd Discourse" (10:1-21), in which he says that he lays down his life for his sheep and takes it back up again (10:11, 15, 17, 18), resulting in much division (10:19-21). We jump ahead a few weeks to the Feast of Dedication, which celebrated the reconsecration of the Temple after its desecration by the Syrians (see 1 Macc 4:36-61). This holiday is still observed annually as Hanukkah. Again Jesus jousts with Jerusalem Jews, and again they try to stone him, this time explicitly saying that they are stoning him for blasphemy. And again Jesus escapes, this time going across the Jordan to John's baptizing place.

They say, "Your beloved is ill." Jesus says that the illness is for God's glory (not unlike what he said to the disciples before healing the man born blind, John 9:3, and what John tells us at Cana, 2:11). John now tells us that Jesus loves Lazarus and his sisters so much…that he stays put two days! What wondrous

Lectionary Loop
Fifth Sunday of Lent, Year A, John 11:1-45

Study Bible
See *NISB*, 1930-32

Sources
See *Word and Soul: A Psychological, Literary, and Cultural Reading of the Fourth Gospel* (Collegeville, MN: The Liturgical Press, 2001), 83-91.

Teaching Tips
Read this story as readers' theatre. Ask for volunteers for the following roles: narrator, Mary, Martha, Jesus, disciples, Thomas, Jews. Again, you may need to direct. After you've acted it out or read it dramatically, debrief the actors or readers: What moved you about your part?

love is this!? Then Jesus decides it's time to go, though his disciples remind him that he nearly got stoned there. (Are they as thick-headed as the Pharisees and the "believing" Jews? Apparently faith in Jesus is no sure gateway to understanding. What is, then?)

Do you have to have read the Prologue? Jesus finally says that Lazarus is dead, and he says he is glad they weren't there so that they may believe. (Don't they already believe? 2:11. Have they fallen from grace?) Thomas says they ought to go with him so they can die with him. (Thomas has this thing about death, 20:23).

Martha, along with many Jews who have come to mourn with her, goes to meet Jesus. She tells him that if he'd been there, her brother would not have died. (So why did you tarry those two days?! You could have healed him!) But I know that even now (the hour is coming and now is) God will give you whatever you ask. (Does she believe that Jesus is going to raise him from the dead?) Jesus tells her that her brother will rise again, which Martha (mis)understands as the resurrection at the last day. But no, don't you understand that the last day is now? Jesus explains with an "I AM" statement: "I am the resurrection and the life," and as previously, he adds a promise: Dead believers will live, and living believers won't ever die. (Ever?! Wow, that's quite a promise in this Roman world of death!) Jesus then asks Martha if she believes, and she says she believes that he is the Messiah-Son-of-God and thus has life in his name (20:31). Martha is the model believer!

Martha goes to get Mary, who goes to Jesus. Jesus sees Mary weeping, the Jews weeping, all God's children weeping, and he is "all shook up," disturbed and moved. He asks where they have laid Lazarus; they say, as Jesus has done, "Come and see." Then he weeps. The Jews think they are tears of love, but are they? The people called "Jews" are the misunderstanders in John.

Is he disturbed by the unbelief of the Jews, who ask if the one who opens blind eyes couldn't have kept Lazarus from dying? (They don't "see" that Jesus is going to raise him!) Is he angry at the prospect of death, both Lazarus' and his own? Later on Jesus' soul or spirit is troubled, first as he contemplates the hour of his death, and then as he tells the disciples that one of them will betray him (12:27: 13:21). Let us enter into Jesus' troubling tears and his life-giving love.

Jesus goes to the tomb, which was a cave with a stone rolled against its entrance, and says to take away the stone; but Mary protests because of the four-days-dead stench! Jesus tells her that if she believes, as she said she does, she'll see God's glory (full of grace and truth...and life!). Jesus then prays, thanking God for hearing him, which God always does, but he speaks so that the crowd might believe (and might have life). Afterward, Jesus yells into the tomb, "Lazarus (you, my beloved sheep) come out into the green pasture of abundant life!" (see 10:3). And that's what he did, bound hands and feet, and wrapped (rapt?) face. Jesus said to unbind him and let...him...GO!

We readers and hearers also come out of our tombs, the tombs of life under Roman imperialism. By entering into this story, we enter into an altered state of consciousness, where we live in that other world, where God is. An altered state of consciousness leads to an alternative consciousness, which is committed to Jesus Christ, Son of God, and not Caesar. Resurrection worship, then, leads to resurrection ethics.

How Is What Is Happening in this Miracle Story Like What Is Happening in the World Today?

I will turn the microphone over to my fall 2005 class in the Gospel of John, for they gave some interesting answers to this question, focusing on the death and new life they saw happening in the church. One said that like Lazarus early in the story, the church is dying because it is not working on economic policy and is not giving sufficient attention to AIDS. Another student commented that as a result of the Hurricane Katrina disaster, there has been a renewed concern for ethnic minorities mired in poverty. A student also noted that the church is beginning to reach out to gangs through ministries such as tutoring. Another student, reflecting on Rosa Parks' recent death, pointed to Parks' legacy of boldness in the face of oppression.

I might add that the story of Al Gore is something of

Reflections

1. Consider whether or not this event actually happened. What are some reasons why someone might say it did happen? What are some reasons why someone might say it did not happen?
2. What difference does it make?

a "raising." After his bitter presidential defeat, he has been raised through his lecturing and "PowerPointing" around the world on global warming. His story is now a major motion picture, entitled *An Inconvenient Truth.* It seems that this truth has set Gore free. Might it also set others free? Might it set the earth free?

How Is What Is Happening in this Miracle Story Like What Is Happening in Your Life?

What kills me? Neglect of my body. Also neglect of my emotional life. In essence, it is neglect of my own humanity. What gives me new life? In other words, where do I see my own "resurrection of the body"? Through paying attention to my flesh. Exercise invigorates me, body and soul, especially when I walk in the early morning around the lake behind our house. Yoga helps me be aware of my body and the energy flowing through it. There is much energy there, much passion, much longing. I often deny it, which kills it, but sometimes I own it, even celebrate it. Become aware of my own body…and bodies broken around the world. Broken, broken. For me. My body is also part of the earth. And it is dying. How can it too live?

Jesus Going, Spirit Coming

Go, Jesus, go! He is going, going, gone! It's a home run…for us! He is going, going to the Father through death, resurrection, and ascension! Go, Jesus, go! Come, Spirit, come! Jesus goes; the Spirit comes. Thus Jesus abides with his disciples after his death, through the Spirit. So come, Holy Spirit, come!

What Is Happening in this Discourse?

I will let my fall 2005 class in John have the first word here. Together, they came up with this statement of what is happening in the text: Jesus is summarizing his ministry to this point and preparing his disciples to carry on his work in love for one another, with assurance that an advocate would be there. Sounds pretty good, huh? First, though, let me set the text in context: Jesus is now in Jerusalem for the Passover (the third one in John, see 2:13; 6:4). Knowing that the hour has come to go to the Father (13:1; see 12:32), he gathers with his disciples. John notes poignantly, "Having loved his own who were in the world [i.e. the children of God, who have believed in his name, 1:12], he loved them to the end" (13:1). This section, even the rest of John, is bathed in love. Jesus shows his love first by washing the disciples' feet, thus setting an example for them (13:2-20). He sends Judas Iscariot off to betray him (13:21-30) and then announces, "Now the Son of Man is glorified" (13:31-33). Jesus gives them a "new commandment" to follow after his departure: Love one another (13:34-35). Jesus then says to Peter that he won't be able to follow him now but later; instead, he will deny Jesus three times (13:36-38).

Lectionary Loop
**Fifth Sunday of Easter, Year A,
John 14:1-14
Sixth Sunday of Easter, Year A,
John 14:15-21
Sixth Sunday of Easter, Year C,
John 14:23-29
Pentecost Sunday, Year C,
John 14:8-17 (25-27)**

Study Bible

See *NISB* 1937-38, especially "Excursus: "No One Comes to the Father Except Through Me." Also see "Excursus: The Spirit in John."

Sources

See *Word and Soul: A Psychological, Literary, and Cultural Reading of the Fourth Gospel* (Collegeville, MN: The Liturgical Press, 2001), 93-104.

Jesus then begins what is often called "The Farewell Discourses" (14:1-16:33, though sometimes it is expanded to include 13:31-17:26). As the *NISB* annotations on 14:1-16:33 state, these discourses are similar to other farewell speeches or last testaments in the Jewish Scripture. The Farewell Discourses as we now have them in John perhaps circulated independently before being placed here. For example, 14:1-31 seems to be a unit and 15:1-16:33 another. We do not see a linear development of thought, but Jesus keeps circling back, sweeping us up in its wake. The poetry of the passage leads us to an altered state of consciousness, into worship, so that we in the Spirit are no longer in this world, but we are with Jesus in the world above.

Jesus tells the disciples not to let their hearts be troubled; they are to believe in God and him. Jesus says that in his Father's house (formerly the Temple but now Jesus' body, see 2:16-21) are many dwelling places (Greek, *monai*, 14:2). Jesus is in the Father, and the Father is in Jesus (14:10-11); and they lovingly make a home, or dwelling place (Greek, *monē*), with those who love them (14:23). Jesus goes to the Father (14:12, 28) through death and resurrection to prepare a place for the disciples (14:2)—a place of powerful practice and prayer (14:12-14), a place of peace (14:27). And after preparing that powerful and peaceful place, Jesus will come again (not at the second coming, about which John has little to say, or at the believer's death, but at Jesus' resurrection, when he comes in and with the Spirit, 20:19-23) to take the disciples to where he is, so that they can see his glory (17:24). And all of this happens while the disciples are still in the world (17:15). Confused yet? Simply dwell with Jesus in the Spirit, and you will get it!

Jesus tells the disciples that they know the way, but Thomas, misunderstandingly, says that they don't know where he is going and they don't know the way. (Know way? No way!) Jesus says, "I am the way [like I am the gate, 10:7, 9] and the truth [gracefully so, 1:14, 17; liberatingly so, 8:32] and the life [eternal life, 3:15-16; abundant life, 10:10; provided by the bread of life, 6:35; light of life, 8:12; and resurrection and life, 11:25]. Jesus provides exclusive access to the Father.

Teaching Tips

1. Sing "Come, My Way, My Truth, My Life" (*United Methodist Hymnal*, hymn #164).
2. Have someone slowly and loudly read this passage, and have one or two people mime it while the first person reads. Ask: What stood out for you as you read or mimed?

Study Bible

See the annotations on 14:1-16:33 in the *NISB*, 1937-42.

Know Jesus, know his Father, see him too. Philip wants Jesus to show him the Father, but that's what Jesus has been doing the whole time he is been with the disciples. See Jesus, see the Father! Jesus is in the Father, and the Father is in Jesus (14:10-11; also 10:38; 14:20). Jesus very truly tells them that they will do greater works because he is going to the Father, and he will do whatever they ask in his name (just as they believe in his name and have life in his name, 1:12; 20:31).

Jesus says that those who love him will keep his commandments, his new commandment to love one another (14:15; see 13:34-35). Jesus will ask the Father to give (or send in Jesus' name, 14:25) them another Advocate/Helper/Comforter (all translations of the Greek word *paraklētos*, probably a legal term, literally "one called alongside"). It's the Spirit of truth (14:17; also 15:26; 16:13) who will guide the disciples into all truth (16:13). He is going to dwell, or abide (*menō*) with the disciples (14:16), teaching them by reminding them of what Jesus said (14:25), while proving the world wrong about sin, righteousness, and judgment (16:8-11).

Jesus assures the disciples that he will lovingly reveal himself to his disciples so that they will see him, but the world won't. Judas (not-Iscariot) doesn't quite get that (14:22), but Jesus says that he and the Father will make a home (dwelling place) with those who love him (14:23-24). The Advocate, the Holy Spirit, will come to this dwelling place, granting the disciples Jesus' (unworldly) peace, which is quite different from the violent, oppressive Roman peace, the Pax Romana. It is non-heart-troubling-or-trembling peace, in him (14:27; 16:33).

Jesus goes and comes, and the result for those who love him is joy and faith (14:28-29). The world's ruler (Satan? Caesar?) comes, but he is completely impotent (14:30) because he has been condemned (16:11). In love, in peace, and in courage (16:33) let us, like Lazarus, rise and be off!

How Is What Is Happening in this Discourse Like What Is Happening in the World Today?

Farewell speeches, common in the Bible, continue in our day. Perhaps the two most famous farewell speeches of the 20th century are Dwight David Eisenhower's presidential farewell address, in which he warned of the influence of the "military-industrial complex" (see http://www.eisenhower.archives.gov farewell.htm), and Martin Luther King's sermon given on the eve of his assassination, "I've Been to the Mountaintop" (see http://www.afscme.org/about/1549. cfm).

John 14:6 is another Scripture, like 3:7, which often has a very public face in our society. I googled "Jesus the Only Way" and came up with over eighty million results! Several were rather bland, wordy, evangelistic tracts defending the proposition that there is no salvation outside of Christianity. One was a blog disagreeing with a 2005 article in the *United Methodist Reporter*, entitled "Wesleyan Wisdom: God's Love Not Confined to Followers of Jesus Christ." (See the article at http://www.reporterinteractive.org/main/Feeds/tabid/116/newsid/227/Default.aspx, and the refutation at http://www.wesleyblog.com/2005/07/is _ jesus_the_on.html.) A few sites I perused prominently featured John 14:6, along with "hot links" that spoke out against such things as Catholicism, abortion, feminism, and homosexuality. As I looked at these websites, I asked, "Where is the love? Where is the respect for those who disagree? Where is the respect for all people's religious experience?" For some, it was there; for others...well..."Where is the love?"

How Is What is Happening in this Discourse Like What Is Happening in Your Life?

Where is the love? Where is the peace—in my writing? It comes from dwelling with the questions, the enigmas, the poetry, and the art of it all. Will you dwell with me—over against the powers of the world? Will you breathe in the spirit of love and breathe out peace?

Reflections

1. How do you interpret John 14:6, particularly in the context of a multiplicity of world religions?
2. Read aloud the Excursus in the *NISB* on p. 1937. What statements seem meaningful to you?
3. How might a Muslim, Buddhist, or Jew interpret John 14:6?

Teaching Tips

Read selections from King's "I've Been to the Mountaintop" and interspersed with selections from John 14. Then ask participants, "What correspondences do you see?"

Teaching Tips

1. Invite a member of another religious tradition to discuss with your group the interpretation of John 14:6. What texts in their tradition are comparable?
2. If there is an interfaith conference in your locale, contact them for resources about interreligious dialogue. For resources online, see the Web page of the Interfaith Conference of Metropolitan Washington, D.C., http://www.ifcmw.org.

Teaching Tips

Have participants draw or write a poem about those places in which they abide in peace and love.

Branching out in Love

Maybe you know this chorus: "Love, love, love/The Gospel in a word is love…" Love. That is certainly the Farewell Discourses in a word. God loves Jesus, Jesus loves us, and we are to love one another. Love, love, love. Let's stay with that.

What Is Happening in this Discourse?

My divinity school class in John came up with the following response to the question: "Using a very familiar symbol, Jesus is saying it's no longer about Israel but about him sent from God. The most important thing is to love with the same kind of love with which I have loved you."

Our passage comes right on the heels of the previous one. Jesus says, "Rise, let us be on our way" (14:31); then he keeps talking! It's interesting that the movie *The Gospel of John* had Jesus leave the room for the last supper and give the rest of the discourse "on the way" through a vineyard! John does not give us any stage direction, so we're not sure what he had in mind. The important thing is to get it in our mind—and body and soul—and stay there, abide, remain. Only then can we branch out—in love.

Jesus has here his final "I AM" saying: "I am the (true) vine," which he says twice (15:1, 5). The vine imagery often occurs in the Old Testament as a symbol of Israel. Jesus seems to echo Isa 5:1-7, "the Song of the Vineyard," which begins: "Let me sing for my beloved my love-song concerning his vineyard" (5:1). The vineyard yields only wild grapes, and the singer says that the vineyard will be trampled down and made

Lectionary Loop
Fifth Sunday of Easter, Year B, John 15:1-8
Sixth Sunday of Easter, Year B, John 15:9-17

Study Bible
See *NISB*, 1938-39.

waste (5:5-6). The vineyard is then interpreted as Israel and Judah, from whom God expected justice and righteousness but got bloodshed and a cry (Isa 5:7). Jesus, however, is the "true vine" over against that of Israel, which did not produce justice and righteousness. (Also see Sir 24:17 in which Lady Wisdom compares herself to a vine that produces "glorious and abundant fruit.")

First he discusses the vine and the vinegrower, whom he identifies as his Father, just as Isaiah identified God as the vinegrower (Isa 5:5-6). This vinegrowing Father removes the non-fruit-bearing branch and prunes (or cleanses, see the marginal note i and the *NISB* annotation [p. 1939] on the wordplay of 15:3) the fruit-bearing branch. Fruit-bearing was an image for being faithful to the Jewish covenant (see Ps 1:3). In the same way, Jesus' disciples bear fruit (and glorify God, John 15:8) by following the commandment of love (see 15:10). So the disciples have been cleansed or pruned through this word, this love commandment.

So now, abide ("stay, remain, dwell," as it is translated elsewhere in John in the NRSV). This word (Greek *menō*) is the key word in this text; it appears ten times in seven verses. It's one of John's favorite words: Jesus stays with the Samaritans, resulting in many more believing (4:40-41), and he stays two days after he hears Lazarus is sick (11:6). Jesus' first two disciples stay with him, after which Philip says they found the Messiah (1:38-41). The Spirit remains on Jesus (1:33), and it abides with the disciples (14:17). In the same way, Jesus' disciples are to abide in him through loving one another. With the numerous repetitions of the word, the mind is "stayed." An altered state of consciousness is nurtured. One is brought into a state of worship. (See the *NISB* "Special Note," 1939.)

A non-abider is thrown away branch-like; it withers, is gathered, and is burned. Yikes! That is, however, part of the imagery in Ezek 19:14, where the entire vine goes into the fire. Jesus doesn't elaborate. We read of no concept of hell in John, though he does speak of condemnation, which happens in the present life (3:18; 5:29). Jesus goes on to speak about the abiders, who will be Father-glorifying, fruit-bearing disciples (15:8). Jesus then speaks of the flow of love:

Teaching Tips

1. Bring in a vining plant as a centerpiece. Before the session formally begins, play John Michael Talbot's song, "I Am the Vine" from his *Master Collection, Vol. 1, The Quiet Side* (Chatsworth, CA: Sparrow, 1989), Disc 2, Track 2. Have the group meditate on the plant while listening to the music. What speaks to you through the plant, the words, and the music?

2. Another possibility is to take your study group outside to observe vining plants nearby. Have people carefully look at them, feel them, and smell them. What does this add to your reading of the text?

3. Ask for a volunteer to read the text and two others to mime it as the first is reading. Ask readers, mimers, and others in turn: What stood out for you as the text was read and mimed?

Study Bible

See the annotations on John 15:1-17 in *NISB*, 1938-39.

See annotations in *NISB* p. 965 for the wordplay involved in Isa 5:7. Jesus also alludes to Ezek 19:10-14 where Judah is compared to a vine that has been destroyed, finally by fire. Note the *NISB* annotation on these verses (p. 1182): "The message is shockingly unambiguous…(T)he Davidic dynasty is no more."

the Father has loved him; he has loved them, and they are to abide in his love. You've been baptized in this lovely water; swim, wade, float in it. How so? By keeping his commandments, just as he has kept his Father's commandments. Jesus tells them this so that they can be completely joyful (15:11), but they won't rejoice until later (16:22; 20:20).

Jesus then reminds them what his commandment is: Love one another as Jesus has loved them (15:12; see 13:34-35) by laying down his life for his friends. He is the good shepherd, who lays down his life for his sheep (10:11, 15, 17-18). Jesus doesn't call them servants anymore but friends, or, translated more accurately, not slaves (*douloi*) but beloved ones (*philoi*). Slaves don't know what the master is up to; they don't have a place in the house (8:35), but the beloved ones do. Jesus has told them everything from the Father; he has "exegeted" God (1:18). Jesus says that he chose them (not the other way around) and appointed them to bear (eternal) fruit, with the result that the Father will grant their in-Jesus'-name requests (15:16; also 14:13-14; 16:23, 26). Fruit-bearing prayers are loving prayers, grounded in God's love for Jesus, his love for us, and our love for one another (see the annotations in *NISB* 1941 on 16:23-24 and 16:26-27).

Read aloud John 15:1-10, then Isa 5:1-7. What similarities and differences do you note?

How Is What Is Happening in this Discourse Like What Is Happening in the World Today?

Where in the world is a community of love, those people who are laying down their lives for one another? My class pointed to local ministries, such as a breakfast feeding program for the homeless and Habitat for Humanity, which builds houses for low-income people. They also mentioned the Howard University students going to New Orleans to assist hurricane victims during the 2006 spring break.

I think of The Friends of Jesus, a church that takes its name from John 15. It is one of several churches that grew out of the ecumenical Church of the Saviour in Washington, D.C., which "emphasizes a commitment to an inward journey—deepening one's relationship with God—and an outward journey—mission and service." Ministries that have come out of Church of the Savior include healthcare and hospice care for homeless men, retreat centers, after school programs, and senior housing and programs. And members commit themselves to disciplines such as prayer, Bible study, and worship attendance.

How Is What Is Happening in this Discourse Like What Is Happening in Your Life?

In response to this question, my class said: "Becoming constant without thinking." "Writing letters to Congress about issues related to children and the elderly." "Working for justice." And as I was capturing some of their thoughts here, I added a few of my own: Being in touch with the source through prayer, poetry, service. No dichotomy between worship and service. Grounding myself in love. Being tender with people and with myself.

Tender. With myself. I'm going to stay with that for awhile. I often have difficulty abiding myself, abiding in myself, with myself. But stay. Do you feel, see, hear, smell, and taste the love in you and around you: the clicking computer keys, the words miraculously appearing on the screen (and as I stop, the blinking cursor—curse that cursor; no, bless it), the sore wrist, the relaxing jaw, the filling breath, the drawings, paintings, and poems on the wall. Stay, dwell—well. Well? Living water.

> **Reflections**
>
> Tell a story about a specific incident in which your church expressed "love for one another."

> **Reflections**
>
> 1. In what specific ways do you "abide in Jesus"? What does it look like, feel like, etc.? How might you put it in non-religious language?
> 2. What kind of people do you have difficulty loving? What things about yourself do you have difficulty loving? How are the two related? What specific ways are helpful in nurturing love for others and for yourself?

> **Teaching Tips**
>
> Conclude by singing "Help Us Accept Each Other" (*United Methodist Hymnal*, hymn #560), and/or "Canticle of Love: Response 1," (*United Methodist Hymnal*, hymn #646).

The Son One with the Father

Jesus is on his way to the Father, and from that vantage point suspended between the world below and the world above, he prays. He prays that the oneness he shares with God might be shared with all believers, all hearers, and all readers of this Gospel. Can I get an "amen" on that?

What Is Happening in this Prayer?

Jesus sums up his Farewell Discourses (14:1-16:33) on a note of peace and courage: "I have said this to you, so that in me you may have peace. In the world you face persecution. But take courage: I have conquered the world" (16:33). Yes, they will face persecution because the world will hate them and even kill them (15:18-16:4*a*)! The Advocating Spirit of truth, though, will convict the world of sin, righteousness, and judgment, and will truthfully guide the disciples (16:4*b*-15). Furthermore, the sorrow that they have over Jesus' death will give birth to joy (16:16-24). And the disciples get it, or at least they say they do. They know that Jesus knows all things (you know?), and they believe that he has come from God (16:30). Jesus is, understandably, a little skeptical, and he tells them that the hour has come for them to be scattered home, with Jesus alone! But he says all of this, the Farewell Discourses, for the purpose of peace.

And for that purpose he prays. The prayer is sometimes called the "High Priestly Prayer," but it is really more intercession than anything else—intercession for the disciples and future believers. It can be divided nicely into three major sections: Jesus prays for himself (17:1-5), for his disciples (17:6-19), and for future believers (17:20-24). (17:25-26 might be looked upon

Lectionary Loop

Seventh Sunday of Easter, Year B, John 17:6-19
Seventh Sunday of Easter, Year C, John 17:20-26

Study Bible

See *NISB*, 1942-43.

Sources

See *Word and Soul: A Psychological, Literary, and Cultural Reading of the Fourth Gospel* (Collegeville, MN: The Liturgical Press, 2001), 104-12.

as a conclusion, in which Jesus returns to his prayer for the disciples.) We, Jesus' beloved, are now entering into the bosom of the Father. We, the readers and hearers, are ushered into the Son's oneness with the Father.

First, Jesus prays for his own glorification. Glory, glory, glory! Jesus has manifested glory through his miraculous signs (2:11; 17:4, 22). Jesus reveals God's and his glory primarily through his death, resurrection, and ascension. It is the hour in which the Son of Man is glorified (12:28; 13:31-32); the Father will glorify his name (12:28). In it Jesus is lifted up from the earth (3:14; 8:28; 12:32, 34), he gives eternal life to believers (3:14), and he draws all people to himself (12:32). In it, all will know that Jesus is "I am" (8:28). Believers now participate in that glory (1:14; 17:24), which is experienced in worship as heightened awareness, an altered state of consciousness.

The hour has come. Jesus (as well as John) has been continually saying that his hour has not come (2:4: 7:30; 8:20), but Jesus now realizes that the time of his death, resurrection, and ascension has dawned (12:23; 13:1). And in this hour Jesus prays that the Father will glorify the Son so that the Son can glorify him (17:1). The Father has given the Son authority (or power, 1:12) to give eternal life to the Father-to-the-Son-given-ones (6:37, 39). Then he defines eternal life: Know the only true God (revealed by the one who is the truth, 14:6) and the sent-one Jesus Christ (the only occurrence in John of Jesus referring to himself in this way). Jesus has constantly been calling God the one "who sent me" (5:23; 6:38; 7:16; etc.) and himself as the one whom God has sent (3:34; 5:38; 6:29; 10:36). So Jesus validates his authority as God's agent, the God-sent-one. As the sent-one, he glorified God through his work on earth; now he is asking his Father to glorify him with preexistent Word-with-God, lovingly-given glory (17:5; see 1:1; 17:24).

The Father glorified Jesus through giving him word-keeping, Jesus-from-God knowing, God-sent-Jesus-believing disciples, and it is for these folks that he now prays (17:6-19). No longer in the world and coming to God, Jesus prays that they might be protected in the Holy-Father-given-to-Jesus name ("I AM"),

Teaching Tips

1. At the very beginning of the session, play a cooperative game. See http://www.learning-for-life.org/exploring/resources/99-720/x08.pdf for suggestions.

2. Follow the same procedure for reading this text as you did with the Prologue. Read it slowly while study participants meditatively move their bodies. See "Teaching Tips" on p. 20.

so that "they may be one, as we are one" (17:11). Jesus has already said that he and the Father are one (10:30). Not a mystical oneness but a functional oneness—not being but doing! Jesus does what he sees his Father doing (5:19). It is in this sense that he says he is in the Father and the Father is in him: his will is in God's and God's is in his (10:38; 14:10, 11); so also the disciples' will is to be one in Jesus, one in love.

The world hates these word-given, non-world-belonging (like Jesus) disciples (17:14, 16; see 15:18-25). Don't take them out of the world (though you will take out some of them later, 21:18-19); just protect them (in your name) from the evil (ruler of this world, 12:31; 14:30) one. Sanctified (set apart, made holy, "holy-fied") in God's-word truth, Jesus, the Father-sent one, has sent the disciples into the them-hating, non-belonging world, and for them Jesus self-sanctifies (17:17-19).

Jesus prays also for believers in him through the disciples' word, that all of them might be one in God and Jesus, so that the world to which they've been sent might believe that Jesus was sent—by God! Jesus has given them glory, one-making glory, making one through God-in-Jesus-in-disciples (though he also speaks of it as disciples-in-Jesus-in-God, 17:21-23). (Reminds me of the Matrushka dolls that nest inside of each other!) Not just one but totally, completely, perfectly one, so the world might know that God sent Jesus and has loved believers as he has loved Jesus. Jesus wants, longs, desires that these given ones might be with him (in that prepared place, 14:3) to see his glory, given lovingly and preexistently (see 17:24).

Jesus concludes by saying that contrary to the world, he knows the righteous Father, whom believers know has sent Jesus, who has made the Father's name known (through his works and word) and will make it known (through his death), so that God's love for Jesus might be in them and Jesus (i.e. his love for God and them?) might be in them.

Amen?

How Is What Is Happening in this Prayer Like What Is Happening in the World Today?

Words from this prayer are often used in the ecumenical movement. The World Council of Churches

> ## Teaching Tips
> Write a conversation between two disciples after they have heard Jesus pray this prayer.

(WCC) has on its homepage this description of its work: "It [the WCC] is a community of churches on the way to visible unity in one faith and one eucharistic fellowship, expressed in worship and in common life in Christ. It seeks to advance towards this unity, as Jesus prayed for his followers, 'so that the world may believe'" (John 17:21). (See http://www.oikoumene.org /en/home.html.)

I grieve, however, at how far Christians are from fulfilling Jesus' prayer that "they may be one." We are divided on issues such as homosexuality, abortion, the role of women, and biblical interpretation. But before we whine (not the fruit of the "vhine") too much, we must note that in local communities congregations are working together. For example, in the county where I live in suburban Washington, D.C., the Community Ministry of Prince George's County is "an interfaith coalition of four hundred congregations...working together to meet the needs of the poor through service, education, and advocacy." Over six thousand volunteers are involved in sheltering the homeless, feeding the hungry, and clothing the ill-clad. (See http://www.cmpgc. org.) I'm sure that many such ecumenical organizations exist across the country, demonstrating ways that Christians are working together in love.

How Is What Is Happening in this Prayer Like What Is Happening in Your Life?

In what ways am I "at one" with others? One, one, one. I suppose this oneness happens most often in worship, as we gather together to center ourselves in love. Friends (Quakers) claim to worship a lot. Even our monthly business sessions are called Meetings for Worship for the Conduct of Business, and decisions are made by consensus. Sometimes we will speak about "being in unity" with a particular proposal, though a long-time Quaker once told me that although a group may have consensus, only God can give unity.

One, one, one. Am I at one with myself? No, that's why my latest book is about the man who said, "My Name is Legion, for we are many" (Mark 5:9). Maybe I better withdraw from people and get my act together so I can be at one with them. Or maybe...

Reflections

What ecumenical efforts are you or your church involved in? In what sense is that effort realizing Jesus' prayer about believers being one?

Teaching Tips

Have group members write a poem beginning with the line: "I in you, and you in me." Share.

Pilate-ing to the Cross

Off Jesus goes to the Father. But how does he go? By death. But it's not a natural death ; rather, an execution, a political execution in which the Roman Empire crushes someone it perceives as a threat. We have a confrontation between two powers, between two worlds, the world above and the world below. We know who is going to win because Jesus has overcome the world (John 16:33). Let us see how it is going to play itself out.

What Is Happening in this Section of the Passion Narrative?

Chapters 18-19 constitute John's version of the passion narrative. At this point, the events narrated are quite similar to those in the Synoptics: arrest, appearances before Jewish and Roman authorities, crucifixion, and burial. John, however, has his own spin. For one, his account of the trial before Pilate is nearly twice as long as that of the Synoptics (see Mark 15:1-15; Matt 27:11-26; Luke 23:2-5, 17-25). Also, throughout the passion narrative, John focuses on two themes: Jesus is king, and Jesus is judge. Let us see how those themes work themselves out in our text for today.

Again, let me give my class the first call in response to the question, "What's happening here?" "Injustice and oppression of the truth," they said. But what is truth? Oh, that's Pilate's line, and we will get to that in good time. First, John structures this story masterfully: he alternates seven scenes in which Pilate goes outside his headquarters (the *praetorium*) to talk with the Jews and inside to talk with Jesus. Out/in/out/in/out/in/out.

Lectionary Loop
Last Sunday after Pentecost, Year B, John 18:33-37

Study Bible
See *NISB* 1941-42.

Sources
See *Word and Soul: A Psychological, Literary, and Cultural Reading of the Fourth Gospel* (Collegeville, MN: The Liturgical Press, 2001), 113-22.

Teaching Tips
1. Sing "O Sacred Head, Now Wounded" (*United Methodist Hymnal*, hymn #286).
2. Read the text aloud as a readers' theatre. Ask for volunteers for these roles: narrator, Pilate, Jesus, soldiers, Judeans. Have them read the text. Ask: What stood out for you?

Who will Pilate choose? We readers and hearers know which he will choose. Alas, he will choose the friends of Caesar, not of Jesus. We know where our loyalties lie too: We are on the inside, with Jesus.

So first Pilate goes outside to meet the Jews (18:28-32, Scene 1). They don't go into his headquarters so that they might not be defiled to eat the Passover. (They are good and righteous, aren't they?) We do have here a problem of chronology. All the Gospels agree that Jesus is crucified on a Friday, but in the Synoptics it is also the day of Passover. In John it is the day before Passover (see 19:31 where it says that the Jews didn't want the bodies left on the crosses for the Sabbath, because "that Sabbath was a day of great solemnity," i.e. it was both a Sabbath and the day of Passover; see also 13:1.) Though the Synoptics and John agree on so much of the events of the Passion, they disagree on the dates that they took place.

Pilate asks for the accusation, and when he hears their vague response, he tells them to judge Jesus by their own law. But the Jews, who have been seeking to kill Jesus (5:18; 8:40), say they're not allowed to put someone to death, that is, crucify someone. Thus is fulfilled Jesus' earlier word about his manner of death; he will be lifted up (and draw all people to himself, 12:32).

Pilate then goes inside to talk to Jesus (18:33-38a, Scene 2) and asks him if he is King of the Jews, a title that will reverberate throughout the rest of the passion narrative (see 18:39; 19:3, 14-15, 19-22). Jesus is king of Israel, not king of the Jews (1:49; 12:13). Jesus inquires about the source of Pilate's question. Pilate says, "I am not a Jew, am I?" (18:35). No, but is he going to side with the Jews concerning Jesus? Jesus says that his kingdom is not from this world. Like Jesus himself, his kingdom is from above (see 8:23). This fact is demonstrated by his followers not fighting to save him. The this-wordly kingdoms (of Rome) use violence to accomplish their ends, but the other-worldly kingdom (of Jesus) does not. Pilate says, "Thus, you are a king, huh?" Jesus says that his task is to bear witness to the truth (which he is full of, 1:14, 17), and truth-belongers listen to the voice of the truly good shepherd (10:4, 16). Pilate throws up his hands, shakes his head and rolls his eyes: "What's truth?" We know: Jesus is! (14:6).

Pilate then goes back outside (18:38b-40, Scene 3) to say to the Jews that he finds no case against Jesus; but he is accustomed to releasing someone for the Passover, and he offers them Jesus. The crowd wants Barabbas, a bandit, a brigand, a non-good shepherd to whom the sheep will not listen (10:1, 8).

Inside (19:1-3, Scene 4, the middle scene), Pilate has Jesus flogged, and the soldiers thorny-crown him and purple-robe him, striking him and hailing him as the Jewish king. Unknowingly they speak the truth, just as soldiers in the garden fell down in worship of "I am" (18:6).

Outside (19:4-8, Scene 5) Pilate presents the crowned and robed Jesus, saying as he has before (18:38) that he finds no crime in him. The chief priests and police call out for CRUCIFIXION!, so they can fulfill Jesus' words (18:32). Pilate repeats: No case (so get off my case)! Jews: Lawfully he ought to die for his Son of God claim, thus making himself equal to God (5:18).

Inside (19:9-1, Scene 6) fearful Pilate (like the blind man's parents and the disciples, afraid of the Jews? 9:22; 20:19) asks Jesus where he is from. (The Jews don't know that either, but like the healed blind man, we know that he is from God, 9:29, 33). Jesus gives him the silent treatment: no words from the Word. Pilate says that he has releasing or crucifying power. Ha! That's what he thinks. But Jesus has power to lay down his life and take it up again (10:17-18). And Pilate's got the power now only because it's been given to him from above, from God, so the hand-over-er (Judas? Caiaphas? God!?) is the greater sinner. Pilate wanted to release him, but the Jews cry from the outside, "If you release him, you're not Caesar's friend. You gotta choose: Are you Caesar's beloved or Jesus' beloved?" (15:15). Anyone claiming kingship is anti-Caesar. Choose, man: Caesar or Jesus. (Hey, we readers and hearers choose Jesus!)

Outside (19:13-16a, Scene 7) Pilate takes Jesus and sits (him? See the *NISB* marginal notes and annotations on 19:13) on the judge's bench, which John emphasizes by saying its Aramaic name *Gabbatha*. Order in the court! Here comes the judge: Jesus! God has given all judgment to him, the Son of Man (5:22, 27). John notes that it is noon on Passover Preparation Day, the time the Passover lambs were killed. Pilate says to the Jews, "Here's your King!"

Jews: "Crucify him away!"

Pilate: "Crucify your King?!"

Chief priests: "We have no king but...but...CAE-SAR!"

Audience: Gasp!

What did they say? Isn't there a Passover hymn that says something like, "We have no king but God"? But they say that their king is...is...Caesar! They're Caesar's beloved. For us, there is no king but God, who is revealed in Jesus! No violent Caesar, just non-violent God! And with that, Pilate hands him over to Caesar's violence: crucifixion.

How Is What Is Happening in this Section of the Passion Narrative Like What Is Happening in the World Today?

My class came up with the following answers to this question: the plight of the poor, those suffering from the powerful in leadership, and the Iraq war. I would like to spotlight the war because Jesus' words in 18:36, "My kingdom is not from this world...," are often used to support a Christian pacifist position, which eschews violence. Yet most Christians are not pacifists, and some have supported the Iraq war. Although Jesus was a victim of state-sanctioned violence, Christians have had a history of both supporting and opposing violence.

How Is What Is Happening in this Section of the Passion Narrative Like What Is Happening in Your Life?

How do I crucify myself? I condemn myself for not being perfect, I tell myself that I'm a loser, a fake.

Is it time to talk about Resurrection now?

Teaching Tips

Have newspapers available so that people can make collages of the Pilates in our world today. Have participants share their creations with the group.

Reflections

1. Why do some churches support war?
2. Why do some churches oppose war?
3. What are some Scriptures that churches point to in order to defend their positions?

Teaching Tips

Have group members write a letter to Pilate. Share.

Appearing Mary-ly, Beating the Tom-Tom

John presents us with memorable characters: Nicodemus, the Samaritan woman, the man born blind, and Pilate. The resurrection narrative presents us with two more: Mary Magdalene and Thomas. They serve as models of faith. Let us enter into their experience—their tears and their demands—so that we too might know resurrection power.

What Is Happening in this Appearance Story?

All four Gospels are markedly similar in the Passion narratives, as they tell of Jesus' arrest, trial, death, and burial. Yet the resurrection narratives are all quite different. Though each tells of an empty tomb and appearances, they differ on where Jesus appeared, when he appeared, and to whom he appeared. Mark has only one appearance, in Galilee, and it is predicted and not narrated; Matthew has two appearances, one to the women at the empty tomb and another to the disciples in Galilee. Luke has two appearances, one to the two disciples on the road to Emmaus and another to the entire group of disciples in Jerusalem.

John has four appearances: one to Mary Magdalene at the tomb, another to the disciples minus Thomas on Easter Sunday night in Jerusalem, another to the disciples with Thomas a week later in Jerusalem, and still another to the seven disciples at the Sea of Galilee. Let us give our attention to these first three appearances narrated in chapter 20.

My class highlighted the movement of the text: death to life, absence to presence, grief to joy, fear to peace, and disbelief to belief. We retrace these journeys.

Lectionary Loop

Easter Sunday, Year A,
John 20:1-18
Second Sunday of Easter, Year A,
John 20:19-31

Study Bible

See *NISB*, 1948-50.

Sources

See *Word and Soul: A Psychological, Literary, and Cultural Reading of the Fourth Gospel* (Collegeville, MN: The Liturgical Press, 2001), 122-133.

Still in the dark (like Nicodemus?), Mary Magdalene comes to Jesus' new garden tomb (see 19:41) early on Sunday to find the stone removed. This is the only time Mary appears in John. (In the Synoptics she is one of a number of women who come to the tomb.) She runs to tell Simon Peter and the disciple whom Jesus loves that she doesn't know where "they have laid [Jesus]." We know, and Mary will know soon. We have previously encountered this "Beloved Disciple" (BD) to whom Jesus runs: reclining next to Jesus at the table (13:23-25, much the same position that Jesus has with God, 1:18), with Peter as they go into the high priest's courtyard (18:15), at the cross with Jesus' mother (19:26-27), and at Jesus' appearance at the Sea of Galilee (21:7, 20-24). When he sees the non-Lazarus burial clothes lying there, he believes, yet John adds the perplexing word that they did not understand the rising-from-dead Scripture. So they go back home.

Mary weeps outside the tomb. (O Mary, don't you weep!) She looks into the tomb and sees two white-robed angels who ask her why she is a weeping woman. She says essentially what she told Peter and the Beloved Disciple (see 20:2, though she says "my" and "I" instead of "the" and "we"). She then turns around and sees Jesus standing there, but she doesn't know it is he (but we know it, and we smile). He asks exactly the same question the angels asked (see 20:13) but adds, like he did at the beginning of his ministry, "What are you looking for?" (20:15, see 1:38). She thought he was the gardener (Ha ha ha!) and tells him that if he has carried Jesus away, she'll take him away. (Boy, is she in for a surprise!)

Jesus: "Mary!"

Mary: "Rabbouni!" (Aramaic for Teacher).

Jesus calls her by name and leads her out of her unknowing (see 10:3). Jesus tells her not to hold on to him. Apparently that is what she is doing, but Jesus is still in the middle of the hour, and he must ascend to the Father; he can't be held back. To loosen her grip, Jesus gives her a commission: Go to the bros. Tell them (and you can quote me on this): "I am ascending to my/your Father and my/your God." (See the *NISB*

Teaching Tips

1. Sing "Breathe on Me, Breath of God" (*United Methodist Hymnal*, hymn #420)
2. Read this passage as a reader's theatre. Have people volunteer to read the following roles: Narrator, Mary, Angels, Jesus, Peter, beloved disciple, disciples, and Thomas. If your group is small, you can have one person play both the angels and the disciples, and if necessary you can have the same person play Thomas and Peter (or the beloved disciple). Tell people to be conscious of how their bodies respond to their lines (how their words become flesh). Encourage people to exaggerate. Then debrief.

Reflections

1. Have you ever been led out of unknowing?
2. What brought you from darkness to light?

Special Note on 20:17.) So Mary goes to tell the disciples, "I've seen the Lord!!!!!!" and tells them what he told her.

That evening, Jesus comes to the disciples (as promised, see 14:3, 18) behind locked doors. He greets them with peace (not as the world gives, 14:27) and shows them his hands/side, and they rejoice when they see him. (Their childbirthing pain is over, 16:20-22.) Jesus repeats peace and sends the disciples as the Father has sent him (sanctified in truth, 17:17-19). Then Jesus breathes on them the breath of life, making their dry bones live (Gen 2:7; Ezek 37:9), and says, "Receive the Holy Spirit," the everything-teaching Advocate (14:26). If you sin-forgive, they're forgiven; if you sin-retain, they're retained. (See *NISB* annotation on 20:23.)

Thomas, "the Twin," wasn't there, though. (Maybe he was out trying to die with Jesus or trying to find the way to where he was going, 11:16; 14:5.) When the disciples said to him what Mary said to them—"We have seen the Lord!"—Thomas said that he wants what the other disciples got: He wants to SEE the handy nail-prints (fair enough!), and he wants to put his finger and hands in the wounds (not fair enough; the disciples didn't get to do that). The next Sunday the disciples were housed with Thomas, and despite shut doors, Jesus again comes, stands, and peaces. Jesus tells Thomas to do exactly what he said that he needed to do in order to believe. And he adds: "Don't be unbelieving but believe" (20:27, my trans.).

Thomas declares, "My Lord (i.e. risen Lord) and my God (i.e. Word in the beginning, the Son revealing the Father, 1:1, 18)!" It is not Caesar (often addressed as "Lord and God"), whom the Jews and chief priests find so beloved and kingly; it is Jesus! Jesus then asks him if he has believed because he has seen (he has certainly not touched!). Jesus then blesses non-seeing believers, that is, those he has prayed for, who believe through the disciples' word (17:20)—in other words, us. Our Risen Lord-God Jesus blesses us.

John adds quickly a conclusion, not just to this story of the Risen Lord but to the whole book (20:30-31). Sometimes some have said that this was the conclusion

Study Bible

See the *NISB* annotation and the Special Note on 20:27 (p. 1949).

Reflections

1. What does it mean to bless someone?
2. How does it affect you to know that the Risen Lord blesses you?
3. Whom do you bless, and how do they bless you?

to the first edition of the Gospel. Perhaps. Nevertheless, it says that Jesus did lots of other signs (so apparently the death-resurrection-ascension is a sign) for his disciples that are unwritten. These written ones (water-wine, paralytic-raising, etc.) are so the non-seers (us!) might believe that the Messiah, the Son of God, is not Caesar (who also was addressed as Son of God) but Jesus, and they might by believing in his name (and becoming children of God, 1:12) have (enlightened, 1:4) life (in this dark Roman world of death).

How Is What Is Happening in this Appearance Story Like What Is Happening in the World Today?

Where in the world is grief turned into joy? One of my students, who had just returned from a mission trip to help Hurricane Katrina victims, said that people were still grieving from the impact of the hurricane, but that some have found new homes and new lives elsewhere. I think of the 118 former death row inmates who, since 1972, have been exonerated. (See a few of their stories at the website of the National Coalition to Abolish the Death Penalty http://www.ncadp.org/fact_sheet4.html.) A recent movie entitled "The Exonerated" tells the story of six such persons. (See information about ordering the movie at http://ncadp.org.) In October each year Amnesty International U.S.A. coordinates the "National Weekend of Faith in Action on the Death Penalty" (see http://www.amnestyusa.org/faithinaction/).

How Is What Is Happening in this Appearance Story Like What Is Happening in Your Life?

Did I really talk about crucifying myself in the last session? Yeah, I guess I did. How then do I raise myself? Or to speak of it from the perspective of the disciples: How do I go from fear to peace? I suffer from generalized anxiety disorder (GAD!) and depression, so I take medication and receive psychotherapy. But my best medication is meditation, in which I sometimes sit (alone or with fellow believers) and focus on my breathing, walk and focus on the surrounding sights and sounds, draw abstract pictures, or write poetry.

> **Teaching Tips**
>
> Have the group members write what Thomas might have said to Jesus following his question and blessing in 20:29.

> **Teaching Tips**
>
> Have recent newspapers and magazines available. Instruct people to make collages of contemporary "resurrection stories," where grief has been turned into joy.

> **Teaching Tips**
>
> Lead group members in a guided meditation. Instruct them to get comfortable in their chairs. Say the following: Imagine that when you are inhaling, Jesus is breathing the Spirit into you. And when you are exhaling, imagine that you are sending that Spirit out into the world. Instruct them to remain focused on their breath. If the mind wanders, simply bring it back to the breath. Share.

The Miraculous Catch of Sheep

What Is Happening in this Appearance Story?

Folks in my class said, "Recognition," "Restitution," "Commissioning," "Validation of the witness of the Beloved Disciple," and "Miracle." Let's start with this last-mentioned item. The story is certainly a miracle (reported also in Luke 5:1-11), but is it a sign? Some interpreters say that it is, but it is really contained in the seventh sign: the death, resurrection and ascension of Jesus.

John 20 is sometimes called the Gospel's Epilogue, corresponding to the Prologue (1:1-18), but it seems very different from the Prologue. It probably should be looked upon as a continuation of the resurrection narratives in John 20. (See the *NISB* annotations on 21:1-25, p. 1950-51.)

It seems like an altered state of consciousness is required to make sense out of this story. Why don't the disciples recognize Jesus when he has already shown himself to them twice? Why are they going fishing? Why 153 fish? Why did Peter put his clothes on before he jumped into the sea? Why did Jesus speak so cryptically about Peter's death and the beloved disciple's non-death? It seems that when a resurrection story is told, we are entering a new plane, a transcendent one. It's like *Alice in Wonderland*, where things don't quite make sense. We have entered into the world above, though the events are happening in the world below. We enter into worship.

Unlike Peter, we've already got our clothes on, so let's jump in! Peter is out fishing in the Sea of Tiberias (another name for Sea of Galilee) with six other disciples, but they have caught nothing. Zilch! Zippo!

Study Bible

See *NISB* 1950-51. Also review the introductory article on John, 1905-07.

Teaching Tips

Use the "playback" method to act out the story. Ask for five volunteers. Explain that one person will read the story, and then four people will act it out using anything except their Bibles. Tell them not to be concerned about delivering their lines accurately as printed in the Bible but rather to act out the story in a way that is meaningful to them. After the reader reads the text, have the others immediately act it out without consulting their fellow actors. After the presentation, ask both the actors and the audience to discuss their experience.

Goose eggs! And just after daybreak, as the light is dawning, Jesus appears, but guess what? Mary Magdalene-like (20:14), the disciples don't recognize Jesus. (Duh!) Jesus tells them to cast the net to the right. They do so and then can't pull in the net because there are so many fish! BD realizes, "It's the Lord!" Of course, he recognizes him; he is the beloved, nestled "at Jesus' breast" (13:23, my trans.), and the man behind this Gospel (21:24). Peter puts on his clothes and jumps in the sea (!?); the rest come in the boat with the fish. (Peter and the BD, the great comedy team of the Gospel, John's Laurel and Hardy!)

Ashore, they see a charcoal fire (just like at Peter's denial, 18:18!), fish and bread (just like at the feeding, 6:9). Jesus tells them to bring some just-caught fish, so Peter drags the untorn net full of 153(!) fish, and Jesus tells them to come have breakfast. Nobody asks, "Who are you?" (Now that would be a stupid question!) They know (unlike previously, 21:4) that he is the Lord. They all have been brought into Jesus' breast, where the BD already is (see 21:7). Jesus does the feeding thing again, though with only seven people instead of five thousand. John adds that this is the third time the risen Jesus has appeared to the disciples, leaving out the appearance to Mary Magdalene. (Doesn't that count?)

After breakfast Jesus asks Peter (calling him Simon son of John, see 1:42) three times if he loves him (one time for each denial) and tells him three times to take care of his flock. Thus, question and commission. In the first two exchanges, Jesus uses a form of the Greek word *agapaō*, while Peter uses a form of *phileō*. But in the third exchange, they both use a form of *phileō*. Sometimes people say that Jesus initially asked for unselfish love, but Peter responds with brotherly love, which Jesus finally settles for. But twice in this Gospel Jesus is said to love the Father, once using *agapaō* (3:35) and once using *phileō* (5:20), so it seems that they are used interchangeably.

Peter is to be the shepherd, taking over for Jesus in tending the sheep (10:1-18), but also, like Jesus, he will be a good shepherd in dying for the sheep. Jesus gives him some perplexing words, which we probably would not understand if John did not tell us that they refer to his (God-glorifying-like-Jesus) death. Peter is now going to follow Jesus, as Jesus told him he would do (13:36) and lay down his life, as he promised he would do (13:37). (Traditions arose in the third century that Peter was crucified upside down. See the Web Gallery of Art, http://www.wga.hu/, for paintings of Peter's death by Caravaggio in 1600 and by Michelangelo in 1546-50.) The gospel will continue to be a threat to the powers! And Jesus adds, "Follow me" (in death! But see 1:43).

Then Peter sees the BD already following. Just in case we've forgotten, John reminds us that at supper the BD reclined "upon Jesus' breast" (21:20; see 13:23). Peter asks about him, and Jesus says, "If I want him to hang around until I come, what of it? You, follow me!" (21:22). John adds that the rumor spread that the BD wouldn't die, but that is not what Jesus said.

But what about the BD? He is the one who wrote the Gospel, or better, caused the Gospel to be written. (The Greek can have either force.) The BD is the Gospel's authority rather than its author. "We" know his testimony is true, that is, the community in which the Gospel was first read affirms his testimony as the one through whom the Spirit speaks, reminding of what Jesus said and did (14:26). It's interesting to note the change of persons in 21:24-25: "This is the disciple…" (third-person singular), "we know…" (first-person plural), and "I suppose…." The "I" here is the author of the Gospel, but he is grounding the Gospel on the authority of the BD, the "true testifier" who was Jesus' beloved bosom buddy. Just as Jesus came out of the Father's bosom to reveal the Father (1:18), so this disciple comes out of Jesus' breast to reveal Jesus. Peter shepherds and dies; the BD writes and lives.

How Is What Is Happening in this Appearance Story Like What Is Happening in the World Today and in Your Life?

In March 10, 2006, Tom Fox, a member of a Christian Peacemaker Team (CPT) in Iraq, was found dead after three and a half months of captivity (see http://www.cpt.org/memorial/tomfox/main.php). Tom was a friend (acquaintance) and a Friend (member of the Religious Society of Friends, also known as Quakers). He went to Palestine and Iraq in order to, in the words of the CPT slogan, "reduce violence by getting in the way." Jesus says, "I am the way" (14:6). Tom Fox got in Jesus' way and laid down his life for his sheep—Iraqi sheep but American sheep too.

Some of us are called, however, to witness and to challenge the powers through writing. My favorites include scholars J. Dominic Crossan, Catherine Keller, and Richard Horsley, and poets E. Ethelbert Miller, Lucille Clifton, and Jay Wright (see http://www.poets.org/).

And me? I try...to testify...to give a witty witness ...for love...for peace.

It's right for me to write. It's a rite. Right/write (spirited, true) worship...and witness.

Reflections

1. What contemporary writers do you think effectively tell the Christian story for our day?
2. How do you give witness? To what do you give?

THE BOOK OF EXODUS

A STUDY BY

FRANK M. YAMADA

Frank M. Yamada is Assistant Professor of Old Testament at Seabury
Theological Seminary in Evanston, IL.

THE BOOK OF EXODUS
Outline

I. Introduction
    A The Structure and Context of Exodus
    B. Major Themes within the Book of Exodus
    C. Interpretative Assumptions

II. Session 1—The Family Story Continues: Exodus 1:1-22
    A. Ancestral Traditions
    B. From Favor to Oppression
    C. Resistance of Faithful Women

III. Session 2—The Birth of Moses: Exodus 2:1-10
    A. The Caring Nurture of a Mother
    B. Past Legacy and Future Hopes
    C. Three Nameless Women

IV. Session 3—The Call of Moses: Exodus 3:1–4:17
    A. The Call and Commission of Moses
    B. Resistance to God's Calling
    C. God's Self-Disclosure

V. Session 4—The Ten Plagues, "Let My People Go": Exodus 7:8–12:36
    A. The Knowledge of the LORD
    B. The Hardening of Pharaoh's Heart
    C. The Passover

VI. Session 5—Deliverance at the Sea: Exodus 14–15
    A. Parting the Waters
    B. Tension between Divine and Human Action
    C. The Response of the People

VII. Session 6—"Is the Lord Among Us or Not?" Murmurings in the Wilderness and God's Provision: Exodus 15:22–17:7
    A. The Hardships of the People and the Provision of God
    B. Manna—Nourishment and Sign
    C. Water—Thirst-Quencher and Sign

VIII. Session 7—Revelation at Sinai and the Meaning of Covenant, Exodus 19
    A. Basis for Covenant
    B. Nature of Covenant
    C. Covenant as Treaty
    D. Covenant as Theme

IX. Session 8—The Ten Words: Exodus 20:1-17
    A. Literary Context
    B. Structure

X. Session 9—The Golden Calf Incident, God Revealed in Judgment: Exodus 32:1-35
    A. Israel's Transgression
    B. Moses as Mediator—Intercessor
    C. Moses as Mediator—Judgment

XI. Session 10—Building the Tabernacle, the People's Faithful Response: Exodus 36–40
    A. Obedience of the People
    B. Completion of the Holy Space
    C. Renewal of the Covenant

Introduction

The Pastor's Bible Study on Exodus

Every social group has core stories, customs, and histories that contribute to its character. These formative traditions are the building blocks of collective identity. As a third-generation Japanese American, I have inherited both national and family stories. Growing up in the United States meant that stories about the Revolutionary War and legislation such as the Constitution serve as essential parts of the American tradition in which I was socialized. Being a Japanese American who grew up on the West Coast meant that I also inherited stories about the struggles of my father's family during World War II, when more than 120,000 Japanese and Japanese Americans were remanded. Core stories and traditions serve as the foundation of any group's identity. The ancient Israelites were no different.

The book of Exodus recounts two such core stories: the miraculous liberation of the Israelites from Egypt and the establishment of God's covenant with Israel at Sinai. Canonically and historically, the traditions within the book of Exodus serve as the core of Israelite theology and identity. Because these stories are so significant, Exodus contains some of the most familiar scenes in the Bible. Religious traditions and popular culture draw heavily from stories such as the deliverance at the sea; the ten plagues; the worshiping of the golden calf; and the covenant at Sinai, including the giving of the Ten Commandments. For centuries, the book has captured the imagination of many religious traditions and cultures. The idea of covenant, including the Ten Words at Sinai, is central to both Christian and

Sources

There are many fine resources on the book of Exodus that will work well within a pastor's library:

Brueggemann, Walter. "The Book of Exodus: Introduction, Commentary, and Reflections" in *New Interpreter's Bible*, vol. 1 (Nashville: Abingdon, 1994) 675-981.

Childs, Brevard. *The Book of Exodus: A Critical, Theological Commentary*. Old Testament Library (Louisville: Westminster, 1974).

Fretheim, Terence E. *Exodus*. Interpretation (Louisville: John Knox, 1991).

Meyers, Carol. *Exodus*. New Cambridge Bible Commentary (Cambridge: Cambridge University Press, 2005).

Pixley, George V. *On Exodus: A Liberation Perspective*. Translated by Robert R. Barr. (New York: Maryknoll, 1987).

Jewish identity. The LORD's deliverance of Israel from the bondage of Egypt has also served as the core tradition upon which African American and Latin American liberation theologies were formed. At the heart of the book of Exodus is God's self-revealing purpose. The LORD is made known to Israel through the liberation of the people from slavery and through the establishment of the covenant with Israel at Sinai.

The Structure and Context of Exodus

The contents of the book of Exodus focus on the liberating work of Israel's God. When one examines the exodus of the Israelites, it is important to note that the LORD liberates the people from their slavery for a purpose: to be able to worship their God freely. Thus, the Israelites move out of the oppressive slavery in Egypt to the service and worship of the LORD. Noting this thematic movement, the book divides into two parts:

- Exod 1:1–15:21   Liberation from Egypt
- Exod 15:22–40:38 Liberation to serve the LORD

The first section begins with a description of Israel's life of bondage in Egypt, and recounts the early life and calling of Moses. The central conflict in Exod 1–15 is between Pharaoh and the LORD, which reaches its climax at the sea (Exod 14–15), where Pharaoh's armies are drowned in a miraculous turn of events. The second section marks the movement of the people out of Egypt and into the Sinai region. This geographical change marks an identity shift for the Israelites as they make the transition from a life of slavery into the covenantal reality of being the people of God. After a series of wilderness stories, in which the LORD provides sustenance for the journey (15:22–18:27), Moses and the Israelites arrive at Mt. Sinai. On the mountain of God, the LORD reveals the Law to Israel, setting forth the covenantal expectations between God and God's people (Exod 20 ff.).

Major Themes within the Book of Exodus

Throughout this series of studies, I will be developing a number of primary themes within the book of Exodus—the liberation of God's people from the Egyptian empire, the revelation of the covenant at

---

Reflections

1. What are the core stories that make up your identity?
2. Consider your family's heritage and background. What are the stories that shape your family's collective identity?
3. What recent or past events contribute to our nation's identity or sense of being? What are your feelings about the direction and shape of that identity?

Sinai, Israel's journey of becoming the people of God, and the abiding presence of the LORD. Common to these themes is the idea of God's self-disclosure to Israel through law and history. Throughout the book of Exodus, this central theme is tempered with human responses of faithfulness and disobedience. The LORD's liberation of Israel from Egypt involves the participation of faithful human beings (e.g., the Hebrew midwives, Moses, Aaron, Miriam, etc.). Human initiative, however, also contributes to the oppression of God's people in the case of Pharaoh's unwillingness to let the Israelites go. Moreover, human actions lead to God's judgment on Israel in the story of the golden calf (Exod 32). Ultimately, covenant is the most complete expression of the LORD's interaction with humanity. It is the place where God's mighty deeds demand human faithfulness (cf. the preamble to the Decalogue in 20:2). Hence, the Law is a holy treaty, which requires a reciprocal response from God's people to the LORD's initial gracious act of liberation.

Interpretative Assumptions

The earliest trace of Israel's presence in Canaan comes from a victory stele erected by Pharaoh Merneptah in the early thirteenth century B.C.E. Israel is mentioned on the stone among a host of other defeated cities and regions. Hence, biblical scholars usually date the exodus from Egypt in the mid-thirteenth century, during the reign of Rameses II. However, the historical data on Israel from this period is lacking and disputed. The present form of Exodus is highly stylized and mythological in character, making historical reconstruction difficult. Moreover, the book is composed of at least three different sources and multiple traditions. The resulting text is filled with overlapping stories, incongruities, and inconsistencies that, nevertheless, tell a powerful story about Israel and its God.

Though the book of Exodus has a complex history of transmission, it has continued to have ongoing significance for readers up to the present. In the following set of studies, I will be working with the canonical or received text of Exodus as it is found within both the

Study Bible

For further discussion on the idea of covenant, see the excursus in *NISB*, 113-14. See also session 7 in this study.

Reflections

1. The book of Exodus points to many different ways that God reveals God's self to Israel. How is God revealed to you, or how has God revealed God's self to you in the past?

2. How do you see God at work in the collective life of your family, your faith community, and/or the nation?

3. The book of Exodus stresses the particularity of Israel's experience of God; but throughout the book, the LORD is also interested in having a reputation among the nations, especially Egypt. How do you see God at work in the world within the lives of other people and nations, including other religious traditions?

Jewish and Christian Scriptures. Moreover, my interpretative method assumes that readers from different cultural perspectives can arrive at diverse interpretations of the biblical material. An interpreter's race, ethnicity, and gender have an impact on the way he or she reads. Thus, the present set of studies will explore these interpretative issues as they arise from the texts of Exodus

Reflections

1. How does your gender, ethnicity, race, and/or class affect the way you interpret the Bible?
2. Do women read the Bible differently than men? If so, what are the differences?
3. The exodus tradition was very important for African Americans in the context of slavery. How would people who have experienced oppression interpret the exodus?

The Family Story Continues

The course of history can change with the smallest of events. A solitary act can often have profound effects that redirect the flow of human life. The opening chapters of the book of Exodus narrate such a shift. Three distinct movements can be traced within this opening episode: 1) the explicit link between the ancestral traditions of Genesis and Israel's life in Egypt; 2) a changed reality from favor to oppression; and 3) the resistance of faithful women within the community. At one end of the chapter, God's promises to the ancestors are remembered through the lineage of Jacob's family (1:1-7). In the middle scene, the paranoid Egyptian empire strikes back against the growing Israelite multitude (1:8-14). The resulting slavery and oppression provide the setting for the last episode in the chapter, in which the Hebrew midwives respond with faithful courage in the face of hostile authority (1:15-22). On either side of the oppression, hope and loyalty remain strong. Though the new realities of tyranny threaten to undo the Israelite community, the promises to the ancestors secure the people's hopes to God's faithful actions in the past. Similarly, the courageous actions of devout people in the present, in this case the daring noncompliance of the Hebrew midwives, serve to give strength and salvation in the present. Divine and human faithfulness work together in the beginning of the book to counter oppression.

Ancestral Traditions

Chapter 1 opens with a brief accounting of Jacob's family lineage. This genealogical introduction pulls

Lectionary Loop

Fourteenth Sunday after Pentecost, Year A, Exodus 1:8–2:10

Reflections

1. The biblical witness often portrays human life as being caught between God's promises and the harsh realities of life. How does one live in this tension between God's past faithfulness and the present struggles?

2. There are many events in our personal lives and in our collective life throughout history that create an abrupt change in the way that we view reality. Some examples in the West include the Holocaust, the Vietnam War, and 9/11. When the world as we know it turns upside down, how do we feel? How do we respond? Give some examples.

3. Talk about the different shades of faith and hope that sustain the people of God especially in times of hardship.

the reader's attention back to the stories of Israel's ancestors as found in the book of Genesis (Gen 46:8-27). Both books number Jacob's descendents at seventy. Moreover, the language that closes the Exodus genealogy hearkens back to the language of creation: "But the Israelites were *fruitful* and prolific; they *multiplied* and grew exceedingly strong, so that the land was *filled* with them" (Exod 1:7, emphasis mine). The three verbs, "be fruitful," "multiply," and "fill," all occur in Gen 1:28 when God blesses the human beings at the climax of creation. Thus, the genealogy functions to tie the events in the book of Exodus back to the creation and ancestral traditions in Genesis. This connection becomes clearer in Exod 3:6, when the LORD announces to Moses: "I am...the God of Abraham, the God of Isaac, and the God of Jacob."

This intentional connection between the world of Exodus and the world of the ancestors is important for at least two reasons. First, this literary allusion has implications for the way one thinks about God. By recalling the family of Jacob, which includes the language of blessing from Gen 1:28, the narrator effectively connects Israel's sojourn in Egypt with God's past promises. The children of Israel have yet to enter into the good land, but they are well on their way to becoming a great nation that lives under God's blessing. With the establishment of this genealogical link, the God who acted on behalf of Israel's ancestors is connected with this young, growing nation in Egypt.

Second, the connection to the ancestors also says something about Israel's continuity with itself. By v. 7, the family clan of Jacob has grown into a great multitude. The Israelite numbers have become so large that the people's presence threatens the pharaoh's sense of national security. The genealogical reference to Jacob's family in 1:1-7 marks the transition from family to nation. It also reaffirms the fact that the nation's roots emerge from the humble beginnings of Israel's ancestors. Remembering one's roots is an important key to identity. Whether a group is a small family clan or a large nation, its character is shaped by its connection to its forbearers. An empire always seeks to have dominion over the minds and hearts of its subjects, nullifying the particularity of different people's cultures and histories. Memory acts as an agent of resistance to such imperialistic tendencies by keeping alive a particular group's connection to its past.

From Favor to Oppression

Exodus 1:6 recounts the death of Joseph, marking a generational transition in the life of Israel. The first generation of Israelites in Egypt has passed away. This development in Israel parallels a transition in the Egyptian empire. Verse 8 reads, "Now a new king arose over Egypt, who did not know Joseph." Under the previous regime, Joseph and his family received favorable treatment because he was a head administrator over Pharaoh's kingdom. The new king of Egypt, however, decides to enforce a policy of oppression upon his Israelite subjects, forcing the descendents of Jacob into slavery. As the text makes clear, Pharaoh's policies are based in both his lack of knowledge of Joseph/Israel (v. 8) and the king's fear of the people's increasing numbers (vv. 9-10). Later in the chapter, Pharaoh's initial dread escalates to a national scale (v. 12). By the end of the chapter, all of Egypt is afraid of the Israelite population growth. With increased fear comes a more ruthless form of slavery. However, as the Egyptian persecution intensifies, the Israelites continue to multiply and spread at a greater rate.

The king of Egypt extends his policies of brutality in the last section of ch. 1. When the ruthless work of slavery does not inhibit the growth of the Israelite people, Pharaoh resorts to more drastic measures. In v. 15, the king instructs the Hebrew midwives to kill all of the male children who are born to the Israelites. The designation, "Hebrew midwives" or "midwives of the Hebrews" is ambiguous, suggesting that these women could be either Israelite or Egyptian. Regardless of their ethnic identity, the midwives act as heroic agents of noncompliance in the face of the empire's decree. In spite of the royal order, these women choose to fear God (v. 17, 21), siding not with Pharaoh but with God and the oppressed.

Reflections

1. How can memory be used to resist the imperialistic tendency, which seeks to erase the particular expressions and histories of diverse cultures (e.g., the Native Americans in the U.S.)?

2. In the U.S., many have used the metaphor of the melting pot to talk about the inherent unity within the nation. This image, however, often does a disservice to the many distinct cultures that have come to the States. What are some potentially harmful effects of grouping all people into a more unified but homogenous whole?

3. How does a dominant culture benefit from the loss of minority cultures through assimilation? What is lost for all parties involved?

Resistance of Faithful Women

The faithfulness and courage of the Hebrew midwives remind the reader that human actions matter in the face of an oppressive culture. God is not overtly present in these early chapters to deliver Israel from its oppression. In Exod 1:1-22, God is only active as a subject in v. 20, where God deals favorably with the midwives, helping the people to continue multiplying. Beyond this one reference, God appears only in relation to the women's conscientious resistance, i.e., they "feared God." In times of oppression and suffering, God may seem passive or only minimally present to act. Even when God's promises are recalled (1:1-7), the present realities of a ruthless empire can overwhelm people at any point in history. The opening chapter of Exodus reminds its audience that God remains present with those who act faithfully on behalf of the oppressed. These skilled women, whose job it was, literally, to handle issues of life and death, made a decision to choose life in the face of a decree of death. Shiphrah, Puah, and the rest of the Hebrew midwives remind the contemporary audience that moments of liberation can take shape in the faithful living of those who fear God.

Teaching Tips

The term, "Hebrew," which is used today to identify the language of the Hebrew Bible or is used synonymously with "Jew," had a different meaning in the context of ancient Israel. In the Hebrew Bible, the term usually refers to the Israelites or their ancestors when others encounter them outside of their territory (Gen 14:13; 43:32) or when others perceive them as outsiders (1 Sam 29:3). The word occurs most often in the Joseph story (Gen 39:14, 17; 40:15; 41:12), the Exodus narratives (Exod 1:15-16, 19; 2:6-7, 11, 13; 3:18; 5:3; 7:16), and in the context of the Philistine battles (1 Sam 4:6; 13:19; 14:11). It also occurs frequently within the context of slavery. In later New Testament usage, "Hebrew," is used to distinguish the Aramaic-speaking Jews from the Greek-speaking Jews (Hellenists). Paul refers to himself as "a Hebrew born of Hebrews" (Phil 3:5), which places him in the former category.

Reflections

1. Give some contemporary examples of people who sought to right the wrongs of oppression (e.g., Martin Luther King, Jr.; Ghandi; Elizabeth Cady Stanton; Sojourner Truth; etc.). How did/do such people make a difference in society? How can a person live a life of advocacy today?

2. Identify strong and faithful women in your lives, who individually or collectively have made a difference. What challenges do women face in trying to be advocates in their communities?

The Birth of Moses

The birth of Moses is told in the style of a heroic folklore legend. In fact, the beginning of Moses' life parallels the miraculous birth of an earlier Mesopotamian king, Sargon the Great, who reigned in the third millennium BCE. Such legends, which involve the miraculous deliverance of the infant hero from death, are common across cultures throughout history. In the New Testament, the Gospel of Matthew uses a similar type of story in recounting Jesus' escape from Herod's decree of death. The use of this genre tells the reader that the birth of Moses represents the birth of a future hero and leader in the Israelite community. In a setting of slavery, a child is born to this oppressed people, one who carries with him the hopes of their future liberation.

The Caring Nurture of a Mother

The setting of this story follows the Hebrew midwives' courageous acts of civil disobedience. After the women resisted Pharaoh's orders to kill the male infants of Israel (1:15-21), the king of Egypt increased the breadth of his command, charging all of the Egyptians, "Every boy that is born to the Hebrews you shall throw into the Nile, but you shall let every girl live" (1:22). Thus, what originally began as a specific command to the Hebrew midwives, Pharaoh now extends to all of Egypt. An empire feeds off of the fear of its subjects. Pharaoh knows this, and so he appeals to his people to carry out this law of genocide. In a time of national paranoia, legislation often coincides with a larger cultural fear within that society. For example, during World War II, President Franklin D. Roosevelt

---

Lectionary Loop
Fourteenth Sunday after Pentecost, Year A, Exodus 1:8–2:10

Reflections

1. Discuss the miracle of birth. Talk about important birth stories in your life (e.g., the birth of your children, grandchildren, nephews, nieces, or some special infant).
2. How can the birth of a child give hope to an individual or community?
3. When death threatens (as it does in this story through Pharaoh's decree), what gives people hope? What stories give you or your community glimpses of hope in the midst of struggle?

signed Executive Order 9066, which authorized the internment of Japanese and Japanese American people within the United States. This legislative move was made within a post-Pearl Harbor culture of fear in the U.S. In such times of national anxiety, legislative acts and cultural ethos can often work synergistically toward inhumane ends. Hence, within the book of Exodus, Moses is born into a culture of paranoia and death. This infant's survival in the midst of a genocidal decree is nothing short of miraculous, a fact that foreshadows Moses' future heroic status as liberator of Israel.

The early stories of Moses contain literary allusions to both Genesis and the later chapters within the book of Exodus. After the birth of Moses, his mother, who is unnamed within this story, sees the child and declares him good (2:2). Though the NRSV translation does not reflect it, the mother uses an idiom that is identical to God's proclamations over creation in Gen 1 (literally, "she saw that he was good," cf. Gen 1:4, 10, 12, etc.). She then hides the infant for three months in order to save the baby from Pharaoh's decree. When she cannot conceal him any longer, she makes a small vessel sealed with bitumen and pitch in order to float her son near the banks of the river (v. 3). The Hebrew word, *teba*, which the NRSV translates in Exod 2:3 as "basket," is found only here and in the Genesis flood narrative, where it is used for Noah's ark. Hence, Moses' mother acts in similar ways to the divine parent in the primeval history of God's people. She gives birth to a new creation, a future leader for Israel, and declares him "good." When his life is threatened because of the judgment of the king, she creates an ark for him and seals it with pitch and bitumen so that he might be saved upon the waters. Thus, the mother of Moses hearkens the reader back to God's providential care for humanity and creation in Genesis. Correspondingly, God's image is aligned with the caring nurture of a mother who responds to her creation within a culture of adversity.

Past Legacy and Future Hopes

The birth of Moses also foreshadows future events within the book of Exodus. When Moses' mother sets

---

Reflections

1. The character of Moses' mother is framed within the image of God as Creator. What images of God sustain your faith? What does the powerful image of a nurturing mother communicate about God (a common image for God in the Hebrew Bible)?

2. There are many parental images of God in the Bible and in our tradition. What are the strengths and limitations of these images?

her child in the water, the narrator makes clear that she places him on the reeds near the riverbank. The Hebrew word for "reed," is *suf*, which is the same term used within the name of the Red Sea (Hebrew, *yam-suf*, "Sea of Reeds"; cf. Exod 13:18 and 15:4). This is a clear allusion to Israel's future deliverance through the waters in Exod 14–15. As Moses is saved among the reeds of the river, so too will the Israelites be saved as they pass through the Sea of Reeds. As the scene progresses, the daughter of Pharaoh sees the basket near the riverbank while she is bathing. She has pity on the infant when she hears his cries (v. 6). In a similar manner, the LORD will respond with divine compassion when God's people cry out in response to their life of slavery (3:7). Finally, Moses' sister, who has been watching this entire scene unfold, suggests to Pharaoh's daughter that one of the Hebrew midwives could nurse the child. In an ironic twist, Moses' mother, who had earlier set her child in the basket upon the river, becomes the infant's wet nurse and gets paid for the task of providing sustenance for her own child! (v. 9). The baby Moses is nurtured and fed after his deliverance from the water. Likewise, the children of Israel will receive in the wilderness manna from heaven and water from a rock after they cross through the sea.

Hence, in the birth story of Moses, God's previous faithfulness to Israel's ancestors meets with God's future deliverance of the Israelites from slavery in Egypt. The story is replete with literary allusions that point both backward and forward in Israel's canonical story. Thus, located in the small package of this miraculous infant is the convergence of Israel's past legacy and future hopes. It is no wonder that when the LORD finally reveals the divine intention and identity to Moses in ch. 3—the LORD's first speech act in the book of Exodus—God's language refers both to the past promises made to the ancestors and to the impending plan to deliver the people from their oppression and lead them into the Promised Land (3:6-8). In the character of Moses, past and present collide. Promises are made real, and dreams of liberation come to pass.

Three Nameless Women

A final comment must also be made about another series of heroic women. In ch. 2, three nameless women play a vital role in the miraculous survival of the baby Moses.

1. Moses' mother gives birth to her child and bravely transgresses Pharaoh's command by protecting him from those who would seek his life. When she can no longer keep him hidden, she makes an ark for her child, setting him among the reeds. This act of sacrifice and desperation, which leaves the child exposed to the natural elements, nevertheless gives the child a hope for survival. Finally, the care of Moses' mother comes full circle as she is given the job of feeding her own son.

2. Moses' sister contributes to the salvation of her brother by keeping watch over the basket (v. 4) and by suggesting to Pharaoh's daughter that she allow one of the Hebrew midwives, Moses' mother, to nurse the child (vv. 7-8).

3. Pharaoh's daughter acts compassionately toward the child, even when her father has decreed death for all Hebrew male children.

All of these heroic women act subversively in an Egyptian culture that fears the Hebrew-other. Their actions, though subtle, point to faithful moments of civil disobedience. Like the Hebrew midwives in ch. 1, these three nameless women find a way to nurture life, live compassionately, and sustain those who are in oppression or danger. Their deeds may not require mighty staffs or involve awe-inspiring miracles, but the resulting salvation is no less powerful. In a world where men like Pharaoh have the power to legislate death, these women respond by "making a way out of no way."

Sources

The phrase "make a way out of no way," is commonly used by womanist theologians to describe the ways in which African American women forge out their own survival and the survival of their communities in situations of adversity. For a representative work on womanist theology, see Delores Williams, *Sisters in the Wilderness: the Challenge of Womanist God-talk* (Maryknoll: Orbis, 1993).

The Call of Moses

For most of the first two chapters of the book of Exodus, God remains silent and minimally active. After Moses flees from Pharaoh to Midian the narrator announces a change in the plot (2:23 ff.). After many years, the king of Egypt dies; but the Israelites remain in slavery. In 2:23-24, however, the cries of the Israelites rise up to God, who hears their groaning and remembers the covenant made to the ancestors. With God's act of remembrance, the movement toward Israel's deliverance moves into a new stage, which begins with the calling of Moses.

The Call and Commission of Moses

The call of Moses begins on Mt. Horeb, another biblical name for Sinai that occurs most frequently in the book of Deuteronomy. In the well-known burning bush story, the future leader of Israel encounters for the first time the God of his ancestors. Moses turns aside to see a bush that is on fire but not consumed. His fascination soon turns to awe as the LORD speaks to Moses, calling him by name, "Moses, Moses" (3:4). After Moses responds with the customary, "Here I am" (3:4), the LORD announces that the ground is holy. Mountains were often places of revelation in the ancient world—liminal spaces where the gods would dwell and where the heavens met the earth. On this hallowed spot, the LORD reveals to Moses, "I am the God of your father, the God of Abraham, the God of Isaac, and the God of Jacob" (3:6). Moreover, the LORD continues in vv. 7-8 to announce the divine intention to deliver the people from their distress. God has heard the cry of the Israelites, and God's desire is to liberate them from oppression and lead them to the land of promise. The LORD commissions Moses for this task in v. 10. Moses responds with an uncertain, "Who am I?" (3:11). God provides assurance to the reluctant liberator through the promise that God will be with him (3:12)—a promise sealed with the sign that the people will worship God on this present mountain.

The call of Moses is similar to the call stories of other prophets or heroes in the Hebrew Bible (e.g., Gideon, Samuel, Isaiah, Jeremiah, and Ezekiel). The LORD's commissioning of Moses has four components common within call stories: 1) the identification of the deity and the reason for the deity's appearance (3:6-9); 2) the commissioning of the individual (3:10); 3) the prophet's objection to the call (Moses' five objections—3:11; 3:13; 4:1; 4:10; and 4:13); and 4) God's assurance to the prophet, including both verbal support and physical signs that authorize the prophet's call (3:12; 3:14-15; 4:2-9; 4:11-12; and 4:14-17).

Resistance to God's Calling

Moses' determined resistance to God's calling identifies this leader of Israel as a reluctant prophet/hero. This reluctance has at least two functions. First, it highlights the humility of the one being called. Second, the prophet's resistance signifies that it is indeed the LORD 's will, not the prophet's, that is operative in the appointed task. By assuring Moses through words of promise and miraculous signs, the LORD both restores confidence to the commissioned figure and authorizes the person's status as a prophet. That Moses objects so many times is likely not a function of the prophet's insecurity but points to the significance and prominence of the one being called. That is, Moses, whom the book of Deuteronomy identifies as the greatest of all of Israel's prophets (Deut 34:10-12), is the most reluctant prophet because his calling is the most important and central in Israelite history.

God's Self-Disclosure

Beyond the burning bush incident, the initial calling of Moses is also marked by an important point of

---

Reflections

1. The prophets were often called in times of difficulty and national distress. How does God respond to the distress of God's people? What human agents does God use?
2. How do we identify God's calling on our life? How do we know when God is calling us to do something?
3. Do we resist the call of God on our lives? For what reasons do we resist?

Teaching Tips

Compare the call of Moses with the call narratives of other prophetic and heroic figures in the Hebrew Bible: Gideon (Judg 6:11-24); Samuel (1 Sam 3:1-14); Isaiah (Isa 6:1-13); Jeremiah (Jer 1:4-10); and Ezekiel (Ezek 2:1–3:11). Look for similarities and differences.

God's self-disclosure in 3:13-15, the revealing of the divine name. Hence, the initial theophany (divine manifestation) of the LORD in fire is coupled with the most intimate and sacred disclosure of divine identity.

In this extended call narrative, Moses' persistent resistance to God's commissioning is paralleled by God's elusive threefold response about the divine name. God first responds with "I AM WHO I AM" (v. 14a). This first reply repeats the same Hebrew verb meaning, "to be," twice in the first person singular ("I") form. It can be translated: "I am who I am" (NRSV), or "I will be who I will be." Thus, God's first answer is elusive, equating God's name with the deity's state of being.

The second response in v. 14b shortens the initial answer: "Thus you shall say to the Israelites, 'I AM has sent me to you.'" Here, the first-person verb is only used once.

The final response (v. 15) uses the Israelites' traditional name for God. Composed of four Hebrew letters, y-h-w-h, it is the third-person masculine singular ("he") form of the same verb, "to be." It can be translated as "he is," "he will be," or "he who causes to be" (i.e., creates). In ancient Jewish tradition, one did not pronounce the divine name and instead used Hebrew words such as "the Name," "LORD," or "heaven" as substitutes. Most English translations use the word "LORD," in all caps, for the name of God.

The elusiveness of the divine name is tied to the mystery of Israel's God. It does not confine God's character into a fixed state or definable identity. Rather, the LORD's name points to the reality of God's presence through an elusive verb of being and presence. God's discernable attributes are not located in a static name but are revealed in God's actions and faithfulness directed to Israel. Hence, the eternal name that will be God's title for all generations (cf. 3:15b) is connected forever with the LORD's deeds of liberation and promises to the people (3:16-22)—God's mighty acts in history.

Reflections

1. In the ancient world, to name something was to have control over it. What's at stake in naming God? Are there other ways that we seek to control God's identity (images, traditional language, etc.)?
2. List some attributes of God. How do these characterizations help us to understand God? How do they limit our understanding of God?
3. How can we work to preserve the mystery of God in our own lives and in the lives of our communities?

Session 4

The Ten Plagues, "Let My People Go"

The conflict between the LORD and Pharaoh begins with Moses and Aaron approaching the king of Egypt. This series of stories, which includes the well-known legend of the Ten Plagues, is framed as a contest story. A similar type of tale can be found in the Joseph narrative (Gen 41). In contest stories, the protagonist's gift—interpreting dreams or performing miraculous signs—is challenged by other officials who have a similar skill. In the conclusion of these tales, the hero is vindicated, and his or her god is recognized as the true god. Though the contest in Exodus begins as a competition between Moses and Aaron with the sages and magicians of Egypt, the real battle is more cosmic—a clash between Pharaoh, the mighty king of Egypt, and the LORD, the God of the Israelites. In summary, the ten plagues are:

1. Water turned to blood (7:14-25)
2. Frogs (8:1-15)
3. Gnats (8:16-19)
4. Flies (8:20-32)
5. Livestock diseased (9:1-7)
6. Boils (9:8-12)
7. Hail (9:13-35)
8. Locusts (10:1-20)
9. Darkness (10:21-29)
10. Death of the firstborn (11:1–12:32)

The plague stories are repetitious and formulaic. They each begin with the LORD instructing Moses to provide Pharaoh with the threat of a disastrous event. After each disaster, Pharaoh eventually disregards the sign, i.e., he hardens his heart or his heart is hardened,

Lectionary Loop
Maundy Thursday, Year A, B, C,
Exodus 12:1-4 (5-10), 11-14
Sixteenth Sunday after Pentecost,
Year A, Exodus 12:1-14

even though at different points he shows signs of sur-rendering. When the plague has passed, however, the king of Egypt eventually returns to his initial position of refusing to let God's people go. Since this session covers a large section of the book, I will focus my attention on three important themes or events within this extended contest narrative: 1) the "knowledge of the LORD"; 2) the hardening of Pharaoh's heart; and 3) the Passover.

The Knowledge of the LORD

The first theme, "the knowledge of the LORD," reflects the divine purpose within the book of Exodus. It is a theme that is repeated many times but is most prominent in the story of the Ten Plagues and the deliverance at the sea in Exod 14–15. It usually takes a form similar to, "that [X] shall know that I am the LORD" (cf. 7:5, 17; 8:22; 9:14, 29; 10:2; 14:4, 18). Within the plague narratives and the Exodus journey itself, this theme serves as a reminder that the LORD 's "signs" and "wonders" are not ends in themselves. Rather they serve a specific purpose in relation to Israel and those who would oppose God's will for the people. In the Hebrew Bible, signs and wonders point to God's activity and extraordinary intervention in the world. They are not intended to prove the LORD 's exis-tence but are signifiers of divine presence and activity in creation. Thus, the LORD 's signs and wonders have the ability to produce a certain knowledge of God's ongoing presence among the people for those who have eyes to see. In the following scene, God's mirac-ulous deliverance at the sea signifies the LORD's defeat of Pharaoh and his chariots, by which "the Egyptians shall know that I am the LORD" (14:4).

Simultaneously, the Lord 's mighty deeds, including God's humiliation of Pharaoh, serves as an indication to Israel and their descendents of what God has done in their midst (10:2). Hence, the knowledge of the Lord cuts both ways. It acts as a further verification of judgment for any empire that would oppose the divine will; and it serves as confirmation of God's faithful action on behalf of Israel that they might know the LORD.

Teaching Tips

1. Compare other retellings of the plague accounts with the stories in Exodus. See, for example, Pss 78 and 105. Note that the traditions do not agree on the order or number of plagues. This suggests that ten is not a reflection of the accurate number of plagues, but is an indi-cation of the stylized nature of these stories. For a helpful chart and discussion of these variations, see Bernhard W. Anderson, *Under-standing the Old Testament*, 4th ed. Englewood Cliffs: Prentice-Hall, 1986, p. 70.

2. You can begin the class by listen-ing to or singing together the African American spiritual, "Go Down, Moses," which appears in many hymnals. It is a good way to set the mood for a session and to get the class reflecting on the tradi-tion of liberation within the Hebrew Bible and beyond.

The Hardening of Pharaoh's Heart

A corresponding theme to "the knowledge of the LORD" within the plague narratives is the perplexing notion of "the hardening of Pharaoh's heart." This prominent motif is complex and reflects a larger tension between human initiative and divine will that is present throughout the book of Exodus. To what extent does God determine the actions of humanity? Similarly, how much free will do human beings have within God's economy? The book of Exodus presents a different range of possible answers to these questions, but, ultimately, does not resolve the tension. Some texts declare that Pharaoh hardens his own heart in response to the LORD 's signs and wonders (8:15, 32; 9:34), suggesting that the king is willfully stubborn in his opposition. Other texts simply describe the state of the king's heart as hardened (7:13, 22; 8:19; 9:7, 35). Finally, others state that the LORD is responsible for hardening Pharaoh's heart, placing the reason for the king's condition squarely within the divine will (7:3; 9:12; 10:1, 20, 27; 11:10).

Theological difficulties result on either end of this unresolved tension. On the one hand, if Pharaoh can act autonomously from the divine will, openly defying God's intention for Israel, how can the LORD be sovereign over all of the earth? On the other hand, if God determines the actions of Pharaoh, how can one hold the king of Egypt accountable for what he does? The beauty and complexity of the biblical text lies in the fact that this difficult theological dilemma is left unresolved. All of the options remain within this story. Pharaoh's heart is hardened in the book of Exodus. This condition is both his own fault and God's determined will.

The Passover

The tenth and final plague within this extended contest narrative combines the killing of Egypt's firstborn with regulations for the celebration of the Passover festival. The Passover tradition, as it has been preserved in Exodus, includes explicit direction for the preparation and celebration of the feast (12:1-28). Instructions for the Feast of Unleavened Bread (12:14-

---

Reflections

1. What "signs" give us evidence of God's presence in our midst?
2. How can we interpret the miraculous deeds in the Bible? Do we tend to rationalize them away? Do we seek scientific verification of them?
3. How can we interpret the LORD's signs and wonders in our present context?

Reflections

1. Is the hardening of Pharaoh's heart his own fault or God's doing, or is it simply a condition that moves the story forward? What is at stake in each position?
2. How much does God give us free will? How much of our actions and lives are determined by a divine plan? Remembering that the biblical story is written from the perspective of God's people (and not the Egyptians), what can this theme—the hardening of Pharaoh's heart—teach us about our lives and about God's will for our lives?

20; 13:3-10) and the consecration of Israel's firstborn (13:1-2, 11-16) are also presented. Hence, this passage combines what were originally two springtime festivals, one agricultural (unleavened bread) and one pastoral (the offering of a lamb). The festivals of the Passover and Unleavened Bread mark two key events within this section of Exodus. The former relates to the passing over of the LORD during the killing of Egypt's firstborn, and the latter to Israel's hasty flight from the land of Egypt. Thus, the celebration of the entire Passover event marks a transition point within the book of Exodus. It corresponds with the tenth and final plague that the LORD inflicts upon Egypt, ironically doing to the Egyptians what Pharaoh had originally decreed for the Israelites—the killing off of the male progeny. It also marks the initial flight of the Israelites from the land of Egypt. Hence, the exodus has begun, and the oppressive yolk of the Egyptians has been broken.

It is significant that this point in the narrative is marked with explicit direction for a festival to the LORD. The major climaxes for both the Ten Plagues story and the exodus ("the Song of the Sea") end with liturgical celebrations. In other words, within the world of Exodus, the proper human response to God's mighty deeds is worship. Therefore, the LORD's initial rationale for allowing the people to go—that they might celebrate a festival to the LORD (5:1)—has been enacted in the narrative memory of Israel through the institution of the Passover. The LORD has freed Israel from its bondage in Egypt with signs and wonders, and Israel responds with worship and song. They are not delivered, however, for the purpose of unrestrained freedom—liberation for liberation's sake—but are freed so that they might worship the LORD unreservedly, serving the God who delivered them from oppression.

Study Bible

For a more thorough exposition of the Death of the Firstborn/Passover section (11:1–13:16), see *NISB*, 101-105.

Deliverance at the Sea

The climactic event within the first half of the book of Exodus, and a key moment in the narrated history of the Hebrew Bible, is the LORD's deliverance of the Israelites at the Red Sea (or literally in Hebrew, "the Sea of Reeds"). This story has inspired people across diverse cultures throughout the centuries and across millennia. While most interpretations of the event focus on the splitting of the sea into towering walls of water, the real drama within the biblical text is centered on the LORD's mythical overthrowing of the Pharaoh and Egypt. Like the plague narratives, the natural wonders that the LORD performs point to the Divine Warrior's overthrowing of the Egyptian empire.

Parting the Waters

The rich descriptions within Exod 14 provide many complex and, at times, convoluted details. Within the story, the divine manifests itself through the angel of God and a pillar of cloud. Moreover, the LORD uses both natural (east wind) and human (Moses) elements in parting the waters. Hence, all of heaven and earth is arrayed against the Egyptians, setting the battle on a cosmic stage. Moses stretches his hands out over the sea (v. 21a), and the LORD drives back the sea by means of a strong east wind. The waters are divided (v. 21b), and the Israelites walk across on dry ground (v. 22). The language of a wind from God combined with the dividing of the waters and the appearance of dry land hearken back to the beginnings of the world in Genesis (1:2, 9) and the re-creation of the earth in the Flood Narrative (Gen 8:1). Thus, the language of Exod 14 suggests that another kind of creation is taking

Lectionary Loop

Easter Vigil, Year A, B, C, Exodus 14:10-31, 15:20-21; Exodus 15:1b-13, 17-18 Seventeenth Sunday after Pentecost, Year A, Exodus 14:19-31, Exodus 15:1b-11, 20-21

Study Bible

See the excursus, "Salvation and the Sea" in *NISB*, 106-107.

Sources

To learn about the exodus from different cultural perspectives, see, "The Exodus: One Narrative, Many Readings," in *Voices from the Margin: Interpreting the Bible in the Third World*, New ed, edited by R. S. Sugirtharjah (Maryknoll: Orbis, 1995), 213-85.

place with the Israelites' passing through the waters. The deliverance at the sea represents the creation of a new people. Moreover, the language within this chapter has strong mythical elements. In other ancient Near Eastern creation stories, the deity slays the watery chaos beast, establishing an ordered creation and the deity's rightful claim to sovereignty over the other gods. Hence, the LORD 's parting of the mighty waters points to both God's rightful sovereignty over the Egyptians and the creation out of chaos of a new people, the liberated Israelites.

Tension between Divine and Human Action

A tension exists within Exod 14 between the LORD's deliverance of Israel and the role of Moses. It is clear that the deliverance at the sea is described as an act of the divine will. Hence, in this last conflict between Pharaoh and the God of Israel, the battle belongs to the LORD. God, like a mighty warrior, fights on behalf of Israel, breaking loose the bonds of Egypt's oppression over Israel in a decisive display of divine and natural power. This climactic scene in the conflict between Pharaoh and the LORD comes to a close with a unanimous acknowledgement from all characters in the story that the LORD has fought for Israel and defeated the empire of Egypt (14:25, 30-31)

Though the theme of the LORD's deliverance is clear within Exod 14, there remains a strong tension between divine and human action in this story. Moses plays a strong mediatorial role within this chapter as elsewhere in the book of Exodus. Throughout this episode, the LORD speaks to the people through Moses, conveying the divine will to the people by means of a human agent (v. 1 and v. 15). At only one point within the story does Israel address God directly (v. 10). Even in this instance, however, the people's cries that follow are eventually redirected to Moses (v. 11). Hence, the pattern of speech within Exod 14, which contains the important movement from human lament to divine response, is mediated through the character of Moses.

Moreover, within the actual act of deliverance, Moses is given a central role. Amidst the powerful images of divine presence and natural force—"angel

Reflections

1. What images do you have in mind when you see the Israelites crossing through the sea?
2. Water is simultaneously the place of salvation and chaos in the exodus story. What meanings does water have for us in our communities of faith?

Teaching Tips

Have members of the class draw the crossing at the sea from their imaginations. Ask them to share their images and interpret them. Ask for feedback from the class on the different illustrations, and compare them with the images within the biblical text.

of God," "pillar of cloud," "strong east wind," and "waters"—Moses plays a crucial part in the orchestrating of the LORD's decisive act of deliverance for the people of Israel. Following the command of the LORD, Moses stretches his hands over the sea to part the waters so that the Israelites can walk through on dry ground (v. 21). At the conclusion of the event, Moses repeats the action so that the waters come back upon the Egyptians (v. 27). The human participation within this passage is not lost on the narrator, who summarizes the awe-inspiring event of deliverance with the conclusion: "So the people feared the LORD and believed in the LORD and *in his servant Moses*" (v. 31, emphasis mine). Thus, this formative event within Israelite history is an act that involves both the mighty deliverance of the LORD and the faithful actions of God's servant, Moses. God's deliverance is made possible through divine natural wonders and human agency. Within this act of salvation at the sea, human and divine will work together to defeat the oppressive force of Pharaoh's Egyptian empire.

The Response of the People

As a result of the LORD's mighty deliverance, the people of God respond with reverent awe and worship. When the Israelites saw Pharaoh's army approaching (14:10), they were afraid, fearing the strength of the Egyptians and the potential for their own death (v. 12). At the end of the chapter, as the Israelites see the once mighty army of Pharaoh dead on the seashore, the people are once again afraid (vv. 30-31). Now, however, their fear has turned into awe, as they marvel at the "great work" that the LORD has done against the Egyptians. This shift in the object of the people's fear points to a transformation in their identity as the people of God. While in slavery under the Egyptian empire, the people were trained to fear the oppressive might of Pharaoh and his officials. Their identity as slaves was cast by the fires of cruel servitude. However, as the people of God, their identity is founded upon the LORD's mighty acts of liberation. Their fear has turned to wonder. They are now free to worship the LORD who has secured their release.

> ## Reflections
>
> 1. To what extent do God's deliverance and salvation involve the participation of human beings?
> 2. How can we be agents of God's purposes for liberation?
> 3. Moses plays the role of mediator in this text; in fact, he is the mediator *par excellence*. What role can/do mediators have in contemporary communities of faith? Do we find the hierarchical aspects of this idea problematic?

Fittingly, in Exod 15, Miriam and Moses lead the people in song, a victory hymn to the LORD. The Song of the Sea, which scholars have identified as one of the oldest texts within the Hebrew Bible, recounts the LORD 's deliverance in rich, mythical images. Within the song, creational motifs, depicting the LORD's victory over Pharaoh in the watery chaos, are combined with the exaltation of the Divine Warrior as highest among the gods (v. 11). Themes emphasizing God's kingship are prevalent within the hymn, including the LORD 's choice of a holy abode (v. 17). Therefore, the people's first act following the LORD 's mighty deliverance at the Sea is worship. Through the waters of deliverance, this once oppressed group of slaves has been re-created as God's people. Israel is transformed as fear changes into awe and lament gives way to praise. In a triumphant hymn to the Divine Warrior, God's people respond by proclaiming the LORD 's victory over the oppressive empire of Pharaoh.

Session 6   Exodus 15:22–17:7

"Is the Lord among Us or Not?" Murmurings in the Wilderness and God's Provision

Immediately following the Song of Miriam, Moses and the Israelites depart from the Red Sea and enter the wilderness. This extended set of stories helps to move the Israelites geographically to Mount Sinai. The wilderness journey itself, however, takes on a larger significance in the ongoing development of God's people. Physical difficulties such as disease, and especially thirst and hunger, figure prominently within these stories. When difficulties confront the Israelites, they complain to the LORD, who responds by providing sustenance for the journey. This section begins and ends with a testing. At the start of the journey, the LORD tests the Israelites to see if they will listen. If the people do what is right, the LORD promises to heal their diseases (15:26), the opposite of what happened to the Egyptians. The wilderness trial ends with the naming of the locations, Masah and Meribah, meaning "test" and "quarrel" respectively; because the Israelites test the LORD saying, "Is the LORD among us or not?" (17:7). Thus, the journey begins with the LORD testing the Israelites and ends with the people testing their God.

Lectionary Loop
**Third Sunday in Lent, Year A,
Exodus 17:1-7
Eighteenth Sunday after Pentecost,
Year A, Exodus 16:1-15
Nineteenth Sunday after Pentecost,
Year A, Exodus 17:1-7**

The Hardships of the People and the Provision of God

The tone for the wilderness journey is set early in the narrator's comments. After traveling for three days, the people find no water. They come to Marah and are unable to drink the water because it is bitter (Marah means "bitterness"). Hence, right from the beginning, the newly released Israelites encounter hardships as they try to leave their old way of life geographically and metaphorically. The people complain against Moses, signaling a recurring motif throughout the wilderness passages. The mediator responds by crying out to the LORD, who shows Moses a piece of wood. The bitter waters turn sweet after Moses throws the wood into the water. Thus, the incident at Marah serves as an initial sign to Israelites that God is with them and will provide for them.

The event represents a reversal of what the Lord did to the Egyptians. Like many of the plague stories and the event at the sea, God uses a human agent, in this case Moses, and the natural elements—water and a piece of a tree—to perform a great deed. However, rather than causing suffering or death, as was the case for the Egyptians, the sign at Marah provides the thirsty Israelites with sweet water to drink. God's provision is emphasized at the end of this first feeding story as the people come to the oasis at Elim, "where there were twelve springs of water and seventy palm trees" (15:27).

Manna—Nourishment and Sign

The LORD's provision for Israel's need is a dominant theme within the wilderness stories of the book of Exodus. God's provision of manna is especially important in this section and within other Israelite traditions (cf. Num 11; Deut 8:3; Josh 5:12; Neh 9:20; Ps 78:24; and Ps 105:40). Though some scholars have sought to rationalize the appearance of manna through natural phenomena, the biblical writers make it clear that the provision of this food is a divine act, even if natural elements are instrumental within the divine sign (quail and dew, vv. 13-14). Similar to the plagues in Egypt, the manna serves as a sign that has as its desired goal: "you shall know that it was the LORD who brought you out of the land of Egypt" (Exod 16:6). Hence, manna, while providing nourishment for the hungry Israelites, also serves as a sign—that the people might know that the same God who delivered them from Egypt will continue to sustain them in the wilderness.

The manna is a mysterious food. The people who gathered much had none left over, and those who gathered little did not run out (16:18). In other words, the

> **Reflections**
>
> What is the difference between a faithful lament and murmuring complaint? When is it appropriate for God's people to cry out; and when does such language cross the line into divisive grumbling?

> **Reflections**
>
> 1. How does God continue to provide "daily bread" for God's people today?
> 2. The dominant images of God's provision in these passages relate to nourishment. How can we actively participate in God's ongoing provision for humanity in a world where famine and hunger persist?
> 3. Who are the hungry in our communities? How can they be fed?

manna provided sufficiently for everyone, whatever their need. Those who tried to leave some over for the following day, disobeying Moses' instructions (16:19), found that the food rotted and bred worms (16:20). Moreover, when the morning sun arose, the leftover manna on the ground melted. In preparation for the Sabbath, however, the people were instructed to gather twice as much. After the manna was prepared and stored, it would keep an extra day only for the day of rest. Hence, the manna was a mysterious and miraculous food that required the people's strict observance for it to feed them. In this way, the feeding stories point to both God's gracious provision and the people's need to observe the LORD's statutes. Within this setting, heeding the word of the LORD is not simply a matter of pious religious observance but is indeed necessary for the people to eat.

Water—Thirst-Quencher and Sign

The wilderness provision stories begin and end with a story about water. At the beginning of the Israelites' journey, the LORD turns the bitter waters of Marah into sweet water. In ch. 17, the Israelites again complain to Moses that they are thirsty. The conflict between Moses and the people, however, is more pronounced in this episode. Moses answers the people's complaint with a complaint of his own: "Why do you test the LORD?" (v. 2). Moreover, when Moses again cries out to God, he adds, "What shall I do with this people? They are almost ready to stone me" (v. 4). Thus, the original testing of the people (15:25b) has developed to include the testing of Israel's leader. Moses concludes that the people have tested the LORD (v. 2), leading him to name this second place of water provision, Massah ("test") and Meribah ("quarrel"). The incident at Massah and Meribah, while also providing the people with water, differs from the LORD's provision at Marah. The first incident involved the transformation of the water from bitter to sweet. Here, however, the water miraculously appears from a rock. Hence, the LORD is able to provide for the people's thirst from an unlikely source, answering the people's test with a positive sign of God's presence and provision. Narratively, the audience receives an affirmative answer to the people's question that ends the story: "Is the LORD among us or not?" (v. 7).

The wilderness is a demanding place for human life. Issues of survival, such as hunger and thirst, can test the fortitude of a people. In the Israelites' journey away from the life of slavery, these conditions challenge their sense of trust in the God who liberated them. The people's complaints point to the realities of a life in transition—the movement away from a life of oppression into the reality of becoming the people of God. In the midst of this challenging new life, the people are reminded continually of the LORD's gracious provision and nurture. Within the reality of God's presence, the inhospitable wilderness is transformed into a place of divine mercy and feeding.

Reflections

What are your "wilderness" experiences? How has God been present for you and nourished you in times of transition?

Revelation at Sinai and the Meaning of Covenant

Within the ancient world, mountains are the dwelling places of the gods. Within the Hebrew Bible, Sinai (or, in some traditions, Horeb) is the numinous place where God reveals God's self to Israel. The LORD originally revealed the divine name to Moses on Horeb (Exod 3). Now that the freed Israelites have been tested in the wilderness, the LORD secures relationship with the people through the covenant at Sinai. This contract between the LORD and Israel, which is based on the initial liberating actions of Israel's God, will govern the interrelations between the two parties. Moreover, the covenant becomes the basis upon which God's community of liberation is built.

Basis for Covenant

The narrative setting of the covenant helps define its meaning. In ch. 19, the Israelites arrive at the mountain of God after having traveled through the wilderness for months. Moses ascends the mountain, where the LORD puts forth the rationale for the covenant. The passage is worth citing at length since the LORD's statement within these verses contains the very logic of the entire Sinai event:

> You have seen what I did to the Egyptians, and how I bore you on eagles' wings and brought you to myself. Now therefore, if you obey my voice and keep my covenant, you shall be my treasured possession out of all the peoples. Indeed, the whole earth is mine, but you shall be for me a priestly kingdom and a holy nation. (vv. 4–6)

Lectionary Loop

Fourth Sunday after Pentecost, Year A, Exodus 19:2-8a

Reflections

1. How do some of our covenanted relationships (e.g., marriage or adoption) help us to understand our relationship with God?
2. The Christian Scriptures are divided into the Old and New Testaments, which is another way to say the Old and New Covenants. How can Christian traditions stress the continuity of the covenanting God of both testaments?

The basis for covenant is located in the LORD's initial gracious act of liberation on behalf of the people. Through the event of the exodus, the LORD has been present in signs and wonders to deliver the Israelites from the oppression of Pharaoh. Now that God has brought Israel to God's self, the people are asked to respond by keeping the covenant. If the people heed the voice of the LORD, they will become God's "treasured possession" among the nations of the earth. Hence, the progression within these preliminary words at Sinai point to the structure of Israel's covenantal life with God. This progression is: 1) God acts on behalf of Israel to liberate them; 2) the people respond to God's gracious acts by keeping the covenant, 3) the people enter into the blessing of being God's treasured possession; and 4) Israel becomes a holy nation, representing God's reign in their midst. Thus, the LORD 's initial words in 19:4-6 summarize the logic of covenant to the people, who accept these terms unanimously by stating "Everything that the LORD has spoken we will do" (v. 8*a*).

Nature of Covenant

Throughout the narrative introduction to the covenant in ch. 19, there are elements that serve to show the holy and awesome nature of the revelatory event. The people must first be consecrated before they can receive the words of the covenant (vv. 10-13). Instructions for purification are given, and proper boundaries are delineated so that the people do not face an untimely death due to the presence of the LORD. Within this initial stage of the mountain event, only Moses (and within a later tradition, Aaron) is allowed to transgress the boundary between the holy and profane. He acts as a mediator, ascending the mountain to meet with God (v. 3 and v. 20) and descending to the base of Sinai to speak with the people (v. 14 and v. 25). In this way, the distance between God and the people is maintained in order to keep the two parties of the covenant distinct (and in the case of the human beings, to keep them alive!). Moreover, elements of theophany—a thick cloud, thunder, lightning, a trumpet blast—point to the awesome display of

> ## Reflections
> 1. Knowing that the Sinai covenant begins with God's gracious act of liberation, discuss how God's grace and salvation has informed your faith journey.
> 2. How do we respond faithfully to God's initial acts of grace, salvation, and liberation in our own lives?
> 3. How do we bear witness to God's reign in our communities, living into the ideal of a priestly kingdom and a holy nation?

God's presence upon the mountain. These combined motifs of consecration and awesome natural demonstration serve to set apart the revelatory event of Sinai both narratively and theologically. The covenant at Sinai represents the preeminent moment of God's self-disclosure to Israel, where the wondrous acts and radical commandments of the LORD are revealed.

Covenant as Treaty

The term, "covenant," comes from the Hebrew word, *berît*, which, though its etymology is uncertain, carries the meaning of a contract or an agreement. Scholars have long recognized similarities between the biblical notion of covenant and treaty forms that were common in the ancient Near East. The legal material most closely parallels suzerainty/vassal treaties. These contracts were made between two unequal parties: the king, or suzerain, and the peoples who were subject to that king's rule. The treaties had a particular form, which could include: 1) an identification of the suzerain; 2) a historical prologue, detailing the deeds of the king on behalf of the vassal; 3) laws governing the rule of the suzerain in relationship to the people; 4) specifications on depositing copies of the covenant in the temple(s); 5) lists including the natural and divine witnesses; and 6) blessings and curses announced as consequences of obedience/disobedience. One can see various elements of the covenant form, especially within the books of Exodus and Deuteronomy. Thus, the biblical writers drew upon this well-known type of document to frame Israel's relationship to its God. The purpose of these treaties was to delineate the ongoing political relationship between a dominant empire and the peoples and nations within it. Hence, issues of loyalty to the suzerain and civil order punctuate this type of legal material. By turning the covenantal form into a theological manifesto, Israel's theologians make an important statement about the LORD's sovereign reign over the affairs of the earth and within the structuring of God's people.

Covenant as Theme

The theme of covenant is prevalent within the Pentateuch. After the flood, God establishes a covenant

Study Bible

For more on the reason for the people's consecration, see the special note in *NISB*, 114.

Study Bible

For more on covenant, see the excursus in *NISB*, 113-114.

with Noah and creation, vowing never again to destroy humanity by a flood (Gen 9:9-11). Later, God makes a covenant with Abraham (Gen 15:7-21), which includes the promise of descendents and land. Moreover, as was noted in earlier sessions, the LORD's compassion was aroused for the Israelites in connection to the promises that God made to the ancestors. In this way, the theme of covenant marks God's continuing presence with Israel throughout the canonical story of the Pentateuch. Hence, within the book of Exodus, the LORD's great deeds on behalf of the people are viewed under the larger thematic ideal of God's *khesedh*, or covenantal loyalty. Israel has been set free from the oppressive life of slavery within Egypt's empire. They have been created anew as they crossed through the waters of the Red Sea. It is only appropriate that the defining event at the center of the book of Exodus should culminate with the establishing of God's covenant with Israel. It is the moment of ratification in which the LORD promises to be Israel's God and Israel swears its allegiance to the LORD. Thus, the covenant at Sinai is not simply a set of legal mandates to keep civil order, nor is it merely a collection of cultic legislations for properly ordered worship. The revelation on God's mountain is indeed grace upon grace. It is founded upon the LORD's mighty acts of liberation on behalf of God's people. It reveals the sanctity and inscrutability of Israel's God. Moreover, the covenant structures Israel's faithful response of worship to their God of deliverance, while serving as the basis for God's newly formed community of liberation.

The Ten Words

W hile the climax in Exodus 1:1–15:21 is the miraculous crossing at the Sea, the central event within Exod 15:22–40:38 is the revelation of the covenant at Sinai. The Ten Commandments are at the heart of this formative experience within the history of Israel. Within later Jewish and Christian traditions, the Decalogue (literally, "the Ten Words") has had enduring significance. In the Hebrew Bible itself, the Ten Commandments are repeated in Deut 5:6-21 with slight differences, especially in the motivation for keeping the Sabbath (5:15). Additionally, when the covenant is renewed after the golden calf incident, the LORD refers to the writings on the newly engraved tablets as "the ten words" (Exod 34:28). Later biblical traditions show that the Decalogue, or some version of it, is at the heart of God's covenant with Israel. The prophets, for example, use elements of the commandments to indict the people for their unfaithfulness (cf. Hos 4:1-2; and Jer 7:9). Thus, the covenant, which is considered to be the foundation of Israel's experience with God, has as its center the Ten Commandments.

Literary Context

In the preceding session, I discussed the narrative setting of the event at Sinai, which includes the LORD's initial proposal of the covenant (19:3-6), the Israelites' acceptance of these conditions (19:7-8), and the consecration of the people (19:9b-15). The first words that the LORD speaks to the Israelites on the mountain are the Ten Commandments. Within their present literary context, the Ten Words are spoken directly to the entire

Lectionary Loop

Twentieth Sunday after Pentecost, Year A, Exodus 20:1-4, 7-9, 12-20
Third Sunday in Lent, Year B, Exodus 20:1-17

Sources

See the detailed study of the Ten Commandments by Thomas McDaniel in *The Pastor's Bible Study*, vol. 2 (Nashville: Abingdon Press, 2005) 157-221.

assembly. Though Moses is the only one who can ascend the mountain (later the LORD also tells Moses to bring Aaron, 19:24), the narrator makes clear that the people are gathered at the base of Sinai to hear the LORD's direct address (19:17). The distancing of the LORD and Moses from the people functions to set Moses apart as mediator between God and the people. However, the narrative section (20:18-21) that follows Exod 20:1-17 reinforces the idea that the Ten Words are spoken directly to the people. In this postlude to the Ten Commandments, the people tremble in fear from the thunder and lightning, which accompany the theophany. Therefore, they ask Moses to relay God's words to them—Moses speaking directly with God, and the people listening to Moses (20:19). Thus, after the Ten Commandments, starting at 20:22, God's instructions about the covenant become mediated through the character of Moses with the words: "The LORD said to Moses...." This setting off of the Decalogue within its literary context serves to highlight the central nature of these words both in the narrated event of Sinai and within the traditions of Israel. In this way, the Ten Words are the core of what makes the people who they are in relationship to the God they serve.

Structure

Within the Decalogue itself, the order of the commandments points to a meaningful structure. The first four commandments (20:3-11) focus on the person and worship of God. The last six (20:12-17) deal with human relationships within Israel. The two sections are related to each other and contain overlapping themes. Hence, the exclusive worship of the LORD structures the way that the people of God live with each other; and the ethical relationships between the Israelites point to their allegiance and devotion to the LORD who delivered them from the land of Egypt and the life of slavery. Both sets of commandments begin with issues of honor and loyalty that are due to God (20:3-4) and the elders within the community (20:12). Moreover, faithful speech about God and one's neighbor will govern Israel's relationships (20:7, 16). The fourth commandment, which focuses on the observing

Reflections

1. How can the Ten Commandments inform our lives today? What meaning and importance do they have within our communities of faith?
2. Is there a difference between making the Ten Commandments normative for a faith community and making them a rule for society?

of the Sabbath, acts as a bridge between the human and the divine, between heaven and earth. Here the people structure their living with each other by remembering the God who created them, resting as God rested on the seventh day of Creation. Thus, the Sabbath command functions literally and theologically as the place where the community's norms and the worship of God meet.

The preamble to the Decalogue in 20:1-2 provides a key to the meaning of the commandments that follow. Verse 2 reads: "I am the LORD your God, who brought you out of the land of Egypt, out of the house of slavery." The first command follows immediately after the preamble. Thus, the Ten Words are rooted in the gracious act of God's liberation of the people from Egypt and the life of slavery. The covenant itself is grace and points to the LORD's identity as the One who liberates God's people. Therefore, the Ten Commandments serve as the center and structuring agent for the Israelite community—a social order that should reflect the liberating presence of the LORD, the God of Israel. The Decalogue is not just a set of ordinances that dictate the proper worship of God and the right living of the people. Rather, it is an alternative manifesto for how the people of God will live as a community of liberation in grateful response to the One who has liberated them.

Read in this way, the first four commandments are not just the mandates of how the community is to worship its divine ruler. More precisely, these first laws signify the people's faithful response of worship to the gracious Liberator. Their response is an act that represents faithful allegiance to the one who freed Israel from a life of slavery. Exclusive worship to the LORD (20:3) is an act of covenantal loyalty, or *khesedh*, directed at the God who delivered Israel. The prohibition of idols (20:4-6) marks off the worship of the LORD as distinctive from the practices of other nations and empires and points to the freedom of Israel's liberating God from constraining representations. The third commandment (20:7), reminds the people of the sanctity of God's divine name—an identity that cannot

Teaching Tips

Not all religious traditions are in agreement on the division of the Ten Commandments. Within Judaism, for example, the first command begins at 20:2, with the LORD's declaration, "I am the LORD your God." The Roman Catholic, Anglican, and Lutheran traditions also start the first commandment here, ending at 20:6, following the prohibition against idolatry. The exposition within this session assumes the pattern within the Protestant and Eastern Orthodox traditions; hence the commandments are as follows:

1. You shall have no other gods before me (20:3)
2. Prohibition against the use of idols (20:4-6)
3. Prohibition against the wrongful use of the LORD's name (20:7)
4. Remember the Sabbath (20:8-11)
5. Honor your mother and father (20:12)
6. You shall not murder (20:13)
7. You shall not commit adultery (20:14)
8. You shall not steal (20:15)
9. You shall not bear false witness (20:16)
10. You shall not covet (20:17)

be bound within the limited framework of human invocation. Finally, the Sabbath observance helps the community of Israel to remember that labor does not have the final word within the rhythm of the calendar. The fourth commandment reminds Israel about the consecrated rest of the Creating and Liberating God (20:11).

Similarly, the last six commandments are not simply a set of arbitrary laws that govern human life. Set within the larger context of God's liberating acts, these six "words" point to the ordering of God's new community of liberation. Within this social order, human beings will resist the impulses of empire, which would seek to exploit human beings (their neighbors) for their own gain. Rather, God's people will practice a life of liberation by honoring and respecting each other as members of the Israelite community. While framed within the form of negative prohibitions (i.e., "You shall not…"), the commandments represent positive ideals, which point to the necessary building blocks that protect the integrity of the community. Hence, the early Christians' later summary of the Law identifies a positive formulation of the unity within the twofold division of the Ten Words: love of God and love of neighbor (cf. Matt 22:37-40; Mark 12:29-31; and Luke 10:26-28).

Reflections

1. What things challenge us the most when it comes to our loyalty to God?
2. What things challenge us the most to live faithfully with our neighbors?

Reflections

1. Discuss how the Ten Commandments represent ideals that can form the basis of a community of liberation. How does the worship of God contribute to the identity of such a community?
2. How can contemporary people live out the ideal of God's liberation in contemporary society? Give concrete examples.
3. What kind of rule should govern worshiping communities? (A rule of love? A rule of discipline and order? A rule of liberation?)
4. How will the community's norms reflect or differ from the norms within larger society? Do these norms reflect the person of God, and if so, what image of God do they reflect?

The Golden Calf Incident, God Revealed in Judgment

The story of the golden calf in Exod 32 is enormously complex and complicated both literarily and theologically. The larger story block of Exod 32–34 interrupts the narrative flow of the book of Exodus. The preceding chapters (Exod 25–31) contain the LORD's instructions for the building of the Tabernacle. Chapters 35–40 describe the construction of the holy place, reaching a climax and conclusion when the glory of the LORD descends upon it (40:34-38). Thus, the golden calf episode disrupts the natural progression between divine command and human response. The digression produces a subplot that requires its own resolution. What happens when the people transgress the covenant? Exod 32 raises important and difficult theological issues about how God is present within the context of sin and judgment. The LORD and God's servant, Moses, prove to be both merciful and severe in response to the people's apostasy. The covenant is renewed (Exod 34) but not without consequence.

Israel's Transgression

Because of the complex literary development of this text, scholars have argued over the nature of Israel's transgression in this passage. Why, for example, do the Israelites ask for gods, but Aaron produces only one calf? Moreover, the calf is not representative of some other deity like Baal in this passage; it is worshiped as the LORD on a festival of the LORD (32:4-5). Regardless of these complexities that clearly point to a complicated history of textual transmission, the canonical text is clear that the people, with the aid of Aaron, violate the

Lectionary Loop
Twenty-first Sunday after Pentecost, Year A, Exodus 32:1-14
Fifteenth Sunday after Pentecost, Year C, Exodus 32:7-14

prohibition against idolatry (Exod 20:4-6). This interpretation of the event is contained within the memory
of Israel's tradition (Ps 106:19-20, cf. 1 Kgs 12:28-30).
Thus, within the present literary context, the incident of
the golden calf points to the people's tendency to fall
quickly into apostasy. Moses has not even descended to
the people with the covenantal tablets before the
Israelites have digressed into idolatry. Aaron's leadership has failed, as he acquiesces to the people's
demands. In addition, the people's conduct has degen-
erated into sexual revelry (32:6). Even in the midst of
Israel's defining revelatory moment, the covenant is
positioned precariously between God's awesome holiness and the people's infidelity.

Moses as Mediator—Intercessor

Throughout this passage, Moses' mediatorial role is
balanced with both his passionate intercession and
severe judgment. When the LORD threatens to destroy
the people because of their rebellion, Moses inter-
venes. In vv. 7-10, God informs Moses about the people's quick decline into idolatry. The LORD creates distance from the people by aligning them with Moses,
calling the Israelites "your people." In his response,
Moses redirects the ownership of Israel back to God by
asking: "Why does your wrath burn hot against *your
people*, whom you brought out of the land of Egypt
with great power and with a mighty hand?" (32:11,
emphasis mine). Moses' intercession in these verses
puts responsibility for the welfare of Israel back in
God's hands. Moreover, he provides the LORD with
two reasons to show mercy rather than wrath.

The first has to do with God's honor and reputation.
Moses suggests that the Egyptians will question why
the LORD brought the Israelites out of Egypt only to
kill them in the wilderness (v. 12). Because of this,
Israel's mediator implores God to have mercy and
change God's mind about bringing disaster on the people. Moses' second reason is based in the LORD's
promises made to the ancestors—to multiply their
descendents and bring them to the good land (v. 13).
Thus, Moses reminds God of the divine obligation to
Israel's forbearers. This intercessory act compels God

Reflections

1. At the heart of the second commandment is the freedom of God
from static human representations.
What are some of the ways that
religious traditions constrain God's
freedom within their own practices
and beliefs?

2. Does our worship vocabulary, for
example the persistence of male-
centered images of God, represent a
form of idolatrous language about
God? Why or why not?

3. Religious symbols and iconogra-
phy can be powerful worship aids
for communities of faith. They are
visible representations of holy realities. How does this practice differ
from idolatry? Explain.

to change God's mind in v. 14 (literally, "the LORD repented of the evil/disaster"). Hence, Moses' daring and passionate intervention on behalf of the people persuades the LORD against destroying them in anger.

Moses as Mediator—Judgment

Despite Moses' faithful intercession on behalf of Israel, he is furious with the people upon his descent from the mountain. He smashes the two tablets as a visible sign that the covenant has been broken (v. 19). After he destroys the golden calf, he questions Aaron about the incident. Aaron's response emphasizes the sin of the people and minimizes his own role, claiming that a calf simply came forth from the fire (v. 24). In this way, the narrator contrasts the two leaders, Aaron and Moses. Moses had daringly interceded on behalf of Israel, standing between the people and the LORD's wrath. Aaron blames the people for the incident, making himself an unwitting bystander to the event.

Seeing that the people have gone wild, Moses asks for volunteers who are "on the LORD's side" (v. 26). The Levites respond, and Moses commands them to kill brother, friend, and neighbor in order to preserve order. Three thousand Israelites fall by the sword. Most shockingly, Moses proclaims that these actions brought a blessing upon the Levites. While originally this legend about the sons of Levi probably served to validate this order of priests, within the canonical context of this passage their actions represent a murderous response to the apostasy of the people. The sin of murder (Exod 20:13) is utilized to extinguish the sin of idolatry. Moses' severe response to the situation points to the reality of judgment among the people. Israel's leader resorts to the use of force in order to restore social order. The executions also point to the consequences of rebellion and apostasy. There is no tidy way for God and God's servant to deal with the chaos created by the people's sin. Thus, Moses' course of action represents the sobering reality of taking the people's transgression seriously. Breaking the covenant is an issue of life and death.

After order is restored, Moses again intercedes on behalf of Israel (vv. 31-32). He, unlike Aaron, aligns himself with the fate of the people, asking God to blot out his name from God's book if the deity is unwilling to forgive the people. In this way, Moses' severe judgment in vv. 25-29 is buffered on both sides of the story with the mediator's intercession on behalf of the people. The LORD replies by stating to Moses that those who were responsible will be held accountable (v. 33). In addition, the LORD sends a plague on the people because of the golden calf incident. Hence, God's actions and words represent both compassion and judgment, similar to the character of Moses. God shows mercy by not destroying the Israelites. Nevertheless, the LORD also looks upon the breaking of the covenant with grave seriousness. Israel's actions have damaging consequences for their well-being. The plague confirms this fact. In the end, however, God's severe judgment is not the final word in the subplot of Exod 32–34. After yet another intercession by Moses (33:12-16), the tablets are rewritten and the covenant is renewed in 34:10-28 (also known as the Ritual Decalogue because of its emphasis on cultic practices). As it would later be for Israel in exile, so it is for them in the narrative at Sinai. Their sin has brought about God's judgment. The LORD, however, remains faithful to the people by renewing the terms of the covenant (cf. Jer 31:31-34), so that God's grace and compassion, and not the people's sin, would have the last word.

Study Bible

For more on the LORD's mercy and forgiveness within this passage, see the "Special Note" in the second column of p. 136 in the *NISB*.

Reflections

1. The idea of God's judgment is not easy for contemporary readers of the Bible. How can we translate this important and yet difficult idea into our present context?

2. Contrast the models of leadership provided by the characters of Moses and Aaron. What distinguishes the two of them as effective or ineffective?

3. The violence in Exod 32:25-29 is problematic. Talk about the dangers and dynamics of religiously motivated violence. How can we resist such ideas theologically? How can we faithfully resist the violence within this text as interpreters?

Building the Tabernacle,
the People's Faithful Response

C hapter 35, which begins with a reminder of the
Sabbath rest (vv. 1–3), resumes the larger narrative flow of the book of Exodus. As stated in
session 9, the incident with the golden calf (Exod 32)
interrupted the progression from command to obedient
response. The apostasy of the Israelites in the golden
calf scene eventually leads to the renewal of the
covenant in Exod 34. In chs. 25–31, the LORD gives
instructions about the building of the Tabernacle. The
story's main plot continues in Exod 35–40 when the
Israelites respond faithfully to the LORD's command.
Thus, this last section within the book of Exodus ends
on the positive note with the people's obedient
response. The renewal of the covenant in ch. 34 suggests that God's grace and forgiveness have the last
word over the people's digression into sin. Similarly,
Israel's obedient and careful construction of the Tabernacle, which is a faithful response to the LORD's original command, ends the book of Exodus with Israel's
careful adherence to the word of the LORD and the
covenant.

> ### Reflections
>
> The end of the book of Exodus empha-
> sizes God's grace in covenant renewal
> and the people's obedience in building
> the Tabernacle. What is the relation-
> ship between grace and obedience in
> our traditions?

Obedience of the People

The people's obedience is characterized in diverse
ways throughout these last six chapters in Exodus. In
35:4-19, Moses instructs the people about the building
of the Tabernacle. The Israelites, all of whom are of
"generous heart," are asked to bring offerings of fine
metals, yarn, cloth, animal skins, wood, oil, spices, and
incense in order to provide raw materials for the Tabernacle, its furnishings, and the priestly garments. The
people, whose "heart was stirred" and whose "spirit

was willing" (35:21), respond to the instruction of the
LORD and Moses by bringing their free-will offerings
(35:20-29). In fact, their generosity is so great that the
artisans ask Moses in 36:3-5 to tell the people to stop,
because the Israelites had already supplied enough
materials for the work. Moreover, the Tabernacle and
accompanying fixtures are constructed with painstak-
ing attention to detail (the description of this work
spans four chapters, Exod 36:8–39:31). Accomplished
artisans and skilled personnel are appointed to the task
of constructing the Tabernacle and creating its furnishings, emphasizing the uncompromising quality of the
workmanship (35:30-35). At the end of the construction, the narrator highlights the precision of the people's obedience with a detailed conclusion (39:32-42).
The conclusion itself begins and ends with the statement that the people had done everything "just as the
LORD had commanded Moses" (39:32, 42). In this
way, the Israelites' generous and detailed obedience to
God's command stands in stark contrast to the golden
calf incident, where the people fail to keep the words
of the covenant. Moreover, when Moses sees the finished work of the Tabernacle, he blesses the people
(39:43)—a pronounced difference from Moses' violent response to the people's idolatry and revelry in
Exod 32.

Completion of the Holy Space

After the Tabernacle's components were finished,
Moses carries out the final assembly of the structure.
Thus, Israel's mediator is assigned the last task of com-
pleting the holy space. Moses' key role has at least two
functions. First, it suggests that the material-gathering,
constructing, and erecting of the Tabernacle was a task
completed by the entire assembly of Israel. God's people act as one in obedience to the command of the
LORD. The people, the artisans, and Moses all contribute to the Tabernacle, where the God who liberated
them will be present. Second, Moses' final task sets
him apart as Israel's supreme mediator. The book of
Exodus began with the birth of Moses and his calling to
lead the children of Israel out of their life of slavery. The
book ends with Moses erecting the Tabernacle, where

Reflections

1. How can we respond faithfully to
the work that God has given us to
do? How can our talents, skills, and
possessions be used to contribute to
this work?

2. Allow the individuals within a
group to write down their specific
gifts, talents, and assets. After giving time for people to reflect on
these things, return to the larger
group and ask them to share their
lists with the larger group. Write
them down and have the group cat-
egorize them. Finally, ask the group
how these things might be used to
further God's work.

the liberating God will dwell among God's people. Similar to the people's obedient response in chs. 35–39, Moses' faithful deeds are punctuated throughout ch. 40 with the phrase: "as the LORD had commanded Moses" (40:16, 19, 21, 23, 25, 27, 29, 32). Thus, the final stages of the Tabernacle are completed through the faithful obedience of Moses, God's servant and Israel's supreme mediator.

Renewal of the Covenant

The themes named throughout this study take on particular significance when one considers that the final form of Exodus took shape within the context of exile. As the prophets suggested, the fall of Judah resulted from the people's infidelity to the LORD. They had broken the covenant and had paid dearly for the consequences of their sin and idolatry. In exile, the judgment of God would have been an all-too-present reality. The ending of the book of Exodus, however, affirms to God's people that the broken covenant can be renewed (Exod 34). Moreover, the people can return to a life of obedience and blessing—a way of being that will result in the LORD's tabernacling presence among them (40:34-38). It is fitting that the book of Exodus ends with the glory of the LORD filling the Tabernacle. God, who liberated the Israelites from bondage in order that they might be a chosen people among the nations, dwells in the midst of the Israelites who have been united by radical obedience to the covenant's demands. The conclusion in Exodus and exile is not bound to the apostasy, death, and judgment of the golden calf incident. The last word begins with God's gracious forgiveness in the renewal of the covenant and ends in the radical obedience of God's people. The resulting effect of covenantal faithfulness culminates with the glory of God being present "before the eyes of all the house of Israel at each stage of their journey" (40:38).

Teaching Tips

The end of the book of Exodus stresses the presence of God among the people. Use this conclusion of the book to have the class reflect upon the different ways that God was present to Israel.

GREAT TEXTS FOR A HEALTHY SPIRITUALITY

A STUDY BY
GLENN HINSON

Glenn Hinson serves as Visiting Professor of Church History at Candler School of Theology at Emory University in Atlanta, GA.

Outline

I. Introduction

II. Session 1—Trajectory of Spiritual
        Growth: Philippians 1:9-11
  A. The Goal
  B. The Way
  C. The Key

III. Session 2—Anxiety's Antidote: Matthew
        6:33
  A. Seek First God's Mysterious Presence
  B. And God's Okaying of You
  C. Other Things Will Fall into Place

IV. Session 3—The Sacrament of the Present
        Moment: Luke 10:38-42
  A. Martha and Mary
  B. "Martha, Martha"
  C. The Better Part

V. Session 4—Making All of Life a Prayer:
        1 Thessalonians 5:17
  A. That Command in Context
  B. Attentiveness

VI. Session 5—Having the Mind of Christ:
        Philippians 2:5-11
  A. The Mind of Christ
  B. Obtaining the Mind of Christ
  C. Humility in an Age of Intimidation

VII. Session 6—Not Conformed but Trans-
        formed: Romans 12:2
  A. Not Conformed
  B. But Transformed
  C. A Sense of God's Will

VIII. Session 7—The Sufficiency of Grace: 2
        Corinthians 12:1-10
  A. Plea about "a Thorn in the Flesh"
  B. "My Grace Is Sufficient."
  C. Power Perfected in Weakness

IX. Session 8—God's Inescapable Near-
        ness: Psalm 139:7-12
  A. The Pain of Presence
  B. Neither Heaven Nor Hell
  C. Attending the Inescapable One

X. Session 9—Whole-Personed Spirituality:
        Mark 12:28-34; Matthew
        22:34-40; Luke 10:25-29
  A. God Love
  B. Neighbor Love

XI. Session 10—Suffering and Hope:
        Romans 5:1-5
  A. It's Hard to Be Hopeful!
  B. But There's Reason for Hope.
  C. Hope in Suffering

Introduction

Great Texts for a Healthy Spirituality

"Our spiritual life is the only precious thing we possess," the great Scottish theologian John Baillie once said. "It is that without which all else is dust and ashes." Then, he warned, "But it is such a fragile thing and it is so easily quenched." Going back again and again to its springs and oases in Scripture may keep that from happening.

The Scriptures have always held a central place in Christian spirituality because the Christian spiritual life, like the Jewish spiritual life, revolves around the covenant that God initiated out of love. As an act of pure grace, God has entered into an intimate friendship with humankind. Through mighty acts in creation and redemption, God discloses to us, to whatever extent we can understand, who God is and what God expects of us.

Persons who take this covenant commitment seriously will realize that developing an intimate relationship with God, the ultimate personal reality in the universe, does not happen easily or automatically. No more easily, in fact, than forging an intimate bond with another human being, as in marriage or a deep friendship. Not surprisingly, throughout Jewish and Christian history, saints have drawn on marriage as the most helpful analogy for interpreting the covenant. Shockingly to some, perhaps, they have mined rich nuggets of insight from the love tryst between newlyweds in the Song of Songs to make sense of the mind-boggling idea that the Eternal God, Source of all that is, should condescend to enter into intimacy with frail and flawed human beings.

Sources

Baillie, John. *Christian Devotion* (New York: Charles Scribner's Sons, 1962) 41.

The centrality of this covenant should make clear why it is important to search the Scriptures (Acts 17:11). Scriptures cradle centuries of testimonies about human encounter with God. The Old Testament contains many examples of how God communicates through nature, through history, and through people's lives. For the Jewish people, their deliverance from Egypt has been the most important of all of these stories. From time immemorial they have gathered at Passover to observe a home seder to commemorate the greatest of God's "mighty acts." Instructions from Jesus' day for the seder direct that, after the meal of lamb and herbs, the youngest child is to ask, "Why is this night different from all other nights?" Then the head of the family is to tell the story of the exodus from Egypt. Rabbi Eliezer added, "Do this as if you yourselves were going out in the exodus from Egypt." That is, like this child who asked the question, enter into the story in imagination, and let it disclose God, God's purpose for this people, God's purpose for you.

For Christians there is another story of stories: the story of Jesus. It is through him that we "aliens" have entered into the covenant with God. By virtue of God's presence in us, as Paul reminded the Romans, we do not come groveling in fear like slaves, but rather, like beloved children, we cry, "*Abba!*" (Rom 8:15). Small wonder, then, that Christian meditation has focused on the Gospels, for it is in them we find our story of stories. Constantly immersing ourselves in that story should help to form in us "the mind of Christ" (Phil 2:5).

The texts that I have chosen to share with you in this series are texts that have contributed significantly to my own spiritual enlightenment and edification.

I. Philippians 1:9-11. Paul's prayer for the Philippians is one I pray constantly for myself, not with my tongue and lips but with my heart. In it, the apostle fingers the engine that propels the spiritual life, God's love, and lays out a trajectory for it. I would encourage you to make it your tacit plea, perhaps self-consciously for a while, until it becomes your soul's sincere desire.

II. Matthew 6:33. Jesus' counsel to the anxiety-ridden of his day addresses just as powerfully the anxiety-ridden of our day. In a day when religion is huckstered like pizza, churches and their leaders would do well to keep at the forefront of their thinking this query of Thomas Merton: "What do we have to offer the world that the world doesn't already have more of than it needs?" Here is Jesus' answer.

III. Luke 10:38-42. Luke's Mary/Martha story challenges us further about our busyness and distractedness. As a career-long workaholic, it makes me ask myself, "How often am I so preoccupied with 'many things' that I miss 'the One who is needful'?" I'm thankful that, when I was a college student at age nineteen, Huston Smith planted in my mind Henry Nelson Weiman's sage comment, "We ought to live each moment as if all Eternity converged upon it."

IV. 1 Thessalonians 5:17. Prayer is the essence of spirituality. The desert fathers and mothers set the bar high for us when they made this verse, "Pray without ceasing," their aim. I think their search resulted not in a superior *method* of prayer but in more fervent love of God and others.

V. Philippians 2:5-11. If what I said earlier is true, Jesus is not just our *example* but our *life in God*. Christian life is, as Paul saw it, "life in Christ." We want in us, therefore, "the mind of Christ"—a humble and self-giving mind. Is that too much to ask even of ministers in our masochistic era? Maybe—but the world may not survive without it.

VI. Romans 12:2. A healthy spirituality requires negotiation with the age and culture in which we live. To some degree we will conform, for the world possesses many godly aspects. If we are to offer something to the world it doesn't have more of than it needs, then we will want God to recycle our attitude and outlook so that we can do what God wants. How are you doing on that?

VII. 2 Corinthians 12:1-10. Christians everywhere sing "Amazing Grace" with gusto, but what Paul says about his experience should cause many to ask whether they have enough of a handle on it. In his most revealing moment he discovered that God shares our vulnerability, and that means everything!

VIII. Psalm 139:7-12. The psalmist who gave us Psalm 139 found God's presence painful, and he did his best to flee. Yet he could not, for he could not escape himself. Though he made his bed in hell, still there God was. Very human, isn't it, to want to make God more convenient?

IX. Mark 12:28-34; Matt 22:34-40; Luke 10:25-29. The two great commandments lay the foundation for any spirituality. God's love should exude from every fiber of our being. Neighbor love should extend to every person everywhere. Are we up to either? Not without God's help.

X. Romans 5:1-5. Ours is a hope-testing age, which has seen many throw up their hands in despair. Healthy spirituality should assist us to get in touch with the hope that is in us in the midst of suffering and grief. There is reason for hope not in ourselves but in a God who has joined us in our weakness.

Reflections

In what ways is your spiritual life the most precious thing you possess? Why is it fragile?

Teaching Tips

Ask the group to list scriptural passages that have special meaning for them. Ask members to describe how these passages remind them of God's love, provide strength to do what needs to be done, or offer comfort.

Trajectory of Spiritual Growth

In this prayer for his favorite saints, the apostle Paul outlines a trajectory for spiritual growth and development. The long-range goal is purity of heart and fruit of righteousness. The way to the goal is to develop a sense of things that really matter. The key to the whole process is God's love in us increasing understanding and sensitivity.

The Goal

Actually, we human beings probably have a goal extending beyond the one Paul indicates here. We want to see God, to participate in the life of God, and to be one with the One. Like the psalmist, we cry, "As a deer longs for flowing streams, so my soul longs for you, O God. My soul thirsts for God, for the living God. When shall I come and behold the face of God?" (Ps 42:1-2).

We must recognize, however, that we humans cannot wave a wand and make God appear. God alone can grant us a vision of God. What we can hope for concerns ourselves—what kind of persons we aspire to be and what quality of lives we offer God. So Paul offers a two-sided plea: that the Philippians may be "pure and blameless" at the return of Christ and have "produced the harvest of righteousness that comes through Jesus Christ."

The first side recalls the beatitude, "Blessed are the pure in heart, for they will see God" (Matt 5:8). That was the central text of devout men and women who went out into the desert to pray in solitude in early centuries. "The ultimate goal of our way of life," said Abba Moses, "is...the kingdom of God or the kingdom of heaven. The immediate aim is purity of heart. For

> **Lectionary Loop**
> **Second Sunday of Advent, Year C,**
> **Philippians 1:3-11**

without purity of heart none can enter into that kingdom." When we approach God at the end, we want to be pure and without reproach.

The other side of our desire focuses on the produce of our lives. The "harvest [literally "fruit"] of righteousness that comes through Jesus Christ" is spelled out as "fruit of the Spirit" in Gal 5:22-23: "love, joy, peace, patience, kindness, generosity, faithfulness, gentleness, and self-control." It is reminiscent of Jesus' parable of the end time in Matt 25:31-46. Those whom the king invited into the kingdom were those who did good without even thinking about it. They fed the hungry, gave drink to the thirsty, took in strangers, clothed the naked, cared for the sick, and visited prisoners. When they protested, the king had to remind them that insofar as they had done it to "the least of these," they had done it to him (25:40).

The Way

How can we attain such transformed character in cultures that pose so many challenges to spiritual growth and development? In Paul's words, God's love in you must grow "to help you to determine what is best" (Phil 1:9). I would translate this segment: "so that you may have a sense of things that really matter."

This petition would seem to have implications of two kinds in our culture. One bears on our ability to distinguish right from wrong, the other on our sense of priorities. In both of these, Americans have an uncommon amount of difficulty today.

Politicians, priests, and business moguls have trouble discriminating between right and wrong. The speaker of the U.S. House of Representatives had to give up his office when he was indicted for violation of election laws in Texas and decided not to run for reelection. Roman Catholic priests have cost the church hundreds of millions of dollars for sexual abuse. Heads of two of America's largest corporations, WorldCom and Enron, were found guilty of numerous charges connected with the way their companies doctored their financial reports to hold up stock prices as they were in process of failing.

This same market economy scrambles priorities,

Sources

Cassian, *Conferences*, 1.4; Library of Christian Classics, 12: 197.

Reflections

What really matters to you?

Reflections

How can a church—from the pulpit and in smaller study/discussion groups—confront unethical activities of political leaders without becoming partisan and without violating a church-state separation standard?

too, in ways Paul could never have imagined. As the late John Kenneth Galbraith demonstrated in *Economics and the Public Purpose*, corporations no longer rely on supply and demand. Instead, they produce what they want at the price they want and then use skillful advertising to convince us we must use their products. Entertainment companies create their shows, set the price, and prove to us that we can't get along without what they offer. We find ourselves caught up in consumption for consumption's sake and activity for activity's sake.

The Key

What is the way out of such a dilemma? Paul posits it in his initial petition: "that your love may overflow more and more with knowledge and full insight." Let me be bold to suggest that Paul is speaking here about God's love in us. He uses the Greek word for love, *agapē*. Early Christians adopted this little-used word rather than the more common words *eros* (romantic love), *storgē* (natural affection), and *philia* (brotherly/sisterly love) to express their experience of God's love in and through Jesus Christ. It is God's love freely given that can transform. So we really want to let that love grow in us.

How do you grow in the love of God? By opening like a flower to the morning sun. God does not force God's self upon you. God doesn't knock your door down or bulldoze you. You have to open from the inside. And if you can open just a crack, God's love will flow in.

I have made it sound simple and easy. *Just open.* Most of us must recognize, however, that it isn't that simple or easy to open. We've experienced storms in life causing us to close our shutters and bar the door from the inside. I'm not speaking so much about physical as about spiritual and emotional storms. You love someone, and that person rebuffs your love or twists and distorts it. You pull in, and it's hard to open again. After such an incident, you are afraid that it might happen again.

If you can open, God's love will cause growth in "knowledge and in full insight" (Phil 1:9), or, as I prefer

Sources

Galbraith, John Kenneth. *Economics and the Public Purpose* (New York: New American Library, 1988).

Teaching Tips

On an overhead transparency, a blackboard, dry erase board, or flipchart, list each of the Greek words for "love" at the top of one of four columns. Have group members think of English words or phrases that could bring each of these four concepts into focus for contemporary Scripture readers.

to translate, "in understanding and in every sensitivity." The development of a proper sense of moral responsibility and of priorities requires not merely greater head knowledge but also greater heart knowledge. In an age and culture in which science prevails, there is a desperate need for love to sensitize, conscientize, and tenderize minds and hearts. As Mother Teresa of Calcutta often reminded us, people today suffer and die more from lack of love than from physical want.

Paul prayed for the Philippians a prayer that I pray constantly for myself and for others—*"that God's love in you may grow more and more in understanding and in every sensitivity so that you may have a sense of things that really matter, in order that you may be pure and without reproach in the day of Christ, filled with the fruit of the righteousness which redounds through Jesus Christ to the glory and praise of God."*

Reflections

How is God's love properly presented and articulated in modern religious rhetoric? How is it misunderstood and even distorted?

Anxiety's Antidote

Jesus spoke to the anxiety-ridden in Matt 6:25-34. Worry will not change your situation. Stop worrying about what you are going to eat or drink or wear. Isn't life more than food and clothing? Take a lesson from the birds and from the flowers, who trust God to provide. Worry puts you in the category of unbelievers.

Good case. Those who heard knew Jesus was on target. Nevertheless, they worried. He knew they worried. How could human beings not worry? So he gave them the antidote to their anxiety. Let me give my paraphrase, which I will proceed to explain and defend: "Seek first God's mysterious presence and God's okaying of you. Then these other things will fall into place."

Seek First God's Mysterious Presence

However we translate the statement, the solution to human anxiety rests in God. "Kingdom" or "reign" (*basileia* or *malkuth YHWH*) does not refer to some ideal government or state, as the English words imply. Quite to the contrary, Jesus illustrated it in ways that strongly underscore the mystery of it. It's like a grain of mustard seed (Matt 13:31-32), like yeast at work in a lump of dough (Matt 13:33, Luke 13:21), like a field bearing fruit of its own accord (Mark 4:28), like a thief in the night (Matt 24:43, Luke 12:39). Nothing expresses this as well as God's Mysterious Presence, God's self.

I'm not comfortable with the word "strive" (NRSV) here. It suggests too much effort on our part. As Rufus Jones, the great Quaker philosopher, emphasized, we

Lectionary Loop
Thanksgiving Day, Year B,
Matthew 6:25-33

are beneficiaries of a double search. God has placed within us a homing instinct, like that of the pigeon taking it to the place of its birth. Our seeking God, Jones insists, is as natural as the retina of the eye responding to the light. "You have made us for yourself, to praise You," Augustine confessed at the beginning of his great classic, "and our heart is restless until it finds rest in you."

Yet, just as surely as our hearts turn godward, so too does God seek us. "Where can I go from your spirit?" a psalmist cries. "Or where can I flee from your presence? If I ascend to heaven, you are there; if I make my bed in Sheol, you are there" (Ps 139:7-8). Every soul seeking God, Bernard of Clairvaux declared, "should know that it has been anticipated by [God], and has been sought by [God] before it began to seek [God]," He added, "You would not seek [God] at all, O soul, nor love [God] at all, if you had not been first sought and first loved."

And God's Okaying of You

Step one in the spiritual life, then, is to seek God. So long as you focus on yourself—what you will eat, drink, or wear—worry will escalate. It will consume you. God alone can okay you and give you shalom, deep down security.

Okaying is what "righteousness" means in Matthew's Gospel. Righteousness connotes not only God's declaration of acquittal to the sinner but also God's making right what is not okay. Not many of us humans feel okay about ourselves. And we are not okay. We are all like Martin Luther crying out for a God who will love us and accept us just as we are in all of our flawed humanity. We may try hard to justify ourselves like the pompous Pharisee of Jesus' parable (Luke 18:9-14), but we will fail. Only Love Divine poured into our hearts and minds will suffice to put to rest our anxiety.

In America I suspect that many suffer from what I would call the "Midas complex." That's the idea that a little more will satisfy this deep, mysterious inner craving. People of my generation who grew up during the Great Depression seem especially to have been

Sources

Jones, Rufus. *The Double Search* (Philadelphia: C.J. Winston Co., 1906) ch. 1.

Augustine. *The Confessions of St. Augustine*. Translated by John K. Ryan (Garden City, NY: Doubleday Image Books, 1960) 1.1.1.

Bernard of Clairvaux, *Sermons on the Song of Songs* 84.2; Library of Christian Classics, 13:74f and 13:77.

Reflections

What worries most consume modern Americans? What worries most consume citizens of the two-thirds world?

afflicted by it. During the Depression, we often didn't have enough. Then during World War II came rationing, and we still could not have what we needed or wanted. After the war we could have anything. We flaunted our ability to practice "conspicuous consumption." But born of our unbridled acquisition came a deception—the notion that acquiring more would satisfy that unfathomable inner longing. Sadly, getting more only whetted the appetite for more. Only God, God's mysterious Presence, can satisfy that longing for God.

Other Things Will Fall into Place

The sequence Jesus has given us is the right one. We must begin from within. Then other things will fall into place. How does that work?

I'm not at all sure Jesus was promising a miraculous increase of food, clothing, and the other necessities. Times and circumstances of his hearers did not permit assurance of cornucopias. The miracle they could expect, rather, had to do with a reordering of priorities from within, not an upping of the supply of things from without (e.g. Jesus feeding the five thousand or the four thousand). Because they had the one who was needful, they had enough to spare.

None of this should be interpreted as implying that Jesus negated or underestimated human physical need. A huge chasm stood between his thinking and that of dualists, such as some ancient Gnostics, who considered matter evil. He knew we needed bread. But he also knew how readily we fall into the trap of thinking that we can live "by bread alone" (Matt 4:4). When that happens, we get our priorities twisted. The right sequence is God first. Here begins an internal simplification that is world-changing. As Thomas Kelly said beautifully, "[God] plucks the world out of our hearts, loosening the chains of attachments. And [God] hurls the world into our hearts, where we and [God] together carry it in infinitely tender love."

God's interior reordering should result in some exterior rearranging of priorities. People, possessions, and projects once critically important might fade into the background. Others neglected, ignored, or unnoticed

Teaching Tips

Divide your group into teams of two to three people. Allow each team ten minutes to come back to the larger group with a report on the topic: Are institutional religious groups (congregations, denominations, etc.) living as if God's presence is the most essential aspect of existence? Or are they more concerned with material gain? Evaluate your own congregation.

Sources

Kelly, Thomas R. *A Testament of Devotion* (New York: Harper & Row, Publishers, 1941) 47.

might step into the limelight. A prime example is Francis of Assisi, whom thousands have imitated.

Son of a wealthy cloth merchant, up to age twenty he paid no attention to the homeless who begged at Assisi's gates. He couldn't stand the sight of lepers. He enjoyed the affluent life his father's wealth afforded. A year spent in solitude as a prisoner of war, however, started a change. Over a period of about five years, a new Francis emerged—one who married Lady Poverty and started begging to help the poor, who kissed lepers he once shunned, and who launched a peace campaign bringing the senseless crusading to an end. He did not compose it, but later generations have attributed to him the magnificent prayer, "Lord, make me an instrument of your peace."

Reflections

Name modern women and men who have sacrificed or are sacrificing material possessions to the point of personal poverty in order to help those in need or to further the cause of justice in the world.

The Sacrament of the Present Moment

ontemplatives stereotyped interpretations of the Mary/Martha story so quickly that it may be hard to slip in another way of looking at it, but I will try. In their view, Mary represented the contemplative, Martha the active life; Mary's way being the superior one. I don't think Jesus, or Luke as preserver of the story, intended to make such gradations in vocation. Quite a few Protestant interpreters, as a matter of fact, have flipped the story over and used it to argue the superiority of the active life.

Notice here that Luke does not associate this pair with Lazarus and Bethany as John does (12:1-3). Jesus entered into "a certain village" and "a woman named Martha" hosted him (Luke 10:38). There is no strong reason not to connect this pair with Lazarus, but leaving it less definite simply enables the reader to pay attention to the story as a kind of acted parable.

Luke wants us to join him in imagination. On the way to Jerusalem, just after passing through Samaria, Jesus and his disciples entered this unnamed village. Details about place are unimportant. We are to fix our attention on the two women who are named and on Jesus. The point of the story revolves around them and their interaction with him.

Martha and Mary

Martha didn't want to grab the center of the stage. She focused on hosting. As at every other party, she intended to see that this guest got Class A treatment. She loved to tend to the details of hospitality. Mary, almost certainly the younger sister, stood near the opposite end of the spectrum. A person-oriented daydreamer,

Lectionary Loop
Seventh Sunday after Pentecost, Year C, Luke 10:38-42

Reflections
Join with fellow learners to recall times when they made preparations to welcome a special guest into a home. What were the dynamics among family members during the process? Who in the home was calling the shots? What would have happened if less preparation had been made?

she did her best to make the most of the moment with their guest, in this case a special guest. She readied herself for an experience of grace that attention to another can supply.

In our age and culture, Martha types abound, and most of us will probably sympathize with her complaint about her lollygagging sister plopped down in front of Jesus, pretending to lap up every word he spoke. Meantime, she left all the work to Martha. If dependent on Mary, the house might have been a shambles, Jesus' tired feet might have gone unwashed, and there might have been nothing to eat!

So we can understand Martha's agitation as she passed by the Jesus and Mary scene again and again. No wonder she was "distracted by her many tasks"; Mary was leaving all the work for her! It's no surprise, then, to see the older sister blow her stack. "She stopped and said, 'Sir, doesn't it bother you that my sister sits there on her can and lets me do all the work? Tell her to get up and help me!'" (my paraphrase).

How readily we Americans empathize. From our Puritan forbears, we have inherited a stout work ethic. In England, the Puritans became what social historian Christopher Hill has called "the industrious sort." Among other things, to facilitate industry, they regularized the calendar by way of Sabbath observance and eliminated the many saints days that interrupted work. They imported this outlook to the American "wilderness" and put it to work, and they engrained it in their descendants. Whereas the Puritans saved themselves from their own obsession with work by insisting on strict observance of the Sabbath as a day of rest, their descendants gradually eliminated even that safeguard to opt for wholesale workaholism.

"Martha, Martha"

Jesus' reply to Martha's demand was not harsh. Repeating her name gentles any criticism. One can visualize a smile as he said, "Martha, Martha." Maybe he reached a hand out to pat her arm, a calming and reassuring touch.

His reply shows, too, that he was not censoring work or her efforts at hosting. No, far from it. Her

Sources

Hill, Christopher. *Society and Puritanism in Pre-Revolutionary England.* 2nd ed. (New York: Schocken Books, 1967) 124-44, 153-9.

problem was getting so caught up in her busyness and distractedness that she was missing what Pierre de Caussade called "the sacrament of the present moment." "Martha, Martha, you worry and fret about a lot of things, but there is need of one" (my translation).

You will observe that I have not added the noun "thing" to "one." The Greek could mean either one *thing* or one *person*. The one who was needful was there, and Mary had chosen "the better part, which will not be taken from her." In her attention to Jesus, she elected to zero in on "the one thing needful."

Is this not close to the heart of our own dilemma? We get caught up in what Thomas Merton called "activity for activity's sake." We run pantingly and frantically through crowded calendars. We live uncollected and fragmented lives.

Years ago, Wayne Oates coined the word "workaholism." He confessed that he didn't know he was a workaholic until his wife and sons started calling him to make appointments to see him. Some don't know they are workaholics until they have heart attacks or nervous breakdowns; or their spouse says, "I want a divorce"; or they find their children in juvenile court. Oates observed that, in our culture, workaholism is more difficult to treat than alcoholism or drug addiction because work is socially approved.

What lies behind this addiction? Obviously it has become habitual. But where did the habit come from? If we look more deeply into the problem, I think we will find that it has something to do with ego. Meaningful employment is very important to self-esteem. Someone who has just lost a job or has been unemployed for a long time feels very low. In our culture, however, a subtle shift has occurred in our thinking. Not just *activity* but *quantity* of activity determines how we feel about ourselves.

Stop anyone and ask, "How are you?" Ninety-nine times out of a hundred you will get a litany of activities. "Oh, I'm so busy. I'm on thirteen committees at church and chair three of them. And I'm working two jobs, one forty hours a week, the other twenty." You begin to feel tired just listening.

Teaching Tips

Model your group session after a 12 Step recovery gathering. Each person in the group who sees herself or himself as a workaholic has a turn to say, "Hi, my name is _____, and I'm a workaholic." Then any group members who will may have a brief opportunity to tell their stories about how work controls their lives.

The Better Part

What is the answer to this dilemma? Jesus posits it in the example of Mary. She attended to "the one thing (or the one person) needful." In this respect, the contemplatives of Christian history have been right: Mary-like attentiveness should be the main business of our lives. Henry Nelson Wieman once said, "We ought to live each moment as if all eternity converged upon it." This surely is what the Mary/Martha story seeks to teach us. "The senses can only grasp the work of man [or woman]," Caussade wrote, "but faith sees the work of divine action in everything."

Sources

De Cussade, Jean-Pierre. *The Sacrament of the Present Moment*. Translated by Kitty Muggeridge (San Francisco: Harper & Row, Publishers, 1966) 84.

Teaching Tips

Ask members of the group to theorize the central reason many Americans allow work to consume them. Discuss ways in which they, as individuals, can find the "one thing needful."

Session 4   1 Thessalonians 5:17

Making All of Life a Prayer

The goal of devout Christians through the centuries has been to fulfill Paul's exhortation to "pray without ceasing." Early on, some Christians sought solitude and silence in the desert to achieve it. Some went without sleep, or at least claimed to do so, so they could pray without ceasing. They called themselves *Akoimitai*, which means "non-sleepers."

Others tried different forms of prayer. Some prayed all 150 psalms every day. Look at Ps 119 to see why it might well take every minute of twenty-four hours to pray them! Some prayed the Prayer of the Heart, also called the Jesus Prayer, "Lord Jesus Christ, Son of God, have mercy on me, a sinner," or some variation of it. They tried to synchronize each syllable with their heartbeat so that, waking or sleeping, they would be attentive to the ever-present Christ. In the nineteenth century, a Russian Orthodox Christian studied the writings of the ancient monks and came up with a formula for synchronizing that he set forth in *The Way of the Pilgrim*. The first week, he instructed, repeat the formula three thousand, the second week six thousand, and the third week twelve thousand times a day. Ever after, he assures us, whether waking or sleeping, your heart will be beating those words.

That Command in Context

No one can say with certainty what the apostle Paul had in mind when he directed the Thessalonians to pray incessantly. His terse two-word exhortation did not include a CD or an mp3 elaborating on a method of prayer. Nowhere else in his letters will you find more than alternate words suggesting that prayer takes quite a number of forms—thanksgiving (*eucharistia*), intercession (*enteuxis*), entreaty (*deesis*), or simply prayer (*proseuche*). The erstwhile rabbi did incorporate quite a few prayers, benedictions, or formulas. Yet none of these tell us how to pray without ceasing.

The context for the command helps. "Pray without ceasing" is part of a series of exhortations about Christian conduct. The chief focus is on attitude and outlook appropriate for a follower of Jesus or for one who lives "in the Spirit." This community of the newly converted needed plenty of guidance in how to get along with one another. That included respecting their leaders (12-13), practicing the art of nudging one another along (14), and loving those who offended them (15). Whether they might achieve such goals would depend on joyfulness, prayerfulness, and thankfulness—qualities Paul identifies as "the will of God in Christ Jesus for you."

Please note, *pace* the *akoimitai*, "praying without ceasing" is for the Christian not an activity to be engaged in twenty-four hours a day, seven days a week. It's an *attitude* and *orientation* toward life in the same way "rejoicing always" and "giving thanks in all circumstances" are. Paul shocked the Philippians when he told them that, his bleak circumstances notwithstanding, he rejoiced and would go on rejoicing (Phil 1:18) during his imprisonment in Rome. He urged them, too, to "rejoice in the Lord always." That they not miss the point, he added, "I will say it again, rejoice. Let your sweet spiritedness be known to all persons" (4:4-5; my translation). The same for thanksgiving and for praying!

Attentiveness

We've thought of prayer so much as an activity, especially petitioning, that we may find it hard to make a shift here to attitude and orientation. I've found very helpful in making my transition the insight born of practice of a seventeenth-century Carmelite lay brother named Nicholas Hermann, or Brother Lawrence. For ten years after entering the monastery at mid-life he tried Carmelite methods of prayer, but they only

---

Reflections

1. How can you live constantly with an attitude or orientation toward rejoicing and giving thanks?
2. What steps can you take to experience every moment in such a way?

frustrated him. Help came from his service as the monastery's cook. Washing dishes one day in the kitchen, he discovered that he could talk to the God of pots and pans or, as expressed in the title of a little book someone put together in memory of him, he could "practice the presence of God."

For Brother Lawrence prayer was, above all, attentiveness. "My commonest attitude," he wrote, "is this simple attentiveness, an habitual, loving turning of my eyes to God, to whom I often find myself bound with more happiness and gratification than that which a babe enjoys clinging to its nurse's breast." Quite clearly, Brother Lawrence's secret was that he fell head over heels in love with God and let that transfuse and transform everything he did. "I turn my little omelette in the pan for love of God," he exulted.

How do we come to love God with all our heart, soul, mind, and strength, as the greatest commandment requires (Mark 12:29-30)? Brother Lawrence was practical on this matter, too. To love God, you must first get to know God. But how do we get to know God, whom no human being has ever seen or will see and who, in truth, remains beyond all human comprehension (John 1:18)? Fortunately, our quest does not depend wholly on us, for God has sought to make God's self known through nature and, above all, through history.

Israel's poets perceived that God has encoded God's self, as it were, in the works of God's hands. "The heavens are telling the glory of God; and the firmament proclaims his handiwork," declared one. "Day to day pours forth speech, and night to night declares knowledge" (Ps 19:1-2) Oh, this bard knew it wasn't literally so. "There is no speech, nor are there words...yet their voice goes out through all the earth, and their words to the end of the world" (19:3-4).

What revelation may come to those who know how to see and to listen, not only about the world and about humankind but also about God's infinite care! "When I look at your heavens, the work of your fingers, the moon and the stars that you have established," another psalmist exclaimed and then asked the question,

Sources

Brother Lawrence, *The Practice of the Presence of God*. Translated by E.M. Blaiklock. (Nashville: Thomas Nelson Publishers, 1981) 45, 85.

Teaching Tips

Give each group member a pot or pan. (If you borrow them from the church's kitchen, be sure you put them back EXACTLY where you found them!) Ask each one to meditate on her or his pot or pan and then share with the larger group how the presence of God might be "practiced" in their own work lives. With what object from their work lives would they replace the pot or pan to tell their story of daily devotion?

Reflections

1. How do you come to know God?
2. In what specific persons, places, or things has God been revealed to you?

"What are human beings that you are mindful of them, mortals that you care for them?" (Ps 8:3-4) Small wonder Jesus would do his best to get the trembling souls of his day to pay attention to the lilies and the sparrows and the hairs of their heads.

As much as we get to know God through nature, we come nearer still to the Mystery at the heart of the universe through God's self-disclosure in history. That's true of all history, for God is in it all. Yet it is especially true of particular moments and stories—for the Hebrew peoples, the exodus from Egypt, and for Christian peoples, the Jesus story. It's true that "no one has ever seen God," the evangelist confesses for us all. Nevertheless, we have no reason to despair. Wonder of Wonders, "God's only Son who is in the bosom of the Father has exegeted God for us" (John 1:18; my translation).

Teaching Tips

Discuss with your study group how you, as a trained theologian, first learned about exegesis. Give specific details about the process and talk about how you apply exegetical principles to the texts from which you preach. Now, ask group members to speculate about the ways Jesus has "exegeted" God for us.

Having the Mind of Christ

You've seen it on bumper stickers, bracelets, rings, dangles in windshields of cars, and lots of other places. "WWJD—What would Jesus do?" It's not new. Francis of Assisi based his movement on such a question in the early thirteenth century. The Social Gospel movement of the late nineteenth century resuscitated it. It was at the heart of Shelton's *In His Steps*. And it has come around again in recent years.

Formulas like that sound awfully simplistic, but this one carries a deeper nuance. To be Christian means to have the mind of Christ (Phil 2:5), to have the living Christ recycle your understanding (Rom 12:2), to exhibit a different way of thinking and acting.

The Mind of Christ

We're talking about something with immense implications for the Christian spiritual life, but Paul did not leave his beloved Philippians guessing as to what the mind of Christ means in essence. They would make him burst with joy if they had unity of mind, heart, and soul, humbly counting others more important than themselves and putting the interest of others ahead of their own—in a word, if they thought and acted as Jesus Christ did.

Here Paul quoted what scholars have recognized as a hymn possibly composed by Paul but just as likely a hymn actually sung in churches at this time, probably at baptism, for it suits the theme of dying and rising with Christ. At a cosmic level and at an earthly level, Christ modeled servanthood, humility, and self-giving.

At the cosmic level he did not consider equality with God something selfishly to cling to, but rather he

Lectionary Loop

**Palm/Passion Sunday, Year A, B, C,
Philippians 2:5-11
Nineteenth Sunday after Pentecost,
Year A, Philippians 2:1-13**

Reflections

How often and in what ways do we try to force our biases and prejudices on Jesus so that we can have him, in our minds, approving what we are about rather than forcing upon ourselves the true radicality of his example?

emptied himself, in his human state taking a servant's form. As the Niceno-Constantinopolitan Creed phrased it, though "very God of very God," he "for us and for our salvation, came down from heaven." He did not come, however, in regal and imperial majesty—surely the way we humans would have expected—but as a menial servant.

At the human level, that of real flesh and blood, he humbled himself and died an ignominious death on a cross. Servanthood in its ultimate expression. Compassion in its ultimate expression. Here, surely, we see how far love will go—trusting himself into God's hands unreservedly, holding nothing back. His was a humble mind, a servant-minded mind, a God-enthralled mind.

Obtaining the Mind of Christ

Notice that Paul's exhortation to the Philippians can be translated in two different ways. "Let the same mind be in you *that was in Christ Jesus*" or "Let the same mind be in you that you have in Christ Jesus." The first would suggest imitation of Christ's example, the second living a life empowered and directed by the indwelling Christ. In his letters, Paul gives support to both ideas. For Paul the Christian life is, above all, life "in Christ." The challenge for us is how the mind of Christ may become our own.

Christians throughout the centuries have not assumed that having the mind of Christ would happen automatically. Take the bus and leave the driving up to Jesus. To be sure, when we open our inner doors and invite God in, the living Christ, the Spirit, makes his dwelling in us, so that our lives henceforth are Christ-controlled. For Christ to take control of our thoughts and actions, however, requires more. It takes some time studying and pondering the Jesus story.

It is not by accident that Christian meditation has focused on the Gospels. Although the faithful have spent time with all of Scripture, they have concentrated especially on the story of Jesus, his life and death and resurrection. From early centuries on, Christians have given special attention to the Gospels in corporate worship by standing when they are read and doing other things to call attention to their importance. Most of the great illuminated manuscripts that monastic artists so lovingly created are Gospels. Entering into these opens to us the mind of Christ.

It's a life-transforming story. Anthony Bloom was a medical doctor in the Soviet Union. An Orthodox priest came and asked him to do something for the church. Bloom said, "But I'm an atheist." The priest responded, "That's okay. Here, read this." He handed him a copy of the Gospel according to Mark. Bloom read the Gospel and became a Christian and soon an Orthdox priest himself.

Humility in an Age of Intimidation

In a culture that has made bestsellers of Robert J. Ringer's *Looking Out for Number One and Winning through Intimidation* and is reprising the Columbine massacre through computer simulation, humility may not seem to make much sense. Not the meek, as the Beatitude asserts, but the proud and aggressive inherit the earth. Not reserved but pushy people get ahead in sales, advertising, management, whatever. Not modest but swaggering athletes and teams win games. The logic seems sound until one asks whether the world's present dire situation of violence and disorder do not have their roots in such logic. Have westerners, including many Christians, fallen prey to the fallacious assumption that the use of force and violence can resolve complex problems in human relationships?

Although one can understand the hesitancy of some who have experienced more than their share of oppression (e.g. African Americans and women), to warm to the word "humility," we must recognize its centrality in Christian spirituality. According to the Hebrew wisdom tradition, God snatches the mighty from their thrones and lifts up the humble (Sirach 10:14; Job 5:11; 12:19; Luke 1:52). In Jesus' parable it was not the proud Pharisee but the self-abasing tax collector with not one thing he could cite to justify himself who went home okayed by God (Luke 18:14). Warning his disciples not to follow the example of the rabbis, Jesus put it pointedly, "The greatest among you will be your servant. All who exalt themselves will be humbled,

> ## Reflections
> What is your first memory of reading the Gospels? What were you thinking as the stories came alive in your consciousness? What impact did they make on your thinking? What impact did they make on your actions?

and all who humble themselves will be exalted" (Matt 23:11-12).

That verse guided early contemplatives. According to Benedict of Nursia, ascending the twelve steps of the ladder toward God depends on lowliness. Humility does not mean a dog-slinking attitude. Rather, as the anonymous author of the fourteenth century classic *The Cloud of Unknowing* explained, "In itself, humility is nothing else but a [person's] true awareness and understanding of himself [or herself] as he [or she] really is." Where pride, egocentrism, stands in the way of intimacy with God, honest owning of your humanity with all of its faults and needs opens the way to God.

Americans seem uncertain which way to turn at this juncture in our history. Could it be that this time of confusion and despair is a good time to do what Benedict of Nursia and Francis of Assisi did in their equally confused eras—to follow Jesus in servanthood?

Sources

Anonymous. *The Cloud of Unknowing*. Edited by James Walsh, S.J. (New York: Paulist Press, 1981) 148.

Teaching Tips

Ask group members to take a few minutes to meditate upon ways that they individually and/or as parts of a church group could do to be servants in your community. After a few minutes of silent reflection, invite three to five volunteers to pantomime an act of servanthood until the group guesses what it is.

Not Conformed but Transformed

A healthy spirituality should affect our relationship with the age and culture we live in. In Rom 12:2 Paul gives us wise counsel, which I paraphrase: "Do not be fitted into the mold of this age but be transformed by a recycling of your understanding, so that you may have a sense of what is God's will—what is good and acceptable to God and contributes to God's ultimate purpose."

Lectionary Loop
**Fourteenth Sunday after Pentecost,
Year A, Romans 12:1-8**

Not Conformed

To a considerable degree, all of us are fitted into the mold of the age in which we live. If that were not true, we could scarcely benefit from or contribute to our culture. From the time of our birth, our parents begin a process of inducting us into the culture's ways. In our schooling, teachers carry the process further. Over time, the whole culture sets to work shaping us in its mold.

Sometimes America's free-enterprise, market-oriented culture does too good a job. It beats, hammers, molds, engraves until we become its captives. Marketers make skillful use of advertising in order to convince us that we must use their product. Intimidating, isn't it, to know that if you want to be a real he-man out in Marlboro country, you have to smoke Marlboro cigarettes? No warning that smoking carries with it deadly consequences.

Here, we get a direct glimpse of the downside of this marketing. Three or four years before he died of lung cancer, one of the models used in Marlboro advertising pleaded with Philip Morris to stop using him as an advertisement because he was dying from their product.

But he was the company's most successful promotion, and they owned his image. Until the cigarette settlement in the U.S. forced them to stop using the ad, I would pass two huge Marlboro Man billboards as I drove from the Richmond airport into the city. The agreement, moreover, did not prohibit Philip Morris from using the ads in other countries. On a visit to Hong Kong three years ago, I passed those same Marlboro Man billboards as I drove from the airport into the city! We do not want to be simply shaped in our culture's mold.

But Transformed

How do we get free from our culture's control? Paul says the answer is being transformed by the renewal or recycling of our understanding. I can think of two means for recycling. One is education. The higher you go up the educational ladder, the more you should develop critical faculties enabling you to distinguish healthy from unhealthy choices. Higher education should enable us to compare our culture's ways with those of other cultures and to discriminate more clearly and readily between good and bad, right and wrong, true and false.

Unfortunately American higher education does not seem to have helped us achieve that critical perspective. Indeed, it has left out an important element of discernment. In *Where the Wasteland Ends* Theodore Roszak charged that American higher education creates "the single vision"—the way of empirical observation and rational reflection—and neglects "the powers of transcendence." A look at the history of American higher education shows why that is true.

When the land grant colleges, now the state universities, were created, they were directed to provide "knowledge for use." They have fulfilled their commission admirably, but at some cost to the humanities, which were once the core of higher education and which cultivated the powers of transcendence. Allocation of federal funds for higher education exacerbates and perpetuates the problem. As apportioned in recent years, 40% goes for military research, 37% for medical, 20% for other sciences, 3% for social sciences, 0% for humanities.

> **Reflections**
>
> What unhealthy products and practices have American marketers caused us to view and use as necessary and normative?

> **Sources**
>
> Roszak, Theodore. *Where the Wasteland Ends: Politics and Transcendence in Postindustrial Society* (Berkeley, CA: Celestial Arts, 1990).

This transformation by the recycling of understanding, therefore, must take place in another way—the way Paul doubtless had in mind when he wrote to the Romans, by conversion. I hesitate to use that word because, in the American context, it often is interpreted as a one-time affair. The apostle Paul had in mind God breaking through in a life-long, life-changing experience.

A Sense of God's Will

Ultimately, the object of our transformation is to have a sense of God's will. Our understanding of the will of God requires some rethinking. In the minds of many, the will of God is like a train track laid out before you. Get on the track, and stay on it. It will keep you in sync with God. When I first heard the analogy of a train on a track in a seminary class, I thought, "There's something wrong with that analogy." It hit me quickly. "I'm not a train. I don't run on a track. There's a big difference between human beings and trains."

Writing a series of meditations for *Upper Room Disciplines* some years ago, I did a study of every reference in the New Testament to the will of God, what pleases God, what is acceptable to God, and other parallel phrases. My research led me to the idea that the will of God has something to do, above all, with what kind of persons we are. God wants us to be persons who, living our lives from the vantage point of a covenant with God, are sensitized, conscientized, and tenderized to make the very best choices we can in whatever circumstances we are in.

In 1 Thess 4:3-8, Paul teaches that it is God's will that men should control their own lustful passions and treat their own bodies and their wives with holiness and honor. In 1 Thess 5:16-18, Paul says that the will of God is to be joyful, prayerful, and thankful in all circumstances. In Rom 12:2, Paul instructs that it is best to orient one's whole life toward God, that is, toward what is good, acceptable to God, and contributes to God's ultimate purpose.

This goal takes us back to the center of Paul's exhortation—being transformed by a recycling of our

---

Reflections

How is the word "conversion" often misunderstood in modern American culture? Discuss the life-long implications of conversion.

perceptions. Here, too, our culture gives us little help, for it tries to keep us on a treadmill of activities diverted from attention to God by an endless array of distractions. It surrounds us with deafening noise and blinding light. What that means is that, if you want a recycling of your understanding to occur, you will have to draw back and retreat, in order to spend time in solitude and silence where the "still, small voice" (1 Kgs 19:12, KJV) can break in upon you.

Our churches could assist us by modeling quiet and attentiveness in corporate worship and in the conduct of their gatherings. In addition, they could make retreats for individuals, families, and various groups within the church one of their chief ministries. Better those than offering the world more of what it already has more of than it needs.

Teaching Tips

This week's session ends in silence. No further explanation. No further discussion. No closing or parting words. The call is to utter silence in the room with a challenge for each person present to listen for the voice of God within. When you say, "Amen," then everyone may leave in silence.

The Sufficiency of Grace

All Christians owe a great debt to the apostle Paul for enabling us to recognize that spirituality is, in essence, a work of grace in Christian life. As a Jewish rabbi named Saul set to bring an end to the Jesus-movement, he bitterly assailed the proclamation of a vulnerable God who has joined us even at the deepest point of our human struggle. Meeting Christ on the road to Damascus dramatically transformed his understanding (Gal 1:13-17) and his person. The persecutor Saul became the Apostle Paul.

As critical as his conversion was, Paul's own experience of vulnerability, which he describes in 2 Corinthians, brought him still greater confidence in God's power working through human weakness. God's grace is sufficient, as we learn from the cross, precisely because God meets us in our weakness.

Lectionary Loop
Fourth Sunday after Pentecost, Year B, 2 Corinthians 12:2-10

Plea about "a Thorn in the Flesh"

No one can say for sure what Paul's "thorn in the flesh" was. At the end of his letter to the Galatians, Paul hints at serious eye trouble that forced him to write with larger print (Gal 6:11). Physical illness brought him to Galatia the first time, and he says to the people there, "Had it been possible, you would have torn out your eyes and given them to me" (4:15). There are also indications that Paul suffered from epilepsy in a day long before there were medications to control epileptic seizures. We can't be sure.

We can be sure that Paul had an intense desire to be healed. Three times, he says, he urged (almost "commanded") the Lord to take it away. Now, "three times" in Hebrew idiom would not suggest that he threw up three little prayers and let it go at that. It means he pulled out all the stops. He put up a stout argument. Like all of us in the circumstances, he demanded to know why. Why he of all people?

Notice that Paul did not toss off any trite and easy answer such as we heard when tsunamis wiped out thousands and thousands of lives in the Indian Ocean basin. "It must have been God's will." This astute theological thinker recognized that there is a mystery about evil. Oh, within the natural order we can talk about an unfinished universe wherein things may go wrong. Within the human order we can talk about human choice to do evil or failure to exercise responsibility. But when it comes down to us personally, however, we can't understand it; Paul called it "a messenger of Satan" (2 Cor 12:7). You may feel like actress Patricia Neal. Her eight-year-old daughter contracted measles and died unexplainably. Her year-and-a-half-old son was struck by a taxi and maimed for life. Then she herself suffered a series of crippling strokes. She said, "I think God must have been looking the other way."

"My Grace Is Sufficient."

So Paul did not get the answer he wanted. We all know his feeling, for we too often do not get the answer we want. But he got the one we need when we are really in the pit, looking up to see bottom. "My grace is sufficient for you" (12:9).

"Grace" must mean here more than "God's unmerited favor," the phrase Protestants have often used to define it. It means, rather, God's gift of God's self, the Holy Spirit. It means what the ancient psalmist declared, "Even though I walk through the darkest valley, I fear no evil, for you are with me; your rod and your staff—they comfort me" (Ps 23:4). When you come up against something with which you cannot cope on your own resources, God alone is enough.

When I first started teaching at Southern Baptist Seminary in Louisville nearly a half century ago, I noticed a loss of hearing. Close on the heels of that, I also began to lose my voice. The loss of one vital faculty is difficult, but the loss of two in quick succession

Reflections

What local, national, or international tragedies have you heard attributed to God's will? What is your feeling about this? Does God will these tragedies? Does God allow them to happen?

can be overwhelming. I felt the floodwaters pouring over me. At first I reacted as we all do, demanding, "Why me?" Then I began to clench my fist and grit my teeth and say, "This will not happen to me." The more I clenched my fist and gritted my teeth, the more I slid backwards, like scrambling up a hill in loose gravel. The harder you scramble, the more you slide back. Then, surrounded by family, colleagues, students, friends, I began to hear these words, "My grace is sufficient for you." It's true!

All too often, I fear, we go through life like people who are afraid of water and don't know how to swim. When we get in the water, we flail our arms around until we wear ourselves out; and then we drown. The saints in all religions remind us that we live in an ocean of love and are surrounded by love. If we will learn how to let down, we will discover a buoyancy that is there to hold us up. God's grace is sufficient.

Power Perfected in Weakness

To Paul also came an explanation as to why that is true: "for my power is made perfect in weakness." How that paradoxical assertion must have puzzled Paul's contemporaries, as at first even Paul himself. How enigmatic it will seem, too, to our contemporaries.

Oh, we know a lot about power. Indeed, future generations will remark that our culture was obsessed with power. We want more power to run larger electric generators so that we can enjoy more comforts and conveniences. We want more power to put up larger payloads into space. We want more power to terrify our enemies. But our power logic is not God's power logic.

Our logic declares: The weak are weak. The strong are strong. In weakness is weakness. In strength is strength. God's power logic says: In your human weakness you may find my power. That, you see, is the logic of the cross. The cross is about the Eternal God joining us in our vulnerability.

None, surely, grasped that more securely than the once bitter enemy of the Jesus-movement. As 1 Cor 1–2 makes clear, he placed the cross at the center of his proclamation. The preaching of the cross may be

> ### Reflections
>
> Has anyone in the group had the experience of finding God's strength and power in a time or experience of utter personal weakness or helplessness?

foolishness to those who are perishing, but it is God's power to those being saved (1 Cor 1:18). Paul parried slashing attacks of his Corinthian critics with an admission of incompetency, but he stood that on its head by asserting that God had made him competent to be a minister (2 Cor 3:4-6). Why does God choose to do things this way? To take away any human ground for boasting (1 Cor 1:29) or, stated positively, "so that it may be made clear that this extraordinary power belongs to God and does not come from us" (2 Cor 4:7). In brief, to say it's all about GRACE!

Teaching Tips

If you have a small group, don't divide it for this activity. In a small group or in small groups, challenge participants to become an ad hoc worship planning committee whose responsibility is to plan a worship service celebrating God's grace from beginning to end. How would the service be structured? What Scripture lessons would be read? What songs would be sung? What would the choral or solo selections be? Who would be involved in worship leadership other than the professional staff? What components would be added to the service not usually included in a "typical" service at your church?

God's Inescapable Nearness

One hears a lot of complaints about devout believers admitting that they sense the absence of God. The unknown author of Ps 139 shocks us with the opposite complaint—the inescapable presence of God. The psalmist was doing his dead level best to flee God but could not. Wherever he went and whatever he did, there God was. Which way would we rather have it—a God far off or a God so near?

Truth to tell, we probably want God on our own terms, by our own choice, but one thing our psalmist and other saints will tell us is that it's better to leave some things up to God. Don't be too quick to rescue strugglers from their pain. More often than we'd like to believe, God is present in an experience of absence, and there is pain in presence.

The Pain of Presence

Many may think an experience of the presence of God is euphoric, pure pleasure. God's presence laid our psalmist completely bare, wholly exposed without a shred of cover. Not even a thought escapes God's notice. Total vulnerability—opening a wound and exposing it for all to see.

Augustine, the brilliant African theologian, would have readily understood. He learned about pain in one of his darkest dark nights of the soul. A deep plunge into life's black vale resulted from the death of an intimate friend while Augustine was away from his hometown of Tagaste. On returning, grief consumed him. "My heart was made dark by sorrow," he lamented, "and whatever I looked upon was death." A member of the Manichaean sect at that point in his life, he could

> ## Lectionary Loop
> **Ninth Sunday after Pentecost, Year A, Psalm 139:1-12, 23-24**

find no salve for his sorrow. Every time he tried to put his burden aside, it hurtled back upon him through the void. He found no solace. "For where could my heart fly to, away from my heart?" he asked. "Where could I fly to, apart from my own self? Where would I not pursue myself?" Yet he elected the geographical solution and fled from his hometown to the big city of Carthage.

As Augustine asked those questions, he was asking something similar to the psalmist's agonizing plea, "Where can I go from your spirit? Or where can I flee from your presence?" For in looking up to see bottom, the great theologian discovered the very truth our vagabond psalmist knew well, that there is nowhere God is not present. Neither the farthest reaches of the sea nor the darkest darkness banishes God. God, the Eternal, confronts us in our souls, yes even in our experience of the absence of God.

Neither Heaven Nor Hell

Verse 8 expresses the psalmist's discovery in its starkest, most condensed form. "If I ascend to heaven, you are there" brings no surprise. That is where, by definition, we expect God to be. Heaven is God's place in human imagination. God should feel at home. Correspondingly, we humans should do our best to make our way upwards toward the heavenly city.

What dashes us awake is the second half of this verse: "if I make my bed in Sheol, you are there." Two things jump out as the psalmist makes his point.

First, he says, "If I *make* my bed in Sheol, you are there" (emphasis mine). He doesn't say, "If I trip and fall in." That says loudly and clearly, "You can't mess your life up to such an extent that God will forsake you." We human beings are very good at jumping to such a conclusion when we sin, err, or fail in some way. "I've messed up. There is no longer any hope for me." Our psalmist found that untrue.

Second, in Hebrew thought Sheol is, also by definition, where God is not. No saint wanted to go down to Sheol, the place of God's absence. The worst curse one might wish upon an enemy was this: "Let death come upon them; let them go down alive to Sheol; for evil is

Sources

Augustine. *The Confessions of St. Augustine*. Translated by John K. Ryan (Garden City, NY: Doubleday Image Books, 1960) 98, 100-101.

Teaching Tips

Would any group members care to share examples of how and where they, at some point in their lives, tried to run away from God?

Teaching Tips

Using daily newspapers, magazines, and other print media, ask members to create collages either individually or in teams. On the left-hand side of the page, the pictures/images/words will represent heaven, where God's presence is known, and on the right-hand side of the page, they will represent Sheol/hell, where God is absent.

in their homes and in their hearts" (Ps 55:15). For our psalmist, not even Sheol lets you avoid God's presence.

Why, then, you may ask, do we so often experience the absence of God? It's amply attested in human history: where there is illness and suffering, injustice and oppression, massive evil as in World War II, a sense of guilt, and death, the ultimate evil. Some argue that the experience proves God does not exist. Others ascribe it to culture. Humans have reached a point where they no longer resort to God. Martin Luther and, in more recent times, Karl Barth insisted that God hides sometimes. Others have pointed to God's self-limitations and entrance into human suffering. In the last analysis, can anyone say for sure?

One observation: Experience of God's absence is the experience of those who take God and the search for God most seriously, as Job, the psalmists, the prophets, or Jesus did. People who have only a casual concern for God are not likely to cry about a sense of desolation, as Jesus did on the cross.

Attending the Inescapable One

Our psalmist's insistence on God's inescapable nearness should make those who hunger and thirst for God wonder how to attune themselves to the Presence. In this frenetic culture we live in, can we improve our seeing, listening, and attending beyond the external?

In a classic entitled *On Listening to Another*, Douglas Steere observed that listening occurs at many different levels. There is the level of the spoken word, but at a deeper level there is "where words come from." Today we make much of non-verbal communication. A sigh, a tear trickling down someone's cheek, may say far more than the words uttered.

Within every conversation, as Soren Kierkegaard reminded his contemporaries, there is the Eternal Listener or the Eternal Spectator. Psalm 139 gives us evidence of that. If we really listen, Douglas Steere insisted, we may listen to another person as a condition of awareness of the Eternal Listener. And, we may also become aware ourselves of the Eternal Listener.

If we are honest, I think we will have to recognize

Resources

A collection of essays edited by Christian Duquoc and Casiano Floristan entitled *Where Is God? A Cry of Human Distress* (London: SCM Press Ltd, 1992), has explored these reasons. See also Elie Wiesel, *All Rivers Run to the Sea: Memoirs* (New York: Schocken Books, 1995) 84, and Dietrich Bonhoeffer, *Letters and Papers from Prison* (New York: Macmillan Co., 1972) 279, 325-26.

Sources

Steere, Douglas. *On Listening to Another* (New York: Harper, 1955).

that we are not doing well with listening and seeing in our noisy and frantic western culture. How can we improve them?

The saints have found two methods helpful. Curiously, they are polar opposites. One is to spend time among people who are hurting. Exposure to others' pains may sensitize and conscientize and tenderize. Yet you will learn quickly that uninterrupted exposure to hurt may also cause you to become calloused. That is why most have imitated our psalmist in choosing a second option—drawing back to spend time in solitude and silence. Solitude permits you to get away from the distractions constantly pummeling your senses. Silence sensitizes.

Reflections

Are there differences of opinion in the group about the value of solitude in spiritual formation? Do single (never-married, divorced, widowed) persons see it any differently than members of busy, full families?

Session 9

Mark 12:28-34;
Matthew 22:34-40; Luke 10:25-29

Whole-Personed Spirituality

The two great commandments, whether cited by Jesus (as in Mark and Matthew) or by his questioner (as in Luke), remind us that a healthy spirituality should be whole-personed. Love of God and of fellow human beings is, of course, its heart. God initiates this love. We love because God first loved us (1 John 4:19). We who have experienced such great love want to respond not simply with one but with every aspect of our being. Not only so, we, the beloved, will love not God alone but everyone and everything God has made even as we love ourselves.

The spiritual life, Thomas Merton has said "is not just a life concentrated at the 'high point' of the soul, a life from which the mind and the imagination and the body are excluded. If it were so, few people could lead it. And again, if that were the spiritual life, it would not be a life at all. If [one] is to live, [one] must be all alive, body, soul, mind, heart, spirit. Everything must be elevated and transformed by the action of God, in love and faith."

God Love

It is worthy of note that, according to the evangelists, Jesus added one extra dimension to the commandment as given in Deut 6:5. The commandment there is: "You shall love the LORD your God with all your heart, and with all your soul, and with all your might." All three evangelists add "with all your mind." Mark and Matthew list it third, and Luke lists it fourth in the sequence. In the addition we may be looking at a Greek context in which the mind, rather than the heart, defined personal being. If so, it underscores the

Lectionary Loop

Twenty-third Sunday after Pentecost, Year A, Matthew 22:34-46
Twenty-first Sunday after Pentecost, Year B, Mark 12:28-34
Sixth Sunday after Pentecost, Year C, Luke 10:25-37

Sources

Merton, Thomas. *Thoughts in Solitude* (Garden City, NY: Doubleday Image Books, 1958) 29.

central point: Every fiber of our being should enter into our devotion to God!

The sequence seems important. *Heart* first. Faith begins in awe. "When mind and soul agree," Abraham Heschel has said, "belief is born. But first our hearts must know the shudder of adoration." Faith is not the end of a step-by-step process. It is not assent to a logical proposition. It is, rather, "a blush in the presence of God." You can never answer all the questions human minds can devise. Yet your heart murmurs yes to Someone in response to an awareness that you are loved with infinite love. As Blaise Pascal, after long and agonized searching, recognized, "The heart has its reasons, of which reason knows nothing; we feel it in many things...It is the heart, not reason, which experiences God. This then is faith: God perceived by the heart and not by reason."

Soul must have intimate connection with the heart in this exhortation. In Hebrew thinking the heart had to do with the mind and will, whereas the soul corresponded to the self or vital life principle. God's love asks for complete self-giving. From the depths of our being, we give ourselves, our very lives, over to God.

Mind probably puts into Greek idiom what *heart* communicated in Hebrew. In modern Western usage, we may think of left and right brain functions as we interpret the terms. The point is, both the rational and the emotional should play a role in our act of loving God. True, the heart makes the crucial decision as to whether you will live your life from the vantage point of a relationship with God. Once you have taken that leap of faith, however, your mind will set to work and do everything possible to unravel the mystery of faith.

Strength reminds us that the physical should not be omitted from our devotion. Hebrew psychology did not compartmentalize personhood. Adam was formed from the dust of the earth, into which God breathed the breath of life, so that he became a living being (Gen 2:7). All through the centuries, saints have taken note of the integral interknittedness of physical and spiritual health and have cultivated ways to praise God in both.

Teaching Tips

Create an interlinear study sheet of the above Synoptic references: Mark in the left-hand column, Matthew in the center column, and Luke in the right-hand column; include each passage's immediate context. Ask group members to study each of these passages side-by-side and bring up any observations that come to their minds.

Sources

Heschel, Abraham Joshua. *Man Is Not Alone* (New York: Farrar, Straus & Giroux, Inc., 1951) 74, 91.

Pascal, Blaise. *Pensées*. Translated by John Warrington (New York: E.P. Dutton & Co. Inc., 1960) 59-60.

Reflections

What happens to a faith effort that becomes all left-brained? What happens to one that becomes all right-brained?

Neighbor-Love

Just as our response to God's love should entail our whole person, so too should it entail love of persons and things God has made. So integral is love of neighbor to love of God that the apostle Paul could declare, "The whole law is summed up in a single commandment, 'You shall love your neighbor as yourself'" (Gal 5:14). How could he gloss over the first and greatest commandment? Only by recognizing that it is fully implicit in the second. As Rabbi Heschel once said, "True love of man is clandestine love of God."

"Love your neighbor as yourself" was not new; it was a part of Torah (Lev 19:18). Where Jesus stretched it was with reference to who "neighbor" embraces. For some it stretched no farther than the people of the covenant. Luke used his presentation of the two great commandments as an occasion to ask whether, in the nature of God's love, it must not include some outside the covenant. In response to a self-justifying query, "Who is my neighbor?" Jesus told the parable of the Samaritan who exhibited rather than prated about what is right.

The parable is quite familiar, but it would seem to have special applicability to the present day when animosities have reached a feverish pitch. Samaritans were not just outcasts and outsiders in the minds of Jesus' contemporaries; they were enemies with whom the truly faithful did not associate. Yet Jesus chose the enemy to illustrate the wideness of God's mercy in much the same way he earned a reputation as a friend of tax collectors and sinners. God is not as fastidious about adherence to the stipulations of the law as were those who confronted Jesus with this question.

If the parable of the Samaritan, as well as Jesus' other words and actions, underscores any point about neighbor love, it is that in God's economy compassion trumps religious and political correctness. Jesus headed a compassion movement that often locked horns with the holiness movement headed by Israel's religious elite. Could this be one of those periods when Christians practice was what Douglas V. Steere called "mutual irradiation"? We let the light of God in us irradiate persons of other

Sources

Heschel, Abraham Joshua. *Man Is Not Alone* (New York: Farrar, Straus & Giroux, Inc., 1951) 139.

Reflections

Who are today's Samaritans? Would they include Muslims, whom we associate so readily with terrorism? Gays and lesbians, whose alternative lifestyles challenge traditional concepts of marriage and family? Immigrants, legal and illegal, who risk their lives to cross America's borders so they can benefit from bounties their own societies cannot supply?

faiths, and we let ourselves be irradiated by the light of God in them. Not since the high Middle Ages has the need for such neighbor-love been greater.

Session 10   Romans 5:1-5

Suffering and Hope

Whether there is reason for hope is one of the pressing questions confronting us in this first decade of a new millennium. We humans can survive without many of life's necessities, but we can't survive without hope.

It's Hard to Be Hopeful!

Persons who lived through much of the twentieth century will know that it is not easy to be hopeful. Two devastating world wars in quick succession, the second of which cost sixty million lives. Wonderful advances in science and technology turning to threatening and sometimes destructive purposes. The Holocaust, followed by continuing inhumanity toward fellow human beings in Rwanda, the former Yugoslavia, and now Darfur in Sudan. Squandering of earth's precious resources and, simultaneously, upsetting nature's delicate balances with global warming. Violent and senseless waste of human life in Oklahoma City, New York City, and Baghdad.

To pile doubt on doubt, in 2005 we witnessed tsunamis that claimed almost two hundred thousand lives in the Indian Ocean Basin, earthquakes taking tens of thousands in Pakistan, and Hurricane Katrina devastating the Gulf Coast and nearly wiping out the entire city of New Orleans.

Few of us will have trouble comprehending the pessimism and nihilism that have captured the minds of many. Samuel Beckett, a Nobel Prize-winning playwright, epitomized the hopelessness of Europeans since the mid-twentieth century. In *Waiting for Godot* one of the characters summed it up: "I've puked my

Lectionary Loop

Third Sunday in Lent, Year A, Romans 5:1-11
Fourth Sunday after Pentecost, Year A, Romans 5:1-8
Trinity Sunday, Year C, Romans 5:1-5

Reflections

What were you thinking as the news presented bit by bit the increasing horror of Katrina? What did you do in response to the danger or to help the victims?

puke of a life away here, I tell you." His dour companion comforted him with, "To every man his little cross. Till he dies. And is forgotten… What is terrible is to have thought."

But There's Reason for Hope.

So it is hard to be hopeful. Yet there is reason for hope that we must find *in the midst of suffering.* As Paul reminded his Thessalonian converts, we should not be as those who have no hope (1 Th 4:13).

Jane Goodall, the authority on chimpanzees and apes and human evolution, cited four things in her autobiography as the bases for hope: the human brain, the resilience of nature, the energy and enthusiasm that is or can be kindled among young people worldwide, and the indomitable human spirit.

I find those hopeful, too. The human brain can and does accomplish marvelous things. Advances in medical science are overwhelming. When I was seven years old, I spent a month in a coma with pneumonia. Today, penicillin will cure pneumonia in a day or two. Although it was invented in 1928, penicillin was not used to cure pneumonia until 1940, two years after I lived through it.

Nature's incredible recuperative powers have displayed themselves in the recovery of human, animal, and plant life from the terrifying destruction wreaked by the bombing of Hiroshima and Nagasaki and the disaster wrought by the nuclear meltdown in Chernobyl, Belarus.

There are ample evidences of the kindling of *energy and enthusiasm for good* not only among youth. "Doctors without Borders" received the Nobel Peace Prize in 1998 for the selfless and risky care they undertake all over the world. Worldwide care extended to survivors of the tsunami, earthquakes, and Hurricane Katrina in 2005-06 reached levels never before witnessed in human memory.

Then we've seen *the indomitable human spirit* manifest itself in persons like Gorbachev, Mandela, M.L. King, Jr., Mother Teresa of Calcutta, and Aung San Suu Kyi of Myanmar. Tom Brokaw made us conscious of that spirit in *The Greatest Generation*, those who

Sources

Goodall, Jane. *Reason for Hope: A Spiritual Journey* (New York: Time Warner Co., 1999) 233.

fought in World War II and who sought to put the world back together when it ended.

Hope in Suffering

I find these hopeful, too. They are rays of light poking through dark clouds. But I think Paul points us to a more secure ground of hope in Rom 5:1-5. Permit me to paraphrase the text:

> Having been okayed by faith, we have *shalom* with God through our Lord Jesus Christ. Through him we have had the door opened to this grace in which we have taken our stand. We take pride in God's glorious hope. Not only so, but we take pride in hardships, knowing that hardship produces toughness, and toughness integrity, and integrity hope. Now hope never disappoints, for God's love has been poured into our hearts through the Holy Spirit which God has given us.

Wow! What a profound analysis of our human dilemma. Ultimately, hope does not depend only on our human brains, resilience of nature, the energy and enthusiasm we human beings muster, or the indomitable human spirit. There is also *God*, the God who ever creates and guides this universe of one hundred and fifty billion galaxies toward some meaningful end. Hope is God's gift. Hope is a consequence of the fact that a God of infinite love has poured that love into our hearts through the Holy Spirit, God's gift of God's self.

This, you see, addresses the ambivalence and fickleness of our human situation where, all our efforts notwithstanding, "The wrong seems oft so strong." Paul, ever the realist, knew that humans see life *now*, as it were, in a mirror as an enigma (1 Cor 13:12). Never, so long as we live, will we have unquestioned clarity about the good and the bad, the right and the wrong, the true and the false that are the makeup of our existence. We may spend our lives in the quest to know and end up in unknowing. So, Paul lays it down as an axiom: *we must live by hope*.

If I understand Paul's purpose in Romans, he is prompting us to recognize that hope lies in God's uniting with us in our vulnerability, pain, and suffering. He will have shocked many of those Christians in Rome

Teaching Tips

If the group is willing and musically inclined, have the group sing one stanza each of four or five familiar hymns that give them hope.

as he shocks us when he says that we have reason to hope not only in "glory" but in "sufferings," afflictions, or hardships. Strange logic? Yes, it's the logic of the cross.

Paul's experience of life taught him that suffering may set off a kind of chain reaction leading to hope. See it?

Hardship produces toughness.

Toughness produces integrity.

Integrity produces hope.

Could it work like this? Chop wood or hoe in your garden for a while. When you start, you will feel pain. After a while, your hands will callous and be tougher, and the work will get easier. So, too, in the spiritual life. I can't think of a single saint who failed to "learn through what she suffered." Hardship—toughness—integrity—hope.

Teilhard de Chardin, the great Jesuit paleontologist and philosopher, said so perceptively, "We must overcome death by finding God in it. And by the same token, we shall find the divine established in our innermost hearts, in the last stronghold which might have seemed to escape his reach." Yes, and we must overcome life, too, for it can often be more frightening than death. We overcome pain, sorrow, sickness, and whatever else life presents by finding God in every circumstance. That's where hope is.

Sources

De Chardin, Teilhard. *The Divine Milieu* (London: Collins, 1960) 82.

Reflections

Ask members of your study group to discuss their greatest hopes and the most powerful facts/forces that would steal their hope.

TEXTS OF COURAGE, FAILURE AND NEW HOPE

A STUDY BY

UWE C. SCHARF

Uwe C. Sharf is an ordained minister of the Christian Church, (Disciples of Christ).
He is the Director of the Pastoral Care Department at Johns Hopkins Hospital in Baltimore, MD.

Outline

I. Introduction

II. Session 1—Peter Walking On Water—and Sinking: Matthew 14:22-34
   A. Introduction: Context of Story
   B. Jesus' Miracles
   C. Prayer in Solitude
   D. "It is a Ghost"
   E. Walking On Water, Sinking in Despair

III. Session 2—"You are the Christ" followed by "Get Thee Behind Me, Satan": Matthew 16:13-28
   A Living Between Extremes
   B. Peter's and Our Own Reluctance to Accept Suffering as God's Way
   C. If Peter's Vision is Our Vision then Whose Vision is Christ's Vision?

IV. Session 3—Washing of Feet—Washing Hands and Head As Well?: John 13:1-20
   A. "You Will Never Wash My Feet"
   B. The Holy Desire to be Close to God and the Demonic Desire to be Closer to God than Anybody Else
   C. Tenderness and Care beyond Acceptance and Redemption

V. Session 4—Defending Jesus with the Sword, Following Him to the Halls of Judgment—and Denying Him: Matthew 26:47-75; John 18:1-27
   A. Cutting off the Servant's Ear: Act of Courage or Act of Desperation?
   B. "I Don't Know the Man": Courage and Bravado Turn into Cowardice and Naked Fear
   C. Betrayal, Bitter Tears, and the Way of the Cross
   D. A Chaplain's Perspective on Transition, Utilizing Kübler Ross's Stages of Grief

VI. Session 5—Peter, Do You Love Me?: John 21:1-19
   A. "Do You Love Me?"—"Lord, You Know, I Love You"—"Follow Me": Renewing the Call into Discipleship at the End of the Gospel
   B. A New Beginning for Peter and for Us—Again and Again—and that Is *Not* Cheap Grace (*Nor* Divine Favoritism)

Introduction

Texts of Courage, Failure, and New Hope

W hen I was looking for biblical texts that exhibited the themes of hope and courage, the life of Simon Peter came to mind. He demonstrated courage, and he had, at times, hope against the odds; but Peter also failed along the way. Of course there are other biblical people who demonstrated these characteristics, too, so why focus on Simon Peter in a study of courage, failure, and new hope? Well, his confession is the rock on which the church is built, for one. He was prominent among Jesus' twelve disciples. And, he was so extreme–quick to talk, slow to think, courageous, cowardly, exuberant, frightened—so human. Simon Peter reminds me of me. I think I have a lot of Simon Peter in me. I would love to be as balanced, as mild, and as saintly as the Johannine disciple who lays on Jesus' bosom and who arrives at Jesus' grave before Simon Peter and who will care for Mary, Jesus' mother, as a son does for his mother—but I am not that saintly. I am not that meek and mild. I have rough edges. I am more the Simon Peter type who can be loud and overly confident (though well-intentioned, of course), who can put his foot in his mouth, who can lop off the High Priest's servant's ear—and who then is too scared to declare his allegiance to Christ in front of a servant girl. The "I don't know the man" or "I don't know what you are talking about—therefore leave me in peace" response is a familiar pattern in my life—and I suspect in your life and in the lives of many people you know, as well.

In my life, I experience not only themes of hope and courage, but also elements of courage, failure, and redemption. In my journey, the redirection from the philosophical (lofty) theology of my doctoral field to the (gritty) theology of clinical pastoral education (CPE) was very important. The change from a systematic or philosophical theologian looking toward a career in academic (lofty, comfortable, theoretical) theology to a chaplain and chaplain educator (CPE supervisor) and administrator of a department of pastoral care in a major U.S. hospital has made me more and more aware of the fact that failure and hopelessness are just as much topics of human life as the themes of hope and courage.

Simon Peter—in most of the stories that are written about him—comes across as a very real person. He's not a caricature or a boring, angelic appropriation of the sanctified life. The portrayal of this particular disciple is realistic, gritty, interesting, engaging, human, hopeful and down to earth. I can see myself, in my own human struggles, better captured in the figure of Peter than in the figure of John or Paul. So, I have chosen to focus on Peter because I find I have a lot to learn from his life.

What are your own associations with the three terms, "courage," "failure," and "new hope"? Is there any one theme that's more dominant in your life than the other two?

I admire people who, like Peter, wrestle with a lot of inner demons, people who have to get up every morning, take anxiety into their own understanding of the holy, and live a faith that allows for doubt and that wrestles with despair. I admire people who know about the demonic (not the little demons that float in the air but the human struggles of sexuality, commitment, immigration, peace, and war), and who know that the divine and the demonic are never far from each other—they are both part and parcel of the "human predicament," as the theologian Paul Tillich liked to say.

Many patients who come to the Johns Hopkins Hospital in Baltimore, MD find their way to the Administrative Building, which used to be the entrance to the hospital. In this old building, with a beautiful dome on

Sources

For more information about Clinical Pastoral Education (CPE) go to the national website of the Association for Clinical Pastoral Education, Inc., http://www.acpe.edu.

Reflections

What do you know about Simon Peter? Are you a fairly balanced person, or are you a person of extremes?

Teaching Tips

Ask participants to define each of these terms. As a second step, ask them to write down associations with each of the terms. Third, ask people to tell a story of courage, a story of failure and a story of redemption.

Teaching Tips

Ask participants to identify themselves with one of the disciples (male or female). What areas of correspondence between the ancient and present-day disciples come up?

top stands a ten-foot marble statue of Christ. The statue is on a platform with an inscription that reads: "Come unto me all ye that are weary and heavy laden and I will give you rest" (Matt 11:28). Many patients receive hope from an encounter with this statue of Christ that, for many, translates into an encounter with the living Christ, or with the Great Physician, or with a power greater than their own. Stories of many of the patients, family members, physicians, and staff whose hope was kindled or rekindled by meditating at the feet of Christ, pondering the message of Christ who invites us with open arms are collected in a beautiful book, *Here is My Hope*. Christ—as pictured vividly in this powerful statue—encourages us to unburden ourselves and to look at him just as Peter looked at him again after he had been frightened by the waves and began to sink (Matt 14:22-33).

These sessions are an invitation to be real, to be honest, to be forthright, and to be courageous as well as hopeful. With God there is always a new beginning—always, always, always—no matter how often they warned you in seminary or a Bible study about "cheap grace." These sessions show that just as Christ admonishes us to forgive our brother, sister, or neighbor near or far, seventy times seven times (Matt 18:21-22), so God through Christ is ready to give us grace and to invite us back into discipleship—if need be on a daily or hourly basis. May you, and people with whom you share these studies, be blessed in the reading and discussing of these sessions from the life of Simon Peter on courage, failure, and new hope.

Sources

Henderson, Randi and Richard Marek, eds. *Here Is My Hope: A Book of Healing and Prayer: Inspirational Stories from the Johns Hopkins Hospital* (New York, Doubleday, 2001).

Peter Walking On Water—and Sinking

Introduction: Context of Story

This is one of my favorites among the five Peter stories that we will study in these sessions. Before getting into the details, let's note the context of the story, as it appears now in our Bible. This story comes on the heels of two stories within ch. 14. Verses 1-12 talk about the beheading of John the Baptist, and vv. 13-21 tell the story of the feeding of five thousand men (plus women and children). Verse 13 reads: "Now when Jesus heard this [the news of John the Baptist's beheading], he withdrew from there in a boat to a deserted place by himself." Reading this verse while in the role of a chaplain, I see Jesus' withdrawal as a grief response. I read Jesus' desire to be alone as coming out of shock and maybe disbelief or anger as well. Later in the book of Matthew, when Jesus faces his own imminent death, he wrestles with God and shouts, "My God, my God, why have you forsaken me?" (Matt 27:46). I would not be surprised if, upon hearing of John's execution, Jesus wrestled with God in prayer and asked, "My God, my God, why have you forsaken *John*?"

John was Jesus' forerunner, and some say his mentor. He clearly was the one who began a reform movement and who baptized Jesus. Jesus' own message of the inbreaking of the kingdom of God was similar to the message of John—namely, repentance and renewal and a new way of living in the anticipation of God's rule. So Jesus withdrew—or tried to withdraw; the crowds gave him no break. Instead of getting angry or impatient with the crowd—as many of us would be—Jesus "had

Lectionary Loop
**Twelfth Sunday after Pentecost,
Year A, Matthew 14:22-33**

compassion for them and cured their sick" (v. 14). In the evening, the disciples wanted to dismiss the people so they could go into the villages to buy food. Jesus, however, had other ideas and told the disciples, "They [the people] need not go away; you give them something to eat" (v. 16). Then follows the familiar story of the five loaves and two fish: five thousand men, plus women and children, were fed, and twelve baskets full of broken pieces were picked up after the meal. Then Jesus dismissed the crowds, sent the disciples off in a boat, and climbed the mountain to pray by himself.

Jesus' Miracles

I don't know about your theology of miracles. I don't know if you take the miracle stories as literal, symbolic, or "myths of a bygone era." I think it would be very difficult to explain the impact of Jesus on his disciples and on the crowds had he not performed many miracles, signs, and wonders. Jesus' preaching alone (though certainly powerful in and of itself) would have presented only half of who God is. God is the healer, the comforter, the one who restores people to health and healthy relationships. And the God who is portrayed in Jesus, the Christ, is certainly a God who does not dismiss physical hunger and thirst as irrelevant. That is why Jesus does not dismiss the crowd as his disciples counsel but asks the disciples to tend to the physical need of hunger, just as he constantly tended to the physical needs of bodily health and wellness. Since becoming a chaplain and chaplain educator, I allow more room for mystery in my theology than I previously allowed when I considered myself primarily a student of systematic and philosophical theology. Some people do get well in mysterious—some would say miraculous, and I will certainly say wonder-full—ways, and I stand in awe when that happens. While I have not figured out why some get healed and many (maybe most) do not—at least not in dramatic, outwardly visible ways—I still think health and healing are gifts that ultimately come from God, and I give thanks to the God of healing, comfort, and restoration. I give thanks for God's presence and healing powers in the lives of my patients and students.

Teaching Tips

Ask group members to talk about times when they have felt that God has forsaken them or someone they love. How did they deal with this feeling in prayer?

Ask group members to discuss ways in which they have experienced miraculous care from God in their lives, when their hunger has been fed.

Reflections

How have you experienced God's healing? Do you feel, deep down, that God wants you to be whole? Ask God in prayer to help you recognize and accept gifts of healing in your life and for others.

Prayer in Solitude

Finally, Jesus was able to dismiss the crowd (after the five thousand men, plus women and children, had eaten). He actually dismissed the disciples as well: "Immediately he made the disciples get into the boat and go on ahead to the other side, while he dismissed the crowds" (v. 22). What does he do then? "And after he had dismissed the crowds, he went up to the mountain by himself to pray" (v. 23). Finally, Jesus gets some solace! As I read it, Jesus needs time to grieve John the Baptist's death. (He tried to withdraw earlier, after he first got the news about the beheading, but he was greeted by a crowd and had compassion upon them [v.14].) Jesus probably also needed to take some rest from the healing of the sick and the feeding of a large crowd. Speculation aside as to how the feeding of the crowd of maybe ten thousand or more was accomplished (whether Jesus set an example of individuals sharing with one another rather than hoarding or protecting the little resources they each had, or whether there was a more spectacular way of assuring that nobody went hungry), Jesus needed some rest.

In CPE we call that "self care." I believe this example of Jesus withdrawing into the wilderness or unto the top of a mountain *alone* to pray is one aspect of his ministry that is least emulated—and we are all paying the price for it. Anyone, but especially caregivers and leaders, who does not practice the art of meaningful self-care, which involves a hefty chunk of solitary prayer in regular intervals, will burn out. The good, old-fashioned "quiet time"—meeting alone with God in a quiet spot and listening for God's voice through the Bible, prayer, meditation, and silence—cannot be overemphasized in its vital importance for the life of ministry, which is the call of all who follow Christ. I have come to the realization that I want to do this more often, not in order to live up to a "spiritual law" or to follow a particular "spiritual discipline" but because my spirit dries out, and I become moody, angry, frustrated, and downright insufferable if I am not refreshed in mind, body, and spirit through regular down time defined as prayer time.

"It Is a Ghost"

The disciples are in the boat, and a storm is brewing. Jesus is praying in solitude on a mountain. When the boat is battered by the wind and waves, Jesus notices the disciples' distress and walks towards them on the water. The disciples are "terrified" and say, "It is a ghost!" (vv. 23-26a). For good measure, their terror is emphasized by the repetition: "And they cried out in fear" (v. 26b). Let us stop the story right here and, for a moment, not speculate whether (and if so, how) Jesus managed to walk on water. Let us rather look at something that may be more helpful as an underlying message or paradigm. It is striking that the disciples do not recognize Jesus as he approaches them in the midst of the storm but instead say, "It is a ghost." The theme of the disciples not recognizing (or, at the least, not understanding) Jesus is a pretty consistent theme throughout the Gospels.

Whether or not the disciples recognize Jesus may have very little to do with Jesus' physical appearance and/or the chemical composition of his body. The disciples may not recognize Jesus as Jesus (or Jesus as Christ, or Christ as the Son of the Living God) because of their focus (or lack thereof) and/or preoccupation. (By "disciples" I do not simply mean the band of the twelve men and handful of women back then, but all of us). In this story the disciples are focused on the storm and their own distress. When they see a figure approaching on the water, this figure frightens them as much, or even more, than the wind and the waves. I take this to mean that we can become so preoccupied with our problems—with our winds and waves, with our storms of life—that we literally will not be able to recognize help when it arrives! Instead of seeing Jesus as part of the solution to their problem, the disciples see him as part of the problem. And that is a problem! When we are unable to recognize Christ as Christ or God as God, we cut ourselves off from help. We are then stuck in our boats in the midst of a storm with no way out.

Walking on Water, Sinking in Despair

We know how this story ended. Jesus speaks to the disciples in the boat; they recognize his voice, and

Teaching Tips

Make a list of ways people can attend to "self care." Discuss obstacles to attending to self and the importance of making time for self care.

Teaching Tips

Act out the story of Jesus walking on the water to the boat, the disciples' fear, Peter's bravery in stepping out of the boat, his beginning to sink and his cry to the Lord to save him. Enact Jesus pulling Peter out of the water with the question "Why did you doubt?" Experiment with the interaction between Jesus and Peter: Is Jesus rebuking Peter? Is he asking a compassionate question of Peter? How does this story help us learn ways to pray?

Simon Peter asks Jesus, "Lord, if it is you, command me to come to you on the water." Jesus says, "Come" (vv. 28, 29a). Peter gets out of the boat, walks on water, and does fine until he notices the strong wind, becomes frightened, and begins to sink (v. 30). In his despair he cries out, "Lord, save me!" (v. 30), and the Lord does, saying: "You of little faith, why did you doubt?" (v. 31). They get into the boat, the wind ceases, the disciples worship Jesus ("Truly you are the Son of God" [v. 33]), and, upon reaching land, they go off to heal even more who were sick in that region. All of this happens with almost dizzying speed!

Notice that Jesus does not ask Peter to try walking on water again. Moreover, he does not declare this a universal lesson of discipleship and does not make the whole band of disciples jump overboard to practice their walking-on-water discipleship skills. So apparently, walking on water as a recognizable and teachable skill of discipleship or as a sign of a mature faith must not be the point.

There are some things that Jesus expected all disciples to do (among the most important are preaching the inbreaking kingdom of God and healing the sick), and then apparently there are some things he expected—or allowed—only *individual* disciples to do. That may be a healthy reminder for us as well not to lump everything together into reproducible and predictable discipleship classes and lessons but to allow for individual and distinct encounters with God and with Christ. I personally am grateful that God has a special way in which God encounters each individual. The divine-human encounters are therefore as diverse and as manifold as the people who experience the encounter. For me, this is one of the gifts of God's creation and is an expression of God's abundance, creativity, and mystery.

Reflections

1 What unique gifts has God given you?
2 What do you think the disciples meant when they said "You are the Son of God"?
3. What do you mean when you confess Jesus as "the Son of God"?
4. Is there a difference in your mind between calling Jesus "the Christ" or "the Son of God," or do you use both terms interchangeably?

"You Are the Christ" Followed by "Get Thee behind Me, Satan"

Living between Extremes

Peter's courageous, insightful confession: "You are the Christ" (the Messiah) and Jesus' harsh "Get behind me, Satan" come in very close succession. It is a living between extremes in the life of Simon Peter—from highest praise to harshest rebuke—within six verses. The life of Simon Peter is one paradigm for discipleship—not *the* one, but one—and the theme of living between extremes is, in my experience and in my understanding of human nature and behavior, one of the universals that goes beyond the particular circumstances of Simon Peter's experience. Living between extremes, as a common phenomenon, is something that binds us together; it is something that is true in the experience of people from many different religious traditions, from many walks of life, and from many cultural and national backgrounds.

In Matt 16: 13-28, which focuses mainly on Simon Peter, we have a considerable tossing and turning of events, and we are hit by the extremes. They keep flying at us with record speed, almost like bullets.

In this text, "the Messiah," or "Christ," is a good thing or good reality, and "Satan" is a bad thing or bad reality. Peter is praised highly as having been inspired by God when he spoke a particular truth about Jesus that Jesus believed to be true about himself, and Peter is scolded strongly when he wants to hinder Jesus from going a particular route that Jesus believed he had to go in order to be true to his calling. Let's be even more blunt in calling out the extremes embedded in these

Lectionary Loop

Fourteenth Sunday after Pentecost, Year A, Matthew 16:13-20
Fifteenth Sunday after Pentecost, Year A, Matthew 16:21-28

few verses: Peter is considered an immensely wise person in v. 17 and an absolute fool in v. 23; Peter is inspired by God in v. 17 and is the mouthpiece of Satan in v. 23; Peter is good, really good in v. 17 and bad, really bad in v. 23; he is triumphant in 17 and defeated in 23; he is joyful and proud in 17 and embarrassed and maybe a bit angry inside in 23. He is on top of the mountain in 17 and at the bottom of the sea in 23. One and the same person, he is divine and demonic, wise and foolish, good and evil, strong and weak, right on target and terribly misguided. That is Simon Peter, and that is, I am convinced, all of us, as well, when we have an honest look in the mirror.

There was a time when I used to think: How could this Simon Peter be such a fool as to miscalculate Jesus' mission so radically when he had articulated a significant divine truth about Jesus' destiny just a few moments ago? How could he have been so dull after he had been so bright? I used to be impatient with Peter and his failure to comprehend Christ's mission. It is not the exception but almost the rule that in our lives we are incredibly smart one moment and make the most foolish mistake the next, that we are empathetic and caring and relational one moment and full of anger, hatred, and rage the next. The forces of good and evil are both familiar inhabitants in our souls and bodies: We love and hate, we save and destroy, we speak the truth and a blatant lie if not in the same breath (sometimes we do) then at least the same hour or the same day. We may very well do both in the same staff meeting, the same board meeting, the same Bible study or prayer meeting.

Over the course of a lifetime and from moment to moment we are no strangers to what we might call the "Simon-Peter Syndrome"—the syndrome of the human condition: in between extremes, left, right, up, down and all over the place, unpredictable, and unstable. And yet in all this unpredictability, there is the good intention of Peter wanting to help Jesus in his mission, and there is the good news that Jesus is building his church on Peter, on the rock. But is it good news that Christ is building his church on top of this particular stone? Is the church like a rolling, slippery stone, built on Simon "Big-talk, quick-talk, quick-betrayal" Peter? How can any religious group, church, or religion be built on such an individual? Honestly, would we want to entrust the keys of heaven to such an unstable person? Would we even consider giving him the keys to our church, sanctuary, home, or car?

In this marvelous story from the Gospel of Matthew, Jesus entrusts his community, the band of disciples, and ultimately the church to the leadership of Simon Peter. In a metaphorical reading of the story, I see in the relationship between Jesus and Peter some truths about the divine-human relationship in general. God trusts us. God puts us—as wavering people who are wise today and foolish tomorrow, strong now and weak an hour from now, believing today and despairing tomorrow—into positions of responsibility and opportunity and power. We can open the kingdom of heaven for ourselves and for others, or we can close it for ourselves and others. The potential for both is there. Knowing that full well, God still entrusts the kingdom of heaven to us.

The text refers to God and Satan as realities—they are the sources of truth and falsehood, of insightfulness and distortion in our text. That may be a bit unsettling to consider: Divine insight and demonic distortion are close to one another, and both will come to expression through us. It may not always look and feel as extreme as in this story, and nobody may actually ever tell us (at least not to our face), "Get behind me, Satan," but we will be perceived as both angel and demon. That seems to be part of the human condition. The good news is that if somebody as fickle, unstable, loudmouthed, and scared as Simon Peter could be called to play a key role in the divine-human interplay, in the drama of eternity and time, then each of us will have a key role to play as well.

The good news in Jesus' acceptance of Peter is that God accepts humanity. God accepts the human condition in all of us when Jesus selects Simon Peter and accepts his complex humanity to become the leader of his church. In Jesus' forgiveness of Simon Peter's betrayal and in his acceptance (see session 5), I see

173

God's forgiveness and acceptance of all of us. When Simon (not the saintly John but the earthy and knotty Peter) is given the keys to heaven, the following message is proclaimed: The kingdom of heaven is wide open. There are no entrance rules, and there is no bouncer. You don't have to fulfill certain prerequisites to be in communion with God. You don't have to be terribly smart or consistently divinely inspired to enter into communion with God. To the contrary, you and I and all of humanity are accepted as we are: divine, demonic, human, strangers neither to suffering nor joy, familiar with triumphs and failures, graced with exceptional insights and mortified in unspeakable embarrassment and shame, a mouthpiece for both good and evil, created in the image of God and accepted for who we are by our Creator, Sustainer, and Redeemer.

"On this rock [on this rolling stone, on this shaky foundation] I will build my church." This is the good, reassuring, and simultaneously restorative and healing news about our common human condition. An old hymn (and a favorite altar-call song in Billy Graham's crusades) is "Just as I Am." Just as I am, I come to you, my Lord, just as I am. Our stones, rocks, bricks and even heaps of sand and rubble are good enough. God values them as building material for the church and for the Kingdom. Could there be a grander vision for our heaps of stones and tons of bricks and bags of sand and dust and rubble than to present them to God as building materials for God's palace? There is not a single stone, person, or being created by God who is beyond God's utilization, affirmation, and blessing. God can put all to good use! That is the marvel, the gem, the precious news of our living in between extremes and still arriving at our destiny.

Peter's and Our Own Reluctance to Accept Suffering as God's Way

The temptation was great to conclude this session with the previous sentence. The text has such an uplifting message when one looks at the bestowal of the kingdom of heaven to Peter that it is tempting to take this message as the whole gospel: God accepts us just as we are. I firmly believe that is true. And yet I also

Teaching Tips

Ask the group to discuss their views of "Satan" and the "demonic." Do they perceive these as real entities or as symbolic of evil in the world? List other persons in the Bible who displayed complex human personalities. (Some examples might be: Sarah, Jacob, Moses, David, the prophets, Paul, Jesus himself.) In what ways did these complex people encounter God? Discuss Paul's statement that the Lord said to him: "My power is made perfect in weakness" (2 Cor 12:9). How does Paul's experience illuminate the story of Peter's extremes?

believe that God wants us to change over time, just as God wanted Simon Peter to change and helped him change time and time again. (The word order in the sentence above is important: "God wants us to change" versus "God wants to change us.")

How does God want us to change? The passage seems to suggest that God wants us to change our perspective on suffering.

If human things or human values (as represented by Simon Peter's attempt at persuading Jesus to abandon his way to the cross) suggest that suffering is bad and to be avoided, then divine things or divine values seem to suggest that suffering is good and to be accepted and embraced. "Now, wait a minute," you may chime in, "Are you suggesting that all suffering is good? Are you saying that God wills the terrorism and the tsunamis and the wars and the inner-city violence and the hunger and the starvation and the disease and the rapes and the killings because it is good for humans to suffer?" Absolutely not. I am sharing Rabbi Kushner's view in *When Bad Things Happen to Good People* that God does not will all kinds of evil to befall us. In my own theology, I have opted for "process theology," a view of an all-loving God who is perfectly related to each of us, suffers with us, and helps us (help each other), instead of a more traditional theology in which God, who has all the powers in the universe and who could stop all senseless suffering but who, out of some mysterious reason, does not chose to do so.

If Peter's Vision Is Our Vision, then Whose Vision Is Christ's Vision?

At issue is not the unavoidable, tragic suffering—whether inflicted by humans or by non-human forces. That kind of suffering is terrible and painful, and we are called to alleviate it and to stop it before it begins (or soon thereafter) if we have any control over it. The suffering at stake here is the individual suffering that *could* be avoided and that Jesus consciously chooses *not* to avoid. Jesus accepted that part of his calling involving suffering and a violent death. That was his interpretation of what God would have him do. Jesus accepted that vision and shared it with his disciples—

Sources

Kushner, Harold S. *When Bad Things Happen to Good People* (New York: Avon, 1983).

For a readable guide to a process theology of suffering and evil, see Suchocki, Marjorie Hewitt. *The Fall to Violence: Original Sin in Relational Theology* (New York: Continuum, 1995).

presumably to prepare them for an outcome they may not have expected and maybe also to get their support since this was, after all, a scary, lonely, and painful truth. The suffering in Jesus' story is defined by his role as a suffering messiah. Simon Peter wants to contradict him by basically saying that "a suffering messiah" is no real messiah.

It may be time for Christians in the West to remember that the risen Christ is the Christ of the Cross. The Messiah is a crucified messiah. And if a crucified messiah is no messiah, then we may have to decide in every moment whether we follow the example of the man who walked willingly to the cross or whether we agree with those who say that suffering and death cannot ever be God's way and that suffering, therefore, must always be avoided. What vision of suffering do we hold, and whose vision of suffering do we follow?

Reflections

Do you think Jesus had to suffer and die in his role as Messiah? If God does not condone violence, why would God call Jesus to this fate? What is the role of suffering in the life of a Christian?

Washing of Feet—Washing Hands and Head as Well?

"You Will Never Wash My Feet"

For me, this is one of the more remarkable stories in the entire New Testament. I don't know of a single story that exemplifies "servant-leadership" more than this story of the foot-washing. According to the story, "Jesus, knowing that the Father had given all things into his hands, and that he had come from God and was going to God got up from the table, took off his outer robe, and tied a towel around himself…and began to wash the disciples' feet" (v. 5). Isn't that amazing? Jesus, after having reached "God consciousness" or fully realizing his origin and destiny as coming from and returning to God did not "initiate" the disciples by asking them to wash his feet. Instead, he washed his disciples' feet. And how did the disciples react? They were stunned; they did not quite know what to do. Apparently they let Jesus proceed, and nobody protested until he came to Simon Peter. Peter questioned Jesus, and his query sounds very much like: "What in the world are you doing? Have you lost your mind? That's a servant's job, not a leader's job. Have you forgotten who you are? This is embarrassing."

It is not clear whether Peter is mainly embarrassed on his own account—i.e. "I am not worthy that my master should wash my feet"—or whether he is taking offense to Jesus' action as not being a fitting or dignified conduct of a leader, a rabbi, or the Messiah. Either way, Peter is thinking that he knows better what Jesus ought or ought not to do than Jesus does. Peter, at times, despaired of his master. The church, often

Lectionary Loop

Maundy Thursday, Year B,
John 13:1-17, 31*b*-35

enough, despairs of its Christ. We are embarrassed when Jesus washes our feet (and even more when he washes our undeserving and obnoxious neighbors' feet); we do not relish the "servant" aspect of "servant-leadership."

It is amazing that the church, in Peter's vein, has continued to assert itself in knowing better than Jesus what the church ought to. Foot-washing, with the exception of the Eastern Orthodox tradition, has not become a sacrament or a practice of the church. We find it occasionally—some Baptist churches offer a foot-washing service during Lent—but it really has not become a standard practice of mainstream, Protestant or Catholic Christianity. It is as if all of us said, "We will never wash each other's feet," and that is that. If Jesus insisted in washing the disciples' feet, that was his prerogative; we don't want to stoop this low. Bread and wine? Yes. Bread and fruit juice? Fine. Bread and water? Acceptable. But water and basin, or water, basin, and towel? No!

Eventually Peter gets the idea that he cannot dissuade Jesus from washing his feet. Oh well, then, why not go the whole way? "My hands and head as well, Lord." Just as the "nothing at all" approach had failed, the familiar "all or nothing" approach failed too. Jesus says to us, "The only thing you need to learn over and over again is *servant* leadership." Let's bow down and serve our neighbor as a servant would serve his or her master. That's a message that neither Peter nor we care to hear. It hurts our pride. It does not fit into our theologies. It embarrasses us. Why does Jesus have to be so unlike any leader we are accustomed to?

The Holy Desire to Be Close to God and the Demonic Desire to Be Closer to God than Anybody Else

Simon Peter's approach was to add head and hands. Was this typical of Peter's exuberancy, the kind of enthusiastic response and all-embracing faith that caused him to say to step out of the boat and walk on the water and to be the first to confess that Jesus is the Christ? Or is Peter trying to distract from the more humbling and embarrassing focus on his and his fellow

> **Teaching Tips**
>
> List qualities of good leaders in various settings, both religious and secular. How is Jesus' example unsettling? How is it helpful (or unhelpful)?

disciples' dusty, sweaty, smelly feet? Let's explore the possibility that he is asking for special treatment from Jesus. The feet alone may have been good enough for the other disciples, but Peter wants Jesus to wash his head and hands, also. With such a request, Peter comes across as "holier than thou." The desire to be close to Jesus is holy, but the desire to be closer to Jesus than anybody else is demonic – is hubris. Let me explain.

I am aware that my interpretation of the text may strike you as unusual. You may accuse me of reading something into the text that isn't there. That is quite possible. For sure, the text does not mention a demonic power behind Peter's request for having his head, hands, and feet washed. However, I see the same demonic quality of wanting to be godlier than God, more messianic than the messiah and more comprehensive than Christ. When we, like Peter and the serpent in the garden (and "the satan" [the adversary] in the Job story) presume to know better how to run God's kingdom than God does, then we fall prey to a demonic—albeit a well-meaning—distortion of the gospel. This demonic distortion is called "hubris," a more polite and nicer-sounding Greek word for the "arrogance," "presumption," and "entitlement" that come from a distorted view of the divine-human inter-relationship.

In this instance, Peter's desire to be closer to Jesus than anybody else is a desire to be holier than the other disciples. Peter wants to be more intimately connected to Jesus. I interpret Peter's action to mean that the washing of head, hands, and feet would go beyond and would thus be superior to the "mere feet" of the other disciples.

Biblical stories of hubris usually portray a power that is not so much contrary to God but wants to improve upon God. The serpent in the garden of Eden wants to help humans become more god-like and presumably wants to help God run the garden more effectively: "You'll be like God, knowing good and evil" (Gen 3:5). When Jesus talks about the cross, Simon Peter rebukes him and Jesus identifies his suggestion as of "Satan." This suggestion is not anti-divine or anti-Christ.

Quite the contrary. The temptation is to improve upon Jesus' messiah-ship by telling him that suffering is not a godly way of ruling the world, just like forbidding humans to eat from the tree of knowledge was not a godly way of running the garden of Eden!

Tenderness and Care beyond Acceptance and Redemption

There is another kind of hubris at work in this story, the hubris of our own tendency to ignore or deny the physicality of the act of foot-washing. Jesus is caring for the disciples not only spiritually, by accepting and redeeming them, but physically, by caring for their bodies. By his example, he asks all of his followers to do the same.

There is an amazing amount of love and tenderness in Jesus' act of foot-washing. It is a humble act, an act that servants and slaves performed, but Jesus took the role of a slave to do it for his disciples.

I would like to explore another dimension of foot-washing that is seldom discussed, that foot-washing could be pleasurable to the recipient. Certainly having one's feet cleansed of dust and perspiration is refreshing, but recall also the woman with the alabaster jar (tradition has often seen Mary Magdalene as this woman, although the biblical text does not say) who poured perfume over Jesus' feet, cried over his feet, and finally wiped his feet dry with her long hair (Luke 7:36-50). This act no doubt created sensory pleasure for Jesus (the sweet-smelling perfume, the sensation of the hair on his feet) and outrage and embarrassment among his disciples. Is it outrageous to think about the foot-washing of Jesus not only as an act of servant-hood but also as an act that gave pleasure (as well as embarrassment) to the disciples?

We are able to tolerate the intimacy of the Lord's Supper, including the slightly embarrassing disciple who lay at Jesus' bosom and whom Jesus loved, but the foot-washing as an intimate act is way too scary for most of us to think about, lecture about, or preach about. Maybe Peter's initial refusal of this intimate act may have come out of the pleasure-denying teaching so deeply engrained in so many religious mindsets.

Teaching Tips

Discuss your reaction to the interpretation of Peter's actions as "hubris?" In what ways do we attempt to be "holier than thou" in our relationship with Jesus and with others?

If we accept the doctrine that Jesus was both fully divine and fully human, I am wondering when we will be ready to accept God's love for our mind, soul, spirit and body? Isn't it time for us to accept the promise that —flesh and bones, blood, sweat, tears, and body fluids—we have been created in God's image? We are deeply uncomfortable with the idea that besides experiencing hunger and thirst Jesus may have had any kind of bodily reactions, that he could both administer physical care and be the recipient of physical care. Jesus washing the disciples' feet, an admiring woman pouring ointment on Jesus' feet, and any suggestion that Jesus may have had any interest in or relationship with any of the men or women among his disciples is too scary for us to even entertain.

What are we afraid of? How do we preach the human Jesus? Do we preach the human Jesus? Or is the Gnostic Jesus as pure Spirit disguised in flesh and blood the gospel we are most comfortable with? Christianity has seldom had difficulties with the "fully divine" part of our confession. The "fully human," however continues to trip us up and embarrass us beyond measure. Perhaps we need to start developing a "body theology" that sees the body not as an enemy to be conquered but as a beautiful gift from God to be cared for.

Teaching Tips

Does the notion of Jesus having physical feelings make you uncomfortable? Why do you think that is?

Describe ministries that involve caring for the whole person—body, mind, and spirit. Explore how the sensation of touch is a powerful means of healing and caring for someone.

Session 4   Matthew 26:47-75 and John 18:1-27

Defending Jesus with the Sword, Following Him to the Halls of Judgment—and Denying Him

Cutting off the Servant's Ear: Act of Courage or Act of Desperation?

In the Gospel of Matthew, the disciple who cuts off the high priest's servant's ear is not named. Neither is the servant. In the Gospel of John, the disciple is identified as Peter, and the servant as Malchus. Whether Peter was the one who drew the sword is not of ultimate importance, but I am including the story here with the discipleship lessons learned from the life of Peter because it certainly fits his profile. Who but Simon Peter would draw the sword?

Was this act an act of courage, or desperation, or perhaps both? Simon Peter may have hoped against hope that this strike would scare off the people who were after Jesus, causing them to flee. He may also have hoped for a real brawl—even a fight to the death—to defend his master and die *with* him or *for* him. The passage depicts Peter as courageous here, but also as angry, disillusioned, and desperate. He does not know how the imminent arrest of Jesus can be averted, but he feels that something needs to be done. So he draws his sword and lops off the servant's ear.

It is interesting that neither Matthew nor John mention what happened to the poor servant and his severed ear. To find out the rest of the story, we have to turn to the Gospel of Luke. In Luke 22:49-51, Jesus touches the man's ear and heals him. Jesus' healing ministry includes his enemies. He is full of compassion until the very end.

Courage, despair, hope, anger and a host of other emotions come together for Peter in this encounter.

183

Towards the end of this session, we will analyze Peter's emotions and actions in more detail, utilizing the well-known stages of grief first recognized and studied by Elizabeth Kübler Ross. For now, let's follow the story.

"I Don't Know the Man:" Courage and Bravado Turn into Cowardice and Naked Fear

Simon Peter, who was ready to defend his Lord and fight to the death, if necessary, witnesses the capture of Jesus and flees with the other disciples. However, with at least one other disciple, he comes back and dares to go into the courtyard of the high priest, where the soldiers had a fire going to warm themselves. According to the Gospel of John, the disciple known to the high priest asks for permission for Peter to come in as well. Thus, the other disciple did not feel that he was in imminent danger. The authorities were after Jesus, not the disciples, because they knew (or thought they knew) that the movement would come to a crashing halt if the leader were captured and executed. The story provides another fascinating character study of Simon Peter. Accused twice by a servant girl and once by a guard of belonging to Jesus' movement, Peter denies Jesus three times, swearing an oath, "I do not know the man" (Matt 27:72). Then the cock crows, and Peter runs away, crying bitterly, remembering the words of his Lord: "Before the cock crows, you will deny me three times" (v. 75). A familiar story. Maybe too familiar. Are we tempted, as we are so frequently when reading stories about Simon Peter, to dismiss him as a loudmouth, a braggart, a windbag, a dog that is all bark but no bite, a coward? Are we ready to proclaim that this would not have happened to us—that we would have been strong, stalwart, courageous, fearless, and death-defying, that we would have answered, "Yes, I am one of them! And what is it to you? Ready for a quarrel? Stand in line. I am taking one after the other." Or, more piously, would we have said, "Yes, I am one of them. I believe in this man. I love this man. And, moreover, he is no mere man. He is the son of God, and he will build his kingdom—and if you want to be part of it you better repent right now, put down

> ## Reflections
>
> Recall times when you have felt such frustration and anger that you lashed out. Recall times when you have been the recipient of someone else's anger. How did you resolve your feelings? Do you think Peter acted with courage or cowardice? Or both? Do you identify with Peter in this story?

your arms, walk down to the river of Jordan with me and get baptized." Would we? I doubt it. I know that I, in all likelihood, would have put my tail between my legs and whimpered off just like Simon Peter. None of us wants to die. Peter didn't. I don't. Jesus didn't. Jesus prayed: "My Father, if it is possible, let this cup pass from me; yet not what I want but what you want" (Matt 26:39). Just like Peter, we would have been scared to death, devastated and heartbroken.

Betrayal, Bitter Tears, and the Way of the Cross

Peter runs away, crying bitterly, ashamed of his own behavior and shocked at the imminent fate of his friend and teacher, Jesus. Peter is a hopeless, broken man.

But we know that the story does not end here. The crucifixion is still to come, and, with the eyes of faith, the resurrection as well. In the end there is a new beginning. Every ending includes a new beginning. After his death on the cross, many disciples will see the resurrected Jesus, and Simon Peter will be the person who proclaims the gospel at Pentecost. Neither Jesus nor Peter will be recognized easily after the cross and resurrection. Jesus will have changed, and Peter will have changed psychologically and spiritually. Peter becomes the rock, the foundation of the fledgling band of disciples. He becomes reliable, sturdy, courageous, and dependable in ways that seem truly miraculous.

What I take from this story is that there had to be a betrayal before Peter could emerge as the leader of the disciples, just as there had to be the crucifixion before the resurrection or Pentecost could take place. In other words, new life comes out of death and no other way. If the seed does not fall into the ground and die, no plant or flower will grow. Without Jesus' death, no new life would have flown into his followers, and without the psycho-spiritual death of Peter who betrayed his master, he could not have been reborn as a truly repentant and reformed leader. We will see in the next session how the revisiting of his betrayal is vitally important for his character transformation and spiritual growth.

Reflections

Take some time to ponder how you might have responded to the accusations of the servant girl and the guard. How far would you be willing to take the role of martyr? Do you identify with Peter in this story?

Teaching Tips

List ways in which you have experienced miraculous rebirth after a time of crushing despair. Think of stories of great leaders and the struggles they have had to overcome in their lives.

A Chaplain's Perspective on Transition, Utilizing Kübler Ross's Stages of Grief

In her 1969 book, *On Death and Dying*, Elizabeth Kübler Ross, a psychiatrist originally from Switzerland, presented groundbreaking studies of her work with dying patients. Based on decades of work with patients at the end of life, Küebler-Ross came up with five stages that most patients go through as they prepare for death: (1) denial, (2) anger, (3) bargaining, (4) depression, and (5) acceptance. She was careful to note that although not everyone goes through all five stages and not everyone experiences the stages in this exact order, most patients experience at least two stages of transition and a majority go through all five. In the decades since her original study, both Kübler Ross and others have expanded upon her work and slightly modified its conclusions. It has been clarified that this five-stage model is not a normative model—in other words, patients do not have to be guided from step one to two and then on to three and so on. Rather, people may go back and forth. They may bargain one day and become very angry again for many days; they may go back to denial, skip the stage of depression, and come to acceptance; they may also drop out of acceptance and return to another stage. The term "stage" has probably been misleading because it suggests a static state of being. The staircase metaphor looks only at a one-movement direction, namely ascension, which belies the more complex reality of death and dying. Nonetheless, when treated as a guideline for understanding the transitions experienced by someone who is actively dying or grieving, the model can be very helpful.

Let's look at Peter's "spiritual dying" with Kübler Ross' "stages" of death in mind. When Peter first hears about Jesus' vision of the way to the cross, he immediately denies it: "Oh no! That can't be true. I will never let that happen. I'll defend you to the death. Don't talk like that. Of course you won't die. What kind of nonsense are you talking about?" (see Matt 16:21-23) That's stage one: denial. We have already looked at Jesus' strong response of, "Get behind me, Satan" (v. 23), which does not give denial much of a chance to linger.

When Peter draws the sword and cuts off the high priest's servant's ear, he is in the stage of anger, and he acts out. He wants to change Jesus' and his own fate by fighting and defeating the powers of death. Stage two is halted when Jesus tells Peter to put his sword away.

When Peter comes to the courtyard to see what will happen to Jesus, he is discovered and accused of being one of Jesus' followers. His denial has the form of bargaining. One might hear his words, "I don't know the man," as, "Please, if I say I don't know him, will you please let me live?" This is stage three: bargaining.

Once the cock crows, Peter immediately realizes what he has done, and he becomes depressed. He cries bitterly and runs away in despair, full of remorse for what he has done. This is stage four: depression.

This particular story does not bring us stage five: acceptance. However, the final step of acceptance is reflected in the story of Peter going fishing again (John 21:1-3). In this story Peter accepts what has happened to Jesus and is ready to pick up the pieces and move on. Having been a fisherman all his life, he goes back to what he knows best: fishing. That is acceptance translated into action. He works through his grief and loss by doing something. Sitting down and waiting (for the resurrected Jesus or for the Holy Spirit or for some sign from God of what to do next) is not his cup of tea. He needs to do something, and his going fishing indicates that he has accepted the new reality that Jesus is no longer with them (at least not in the old and familiar ways) and that, therefore, life needs to go on.

This is stage five: acceptance. Peter has worked through disillusionment, anger, and frustration and has truly become a new man. With the help of the Spirit of God, we too will be able to become renewed and refreshed as well to find a new level of acceptance of the tasks in front of us and the realities around us.

Reflections

How do the "stages of grief" help illuminate the story of Peter's experience? How do they help us deal with our own grief and despair?

Peter, Do You Love Me?

"Do You Love Me?"—"Lord, You Know I Love You"—"Follow Me": Renewing the Call into Discipleship at the End of the Gospel

Lectionary Loop
**Third Sunday of Easter, Year C,
John 21:1-19**

We end our five-session study on Peter (as a *concrete* disciple and as *one* possible paradigm of discipleship) with this marvelous text of a post-resurrection encounter between Jesus and his disciples. This text features a call to leadership and a renewed call to discipleship for Simon Peter. What fascinate me here are a number of story details that connect Peter's life as a disciple of Jesus with his life as an apostle of the living Christ. One interesting detail is that Peter goes fishing. That's what he did before he knew Jesus; that's what he's (presumably) good at even now. "I am going fishing," says Simon Peter. "We will go with you," say the other disciples. Peter is in a leadership role. Here he is leading by example. He does not ask the other disciples, "Hey, do you think it's a good idea that we all go fishing?" He simply states his intention, "I am going fishing." This gives the others a chance to respond as they wish— "Good luck," or, "Oh, but you shouldn't," or, "How can you think of fish/food at a time like this?" or, "Ok," or, as it turns out, "We will go with you." As a leader, it is sometimes not a bad idea to state your intention, not seeking approval, not inviting an argument, not trying to persuade others to join you, but simply saying, "I am going to do this now," and then do it. It is clear from the story that the other disciples thought this was a good idea, because they went, too.

Ironically, the disciples do not catch a single fish. If you have ever thought, "Everything is going wrong," this was probably such an occasion. (I am assuming for a moment that ch. 21 may have been an independent resurrection narrative that is not chronologically related to ch. 20 but comes from a different tradition of post-resurrection appearances of Jesus.) Jesus had been crucified, and his body had disappeared from the tomb. The disciples' hope for a new reign of God among them had not come to pass, and no new leader of the group had emerged. The disciples had no idea what they ought to do from this point forward. Fishing seemed like the only thing to do. But the results were as disappointing as the hope for the kingdom. There was no kingdom, and now there were no fish either! They may have thought, "Nothing is going right. If we are not even good at fishing anymore, what in the world are we to do?"

Jesus interrupts all of this and calls out to the disciples, giving them instructions on how to fish. They follow his advice without so much as a murmur, and they make a huge catch of fish. Simon Peter, once again, thrusts himself overboard when he recognizes Jesus. This time he does not walk on water; instead, he swims toward shore. But the same motivation that was present in the storm encounter (Matt 14:22-34) seems to be present again. Peter is drawn to Jesus. He wants to be close to him, and he wants to get there first. There is competitiveness in Peter throughout the stories we read in the Gospels.

Jesus has breakfast cooking already (including some fish), and he invites the disciples to eat. When they have finished, Jesus asks Simon Peter the three-fold question about whether Peter loves Jesus. Peter answers all three questions affirmatively, "Yes, I love you." (The obvious parallel of the three questions is Peter's previous threefold denial, "I don't know the man.") In response, Jesus gives Peter the task of feeding his sheep.

A New Beginning for Peter and for Us—Again and Again—and that is *Not* Cheap Grace

"The LORD is my shepherd, I shall not want." I imagine Peter may have prayed Ps 23 in his heart in response to Jesus' invitation to tend his sheep and look after his lambs. What a task! Doing the work of the Lord by becoming a shepherd like God, Moses, Abraham, Israel, and David—looking after the sheep like Jesus did. Peter must have felt that he was not worthy. Why him of all the disciples? Why not the "beloved disciple"? Why not one of the eleven—any one—who had not sworn loudly, "I will never leave you," and then failed miserably, publicly with, "I don't know the man"? There are no clear answers why Jesus picked Peter as the rock of his church. Sometimes there is only awe and wonder, and there is no clear explanation that can dissolve the mystery and grace.

Maybe we have become a little too scared to assert God's choice and God's sovereignty. Maybe process theology's beautiful assertion that always at any given time God does everything God can possibly do to draw people closer to each other and closer to God's self in a non-coercive way has been misunderstood to mean that God does exactly the same thing for every person without distinction or that God does nothing (out of the ordinary) at all. Maybe we are so afraid that we could be labeled "arrogant" or that God could be accused of "having favorites" that we can no longer find meaningful ways of asserting God's choice, God's actions, and God's free reign. Are we so afraid of our God being accused of doing things for some and not for others that we would rather settle for the belief that God is doing nothing for anybody? Nobody is getting anything from God, so there you have it—justice is served! I am no longer satisfied with a vision of God who largely stays out of our affairs and lets us mind our own business while God attends to a higher calling. I believe we *are* God's calling. And I believe, in turn, that God has a calling for each of us.

I believe God has a mission for each of us. The mission is *the same* in its universal orientation—love God, love your neighbor, love yourself; work for justice, love mercy, walk humbly with your God. However, this mission is *different* in its specific application to each person. For Peter, the specific mission was to become the rock for the church, whatever that meant. For the beloved disciple, the particular mission was to care for Jesus' mother after Jesus' death. For the women at the tomb, the mission was to proclaim the message of the resurrection of the one who had been crucified. My specific mission involves many roles: to be a husband, a father, a son, a brother, a friend, a chaplain, and a CPE supervisor to the best of my ability—while following Christ in Christ's mission of reconciliation, healing, and justice. These are the specifics joined with the universal. The specifics differ. I do not think of the specific differences in our calling as divine favor or disfavor. I believe God wants to use us with the fullness of our gifts in specific areas.

Some of us will pastor churches, others will work in hospitals, still others will teach, some will write, others will build, plan, landscape, weed. Besides his betrayals, impulsiveness, and bravado, Jesus saw something in Peter that would make him a good "rock." And besides our growing edges (the euphemistic CPE word for limits or weaknesses), God sees something in each of us. I am, frankly, grateful and thrilled that I have been invited to be a laborer in God's vineyard—aren't you?

Teaching Tips

Discuss ways that we are called to feed Jesus' sheep.

Reflections

1. What are your specific gifts for ministry? How has God chosen you to serve?
2. Reflect on 1 Cor 12:1-31, where Paul describes a variety of spiritual gifts and the necessity for all to serve as members of the body of Christ.

A PARTY CALLED FAITH

A STUDY BY

KANDY QUEEN-SUTHERLAND, PH.D.

Kandy Queen-Sutherland is Sam R. Marks Professor of Religious Studies,
Stetson University in DeLand, FL.

Outline

Introduction

A Party Called Faith

It is probably fair to say that the church is known more for praying than for partying. There could be many reasons for this reality. Perhaps religious types are just not effective partiers. After all, Amos had to scold the religious folk of his day for drinking wine in bowls (Amos 6:6), and Paul had to deal with people getting drunk at the eucharist, a first-century "super-size-it" enthusiasm (1 Cor 11:20ff.). Remember Hannah praying for a son and old Eli, the priest, thinking she was drunk (1 Sam 1:12ff.)? Now that was certainly a misunderstanding that deserved clarification! There is something to be said for living life as both prayer and party. Although the present lessons will focus on the party part, in many ways prayer and party are the same.

A Party Invitation

Jesus will set the stage for our thinking about a party—a party called faith. In John, as you saw in the study of John earlier in this volume, Jesus' ministry begins at a wedding where he turns water into wine. Now by any standards, that's a cool sign. And as we know, the end comes with a supper—a Passover celebration of wine and bread. In between there was dinner with the despised tax-collector, Zacchaeus; lunch with the squabbling siblings, Mary and Martha; and a picnic supper of loaves and fishes shared by five thousand men and their families. Each instance provided the context for fresh teaching about the Kingdom, and each would be met with incomprehension ("for they did not understand about the loaves" Mark 6:52). It would take the events of Good Friday and Easter

> ## Reflections
>
> The present marketing of the church as a fun place to be finds the church laboring mightily to capture the appeal of non-religious rituals—from Trunk-or-Treat to Valentine Banquets, Fifth Quarters to Souper Bowls—while the religious rites of weddings and funerals, or at least the party parts, are moving out. What is the impact of such movement on the church? Should we be concerned?

morning for those who had spent their days with him to understand. When they did, "they devoted themselves to the apostles' teaching and fellowship, to the breaking of bread and the prayers" (Acts 2:42).

A Party Calendar

Though Judaism and Christianity parted ways, the two share the bulk of the Bible: the Hebrew Scriptures, or, in Christian terms, the Old Testament. Within that literature we find reference to numerous festivals that celebrated the presence of God in the life of the people. From weekly (the Sabbath) to monthly (New Moon) to annual festivals (Passover, Festival of Weeks, and Festival of Booths), the people ordered their lives around religious observances that remembered the faithfulness of God throughout their history and called them to a faithful response.

Party Books

According to Hebrew tradition, five books of the Old Testament are known as festival scrolls. Collectively they are called the *Megilloth* or Scrolls, and they are grouped together in the third part of the Hebrew Bible known as the Writings. The present ordering of the books reflects the sequence of the respective festivals to which each of the five books became attached in Judaism: Song of Songs at Passover, Ruth at Pentecost/Weeks, Lamentations on the Ninth of Av (commemorating the destruction of the Temple in Jerusalem), Ecclesiastes at the Feast of Booths, and Esther at Purim. Although there are other festivals, these five stretch from the beginning to the end of the annual Jewish festival calendar.

Although the five books are the same, whether as a part of the Tanakh (the Jewish Bible that consists of the Law, the Prophets, and the Writings) or as books in the Old Testament of Christian Bibles, the placement of the books differs. They are neither grouped together nor tied in Christian tradition to the festivals that Judaism observes. In fact, for Christianity, many of the festivals were transformed or simply lost over time.

The present study will look to the individual texts of the Scrolls, listening for the message that each brings

---

Study Bible

See also Lev 22-23 and Num 28–29 in the *NISB*.

Reflections

In Hebrew tradition, the number seven symbolizes wholeness, completeness, and perfection. God's creative activity was completed in seven days, and the seventh day of each week, the Sabbath, was a joyful reminder (Isa 58:13-14) of God's own rest in creation (Gen 2:3). The seventh month observed four national festivals, with two lasting for seven days—Passover and Booths. Seven days were given to the wedding feast (Judg 14:12, 17) and in the seventh year the land was given rest (Lev 25:2-7), allowed to lie fallow for rejuvenation. The Festival of Weeks, or Pentecost, was celebrated on the fiftieth day, seven complete weeks after Passover; and the fiftieth year was the year of Jubilee. The completion of seven cycles of seven years commanded the release of bondslaves and the return of bought land (Lev 25:8-55). The symbolic understanding of seven is carried into the NT where the idea that forgiveness has no limits is expressed by Jesus' teaching to forgive seven times seventy (Matt 18:21-22).

1. How does this ancient ordering of worship find meaning in our modern world?
2. Which observances remain, which have been transformed, and what has been lost along the way?

to the understanding of what it means to live faithfully. Bringing to light the Jewish festivals to which they are tied, the Scrolls will be read for insight into their meaning for the Christian life.

Sources

For an understanding of how ancient Israel's religious festivals show Canaanite influence and how Israel developed as an agricultural society around the three major harvest seasons, see Anderson, Gary A. "Introduction to Israelite Religion" in *New Interpreter's Bible*, vol. 1 (Nashville: Abingdon Press, 1994) 272-83. "The Agricultural and Civil Calendar" on p. 275 is particularly helpful. See also Rylaarsdam, J.C., "Feasts and Fasts" in *Interpreter's Dictionary of the Bible*, vol. 2 (Nashville: Abingdon Press, 1976) 260-64.

Teaching Tips

To acquaint participants with the differing biblical traditions of Judaism and Christianity, examining various Bibles would prove useful. You might show a Hebrew Bible and a Greek New Testament. Participants could examine a Septuagint (the Hebrew Bible in Greek), paying special attention to how the order of the books in the Old Testament of Christian Bibles follows it rather than the order of the Hebrew or Jewish Bibles. Equally helpful would be to compare the Bibles of Christian traditions, noting the additional books of the Apocrypha or Deuterocanon found in Catholic and Orthodox Bibles that are not a part of Protestant Christianity.

Study Bible

The Canons of Scripture, *NISB*, pp. xxvii-xxxi

Sources

Webb, Barry G. *Five Festal Garments: Christian Reflections on The Song of Songs, Ruth, Lamentations, Ecclesiastes and Esther* (Downers Grove, IL: InterVarsity Press, 2000).

Dosick, Wayne. *Living Judaism: The Complete Guide to Jewish Belief, Tradition & Practice* (San Francisco: HarperSanFrancisco, 1995).

Session 1

Song of Songs

There are some parts of the Bible that we just don't know what to do with, and unfortunately too many are found in the Old Testament. There are laws for the removal of unclean persons from community (Num 5:1-4) that, thankfully, we no longer apply and expressions of vengeance that are hard to reconcile with a "love your enemy" command. There are rituals and practices whose meanings, we may surmise, have simply been lost to history (for example, the saving of Moses by his wife, Zipporah, through an act of circumcision in Exod 4:24-26). What are we to do with the sacrificial laws of Leviticus, the sending away of foreign wives and children (Ezra 10:44), and a God who would command a father to sacrifice his own son (Gen 22)? To understand the biblical witness is at times a struggle. The Song of Songs troubles us even more than most portions of Hebrew Scripture!

We're not sure what to call it—The Song of Songs, The Song of Solomon, or Canticles? Poetry in general is tough enough, but how is poetry that seethes of male/female sexuality to be read in church? Historically, both Judaism and Christianity found it easier to handle the Song's eroticism by allegorizing the Song's two young lovers as either the LORD and Israel or Christ and the church. Over time, Judaism would read the poems as a reflection of Yahweh's covenant relationship with Israel that moved from the exodus and entry into Canaan, through exile and return, to the Roman Diaspora and the coming of the Messiah. Eventually the book found a liturgical home as a reading at Passover, the annual Jewish celebration of

Lectionary Loop

Twelfth Sunday after Pentecost, Year A, Song of Songs 2:8-13

Study Bible

See, for example, Ps 58 with note in the *NISB*.

redemption and freedom and as a lectionary reading of the Christian observance of Passover that regards redemption as an act of love and sees love as a proper response. While traditional interpretations of the poems as allegory helped keep the book as Scripture, modern interpreters are teaching us to be more comfortable with the text's celebration of human sexuality that finds expression in the giving and receiving of love.

The Scroll of Song of Songs

From opening to closing lines, the Song of Songs assaults us with its language of love—a passionate, emotional, roller-coaster ride of longing and wanting that leaves us a bit embarrassed. We are the watchers, with love play happening before our eyes. As eavesdroppers, hearing each lover's appraisal of their beloved's body (4:1-7; 5:10-16; 7:2-5), we're not sure whether to look or turn our heads away. If we presently know such love, we probably giggle at love's self-absorption. If we've known such love in the past, memories might draw us back to a time when we couldn't keep our hands off the other. If we're awaiting love, the longing for intimacy blatantly expressed throughout the book will surely tug at our hearts. How can we not be captivated by those "drunk with love" (5:1)? The intensity of such passion is intoxicating. It isn't necessary to know all the ins and outs of ancient Hebrew poetry nor does one have to appreciate fully what it means to compare a woman's hair to a flock of goats, her teeth to pregnant ewes (4:2), or a man's arms and legs to rounded gold and alabaster columns (5:14-15) to recognize two people with the "hots" for each other. There's no way to miss that in the Song!

To a certain extent, it matters little that the Scroll's lovers are not known to us by name nor are we always sure who is speaking, whether the male or the female lover. Scholars debate the unity of the book, whether it should be read as a collection of love lyrics or as a single poem. There's a reference to King Solomon in chapter 3, but any historical connection of Solomon to the Song is debatable. Of course, should discussion drift to men who love women, King Solomon would

Study Bible

See the Introduction to the Song in *NISB*, p. 943. See also the "Excurses: History of Interpretation of the Song of Songs" on p. 953.

Study Bible

Read Song 1:2-2:7 for an initial feel for the Scroll.

definitely come to mind (1 Kgs 11:1-3). For all that we don't know, what we do recognize from the Song is the intoxication of love, with all of its desire, longing, and intensity. A country girl (called the Shulammite in 6:13) and a shepherd boy are head over heels in love. Their kisses and fondling are spoken of openly. There is no shame in their longing. So natural is their union, the very air is heavy with the scent of love (1:12-14).

The Ache of Love. A world that relegated females to the protection of males, whether fathers, husbands, or sons, is met head-on in Song of Songs by a woman driven by the claims of love. Every waking and sleeping moment is consumed by her desire to be with her lover. She talks about him, dreams about him, and chases after him. He matches her desire. Here are two people drunk with love yet who also know its pain. Song of Songs knows that love hurts, that the pleasure of being with the one you love stands in tension with the pain of separation (3:1-5). Everyone who has ever waited for a loved one, spent agonizing hours apart, knows like the lovers the ache that comes with separation. Love may be wonderful, but it isn't easy. Nor can it afford to be blind. In the Song, both longing and fear accompany love. The female lover is free to love, yet she is also reminded that real life is not a fairy tale—her sweet dreams of love are balanced by nightmares of rape (5:7). Minor characters in the Song (brothers, mother, women of Jerusalem) serve to underscore the point that love must be worked at, in the face of hostility and meddling (8:8-9; 5:8-9).

Love Strong as Death. Whether we are dealing with one Song or many smaller ones woven into the present text, or whether the lovers are one particular pair or the voices of all people in love, the Song of Songs draws us to see that "love is strong as death, passion fierce as the grave" (8:6). We cannot escape death nor should we try to elude love. Love and passion are the fabric of life, which we are to enjoy and celebrate.

The Festival of Passover (*Pesakh*)

Pesakh is the Jewish celebration of Passover, a seven- (or eight-) day celebration commemorating the exodus of the Hebrew people from slavery in Egypt.

Beginning on the fifteenth day in the Jewish month of Nisan (usually in April), the festival also celebrates the "rebirth" of the earth associated with the coming of spring. Based on the exodus tradition that the slaves fled Egypt before their dough could rise, unleavened bread, or matzah, became the first food of freedom, and nothing that is leavened (*khametz* in Hebrew) may be eaten during the days of *Pesakh*. Observant Jewish families "spring clean" their homes, ridding them of all traces of *khametz*, and on the night before *Pesach* a last ceremonial search for the *khametz* is held. The major observance of the festival relates to the blessings followed by the eating of foods that symbolize the exodus, particularly the *matsah* (unleavened bread). Passover recalls both the misery of slavery and the joy of redemption and freedom. A cup of wine set out for the prophet Elijah symbolizes the continued Jewish hope of ultimate redemption and peace.

On the Sabbath of the days of Passover, the Song of Songs is read in the synagogue. Rooted in allegorical tradition, the Song is heard as an expression of the romantic beginnings of the God-Israel relationship that is "consummated in marriage" at Sinai with the giving of the Law. The Festival of Weeks, seven weeks after Passover, will mark this union, and the Scroll of Ruth will be read.

Celebrating Love

The Song of Songs is a celebration of love. Like the song of creation, bone of bone and flesh of flesh (Gen 2:23), male and female meet as equals and awaken love in each other. The Song is erotic, not pornographic, sensuous rather than sexy. The Song celebrates the tenderness of love and approves of love that is openly passionate. There should be no embarrassment here, for such love is truly a gift of God. We cannot deny that the Song brings to mind the passion God has for human beings nor should we refrain from speaking of Christ's love for the church. What we must not do, however, is deny the lovers their love. Love that is passionate, sees beyond its own needs, and seeks fulfillment in the face of risks and disapproval demands not to be whitewashed in religious language. Attempts to

Sources

For a more detailed description of Passover, see Dosick, Wayne. *Living Judaism: The Complete Guide to Jewish Belief, Tradition & Practice* (San Francisco: HarperSanFrancisco, 1995).

Reflections

The book that is used for the Jewish Passover is called the *Haggadah*. It contains biblical quotations, rabbinic interpretations of the exodus, songs, prayers, and directions for the rituals of Passover. Over the centuries, Jews in various communities around the world have added their unique experiences to the tradition. With an emphasis on freedom, new lines have been added as the struggle for civil rights was affirmed in the 1960's, the call for the emancipation of Soviet Jews came about in the 1970's, and feminists have struggled for equality in more recent years. Each new interpretation reinforces the belief that human dignity and freedom are to be actively pursued (*Living Judaism*, pp. 166-68).

1. What role does the church have in the struggle for human dignity and freedom? (In assessing this question, you might ask participants to name groups of oppressed people with which they are familiar, identify the circumstances that keep them in marginalized or powerless positions, and come up with concrete suggestions for how the church might participate in their liberation.)

reign in such erotic passion will not do away with love. The Scroll remains. The question is: Will we through embarrassment find ourselves on the sidelines, left as minor players in the story, or will we recite with the poet, "Love is strong as death, passion fierce as the grave"?

Reflections

Song of Songs is a sensuous work that celebrates the passion of lovers.

1. How might the church tell people that it is okay to love passionately, sensually, with all your heart and body?
2. What do we lose if we opt out of such discussions? What might we gain?

Reflections

Allegorical interpretations moved away from discussion of human love and spoke instead of divine human love.

1. How might the idea of loving passionately for the goodwill of the other be a talking point of the church?
2. Is it possible to celebrate love beyond that of male-female love?
3. Is it the love for others that is to be celebrated?

Sources

Weems, Renita J. "The Song of Songs" in *New Interpreter's Bible*, vol. 5 (Nashville: Abingdon Press, 1997) 363-434.

Session 2

Ruth

R uth is one of two biblical books that bear a woman's name. The other is Esther, and both are festival scrolls. Ruth is the kind of sweet little story with a happy ending that we expect to find in the Bible. Unlike stories that begin in life and end with death, Ruth moves from death to life—from the death of a family to the birth of a nation, or at least the promise thereof. The young heroine is a Moabite woman who against all odds casts her fate with Naomi, an old woman from Judah, Ruth's widowed mother-in-law. It is their story that the book tells, and it is the faithfulness of Ruth that calls for the story to be read annually at Pentecost (the Festival of Weeks).

Lectionary Loop
Twenty-first Sunday after Pentecost, Year B, Ruth 1:1-18
Twenty-second Sunday after Pentecost, Year B, Ruth 3:1-5, Ruth 4:13-17

The Scroll of Ruth

In Protestant Bibles, the book of Ruth takes its place between the book of Judges and 1 Samuel. The beginning and ending of the book demands that we read both backwards and forwards to understand its canonical placement. Opening with the words, "In the days when the judges ruled, there was a famine in the land," knowledgeable readers hear a double foreboding. For female listeners, the warning is particularly haunting. The first phrase takes us back to the parting words of Judges, "In those days there was no king in Israel; all the people did what was right in their own eyes" (Judg 21:25) This judgment follows the story of the rape and mutilation of one woman, the Levite's concubine (Judg 19), which led to tribal warfare (Judg 20). The subsequent abduction of four hundred virgins of Jabesh-gilead and kidnapping of thirty young female dancers at Shiloh as wives (Judg 21) for the men of Benjamin, the tribe responsible for the initial rape in Judg 19 brings the story full circle. Female hearers know that "in the days when the judges ruled," there was no safe place for a woman.

This truth is underscored by the phrase, "There was a famine in the land." While readers might naturally move to the Joseph stories of Gen 37-50, recalling the famine that encompassed the whole land (Gen 41:53-57) and brought the family of Jacob from Canaan to Egypt where there was grain thanks to the preparations of Joseph, there are other stories in Genesis that use this line as well. Three different passages in Genesis tell a story of a wife being passed off as her husband's sister (Gen 12:10-20; 20:1-18; 26:1-11). Although the plot is basically the same, names and locations change between the three versions. The first two tell the story with Abraham and Sarah as the main characters while the third jumps to the next generation, using Isaac and Rebekah. Both the first and third telling set the stage for the story with the phrase, "Now there was a famine in the land" (12:10; 26:1). Whether one reads the story as a historical event that happened three different times or regards it as a stock story (the way we might today use a Cinderella plot, interchanging names and locations to fit a particular thematic need), the fact that women are considered expendable in a patriarchal world cannot be overlooked. The opening of Ruth reminds us of that truth as well.

The Story. To escape famine, a family of four (Elimelech and Naomi with their two sons, Mahlon and Chilion) leaves Bethlehem (in Hebrew, "house of bread") and journeys to the neighboring country of Moab. The move proves disastrous. Rather than life, death awaits. The first to die is Elimelech, leaving Noami a widow with two sons. The two sons take Moabite wives, Orpah and Ruth, but the family increases no further in size. When the two sons die, Naomi is left as a childless widow; there was no worse state for a woman.

News that there was food once again in Judah leads Naomi to head toward home with her Moabite daughters-in-law. Along the way, Naomi stops and seeks to

Teaching Tips

Have members read Judg 19–21. How is a woman's experience of the world different than a man's, both then and now?

Teaching Tips

Have members read Gen 12:10-20; 20:1-18; and 26:1-11; noting their similarities and differences.

turn the two women back towards Moab. Only their own family homes hold the possibility of a woman's hope, that of becoming a wife and mother of sons. Naomi has nothing left to offer. Orpah accepts the older woman's advice, but Ruth casts her fate with Naomi; her stated pledge of devotion, "Where you go, I will go; where you lodge, I will lodge; your people shall be my people, and your God my God," (1:16) becomes one of the most memorable lines in Scripture.

The return to Bethlehem finds Naomi a "bitter" woman (1:20). Famine for her was not a lack of bread but rather the loss of husband and sons. She is indeed an empty woman (1:21), and in good, Hebrew theological fashion, the one responsible is God. Life goes on, however, and daily existence requires daily sustenance. Ruth may have followed Naomi home, but it is Ruth who now takes the lead. A Judean, Naomi is an insider among her own people with Ruth, a foreigner, the outsider. In the interest of survival, however, the two immediately switch roles. Naomi remains at home in the private sphere while Ruth finds her place outside in the fields, gleaning with those for whom work in someone else's fields is the key to life. As it would happen, the field belongs to a rich relative of her in-law, Boaz, and Ruth wins his favor (a circumstance we will find in Esther later on). Two chapters (Ruth 2 and 3) are given to a developing, unspoken romance, at least on the part of Boaz (totally opposite the outspokenness of the lovers in the Song of Songs). All motives are honorable, whether those of Ruth, devoted to the well-being of her mother-in-law; Naomi, who has Ruth's best interest at heart; or Boaz, who protects the unprotected women, but always from what would be considered a respectable position. The end of the day discussions in chs. 2–3 not only keep Naomi in the picture but also give sanction to the actions of the younger woman. Ruth may be foreign, but under Naomi's tutelage, she will be "raised right."

The women's arrival had been at the beginning of the barley harvest (1:22). It is at the end of the barley and wheat harvests (2:23) that a more permanent existence must be sought. Naomi hatches a plan that will be carried out in darkness. Like most events that transpire in the dead of night, what happens between Boaz and Ruth on the threshing room floor is left in shadow. What we do know is that Ruth did as she was told, and Boaz acted as he should have. Slipping back home before dawn, the two women await the story's next event. Their future rests in Boaz's hands.

Seemingly complicated issues involving the transferal of land and name, rightful inheritance, and legal heir are settled speedily. A relative closer in kin than Boaz declines the role of redeemer, leaving Boaz in the position to acquire the land and to acquire Ruth as his wife (4:9-10). The events have taken place at the city gate with the elders and townspeople as witnesses. Caught up in the promise of the transaction, they offer a blessing for the impending union. The promise of land and a great nation made to Abraham in Gen 12:1 and worked out through the stories of the ancestors (Gen 12-36) is heard in the mentioning of Rachel and Leah (4:11). Together with their handmaids, Bilhah and Zilpah, Leah and Rachel had borne twelve sons to Jacob (Gen 29:31-30:24; 35:16-26), symbolically birthing the nation of Israel. (One should note the changing of Jacob's name to Israel in two traditions: Gen 32:22-32 and 35:9-15.)

The one-line blessing, "May your house be like the house of Perez, whom Tamar bore to Judah," (4:12) encapsulates another Genesis story. A side episode in the Joseph novella of Gen 37-50, the story of Tamar and Judah in Gen 38 struggles with the continuation of a family line accomplished by the bold actions of a widowed woman. The basic story line involves Judah, Jacob's son, who marries a foreign woman. They produce three sons, and the first one marries Tamar. He "was wicked in the sight of the LORD, and the LORD put him to death" (Gen 38:7). The second brother is to produce a son through sexual relations with his brother's widow. Applying his own method of birth control through early withdrawal, the coupling is futile, his actions judged wicked, and he too dies at the hands of a displeased God. With two sons dead and fearful for the third, Judah uses the ruse that the youngest is not

Study Bible

See Excursus: "Puns and Innuendos in Ruth 3," *NISB*, pp. 387-388. See notes 4:1-10 *NISB*, pp. 389-390.

Sources

McCown, C.C. "Gate" in *Interpreter's Dictionary of the Bible*, vol. 2 (Nashville: Abingdon Press, 1962) 355.

old enough to perform the act of brother and sends Tamar back to her family. Time and events speak to Tamar's abandonment. Applying the art of deception perpetrated on her by her marriage family, Tamar takes steps that lead to her impregnation by Judah. In the face of death (Gen 38:24), Tamar is judged to be "in the right" (v. 26) and survives in the tradition as a matriarch of Israel. She will be joined by Ruth. Her twin son, Perez, will be an ancestor of Boaz (Ruth 4:18-22) who with Ruth, the Moabite, produces Obed, the father of Jesse, the father of David.

The Festival of Weeks

The book of Ruth is tied to Pentecost or the Festival of Weeks (*Shavuot*). Like many religious festivals with ancient roots, the traditions for observing the holiday changed over time. Initially an agricultural festival, the holiday was to occur on the fiftieth day, seven weeks past Passover, marking the end of the barley harvest and the beginning of the early-spring wheat harvest (Deut 16:9-10). In biblical times the festival was observed through the offering of first fruits (wheat, barley, figs, dates, grapes, pomegranates, and olives), the produce of late spring. With the passage of history, a pilgrimage festival to the Temple in Jerusalem struggled for meaning in the face of the diminishment of an agrarian lifestyle, the destruction of the Temple, and the scattering of Jews. Judaism sought to hold on to the festival through a connection that was made between *Shavuot* and the giving of the law at Sinai. The festival was thus historicized into the very heart of Judaism, celebrating the revelation of God at Sinai in the giving of Torah. While Passover commemorated the exodus from Egypt and through the reading of the Song of Songs the pledge of God and people to each other, Judaism came to see *Shavuot* as the moment of commitment, the marriage between God and the Jewish people, with Torah (the Law) being God's wedding gift to them. The reading of Ruth during the festival is fitting for its setting in the time of harvest and for the example set by a non-Jew who accepts God and Torah.

Study Bible

See notes on Gen 38 in *NISB*, pp. 67-68.

Teaching Tips

Compare the stories of Tamar and Ruth. How are they similar/dissimilar?

Sources

Dosick, Wayne. *Living Judaism: The Complete Guide to Jewish Belief, Tradition & Practice* (San Francisco: HarperSanFrancisco, 1995).

Celebrating Kindness

Try as we may, some traditions are hard to keep alive. Such is the case with Shavuot, or Pentecost (Festival of Weeks). Over the years, non-orthodox Judaism (Orthodox Judaism continues to observe all holidays) has made numerous attempts to help people find meaning in a festival that no longer speaks to them, from transforming older customs to the introduction of new ones; yet "no Jewish holiday is more ignored and less observed than Shavuot" (*Living Judaism*, p. 179).

Within Christianity, Pentecost was redefined through the Lukan tradition as the time of the coming of the Holy Spirit (Acts 2:1-4) and continues to be observed in churches that hold to a liturgical calendar. But what should we really celebrate? At the core, Ruth and the Festival of Weeks are tied to daily survival. Pure and simple, human beings need food. We are taught to pray, "Give us this day our daily bread," and mealtime prayers remain a constant for many people of faith, giving thanks for what we have been given. Yet, for so many of us, the issue is not whether we will eat but whether we will stop eating when we're full. In dealing with the text, we have to come to terms with whether we're the haves or the have-nots. Do we own the fields, that is, have the means to assist people who are in need, or are we among the poor of the land? It is absolutely essential that we are honest and identify ourselves correctly. When trouble comes our way, do we like Naomi become paralyzed through bitterness? Can we be like Boaz and respond with what we have to those in need? And should we not be like Ruth, the foreigner, whose acts are as exemplary as Jesus' "Good Samaritan," setting the standard for faithfulness?

The connection Judaism made between Ruth, the Festival of Weeks, and the giving of the law is especially worth consideration. Living in a time when the Ten Commandments have been reduced to something to fight about (should they or should they not be posted in public places?), foreigners of certain regions are immediately suspect, and "illegal aliens" are at the top of the national political agenda, the story of Ruth challenges us not to act before we think. Ruth was a

Study Bible

See Ruth "Introduction," *NISB*, pp. 383-84.

Moabite. The letter of the law forbade a Moabite from being admitted to the "assembly of the LORD," (Deut 23:3-4) and in the post-exilic reforms Moabites were excluded from the community (Neh 13:1-3). Yet, Ruth was also a widow and a landless alien, and the law spoke to that situation as well (Deut 14:28-29). The law gives background to the story but does not limit the actions of the characters towards each other. More than the law is at stake. The real issue is kindness (in Hebrew, *khesedh*,) The words of Mic 6:8 come to mind with the requirement to "love kindness," a kindness shown by Orpah and Ruth to their husbands and Naomi (1:8), by Boaz to Ruth (2:20), and especially by Ruth to Naomi (3:10,). The words of Naomi's departing blessing prove prophetic. The kindness of Yahweh that she wishes for her daughters-in-law (1:8-9) plays out in the actions of a young foreign widow willing to risk death itself for the sake of an old woman (1:17), and in the end Ruth will know the kindness that Naomi wishes for her (4:13).

Acts of kindness should be celebrated. They call for a party! As the women celebrated with Naomi at the birth of Obed (4:14-15), people of faith are called to celebrate the moments when *khesedh* occurs in our midst, and Pentecost is a fitting time. Tradition ties the actions of foreign women to the birth of David, Israel's ideal king, and to Jesus, the Christ (Matt 1:1-16). The coming of the Holy Spirit at Pentecost breaks the barrier of language that separates people from one another (Acts 2:1-13). The breaking of barriers is the first step, and the second is committing acts of kindness, with a party to celebrate.

Sources

Baab, O.J. "Widow" in *Interpreter's Dictionary of the Bible*, vol 4 (Nashville: Abingdon Press, 1962) 842-43.

Study Bible

See note on 1:8-9 *NISB*, p. 385. See Special Note, *NISB*, p. 388.

Reflections

How might the church encourage true acts of kindness?

Teaching Tips

Have class members plan a party with "Celebrating Kindness" as the theme. Come up with a design for invitations, decorations, and party favors. Create a program and menu, and draw up an invitation list.

Sources

Farmer, Kathleen A. Robertson. "The Book of Ruth" in *New Interpreter's Bible*, vol. 2 (Nashville: Abingdon Press, 1998) 891-946.

Nielsen, Kirsten. *Ruth* The Old Testament Library (Louisville: Westminster John Knox Press, 1997).

Session 3

Lamentations

Lamentations is a dark, dark book for it speaks from the rock bottom of life. Like all laments, those of Lamentations speak to life's hurts, sorrow, anxiety, and uncertainty. Surely all know what it means to suffer loss, in one form or another. We also know what it means to find comfort in the words of those who have turned their suffering over to God. The words of Ps 23:4, "Even though I walk through the darkest valley, I fear no evil; for you are with me; your rod and your staff—they comfort me," are found in funeral homes and on hospital walls. Laments are the cries of an individual struggling with illness, old age, personal calamity, or impending death (Ps 22); a community confronted with famine; or a nation in the face of the enemy (Ps 74). The experiences of uncertainty, helplessness, and sorrow that drive people to pour out their hearts to God are heard in their mournful pleas.

Lectionary Loop

Eighteenth Sunday after Pentecost, Year C, Lamentations 1:1-6

The Scroll of Lamentations

The Scroll of Lamentations is a collection of five laments, each of which mourns the fall of Jerusalem to the Babylonians in 586 B.C.E. In its liturgical home as the festival scroll for the Ninth of Av, Lamentations commemorates the loss that strikes at the core of ancient Israel's identity, recalling both the destruction of the Solomonic Temple by the Babylonians and the Second Temple in 70 C.E. by the Romans. The expression of grief in the form of an acrostic characterizes the first four of the five laments. Starting with the first letter of the Hebrew alphabet and moving to the last, the initial word of each verse or, in the case of Lam 3, three verses, begins with a letter that is followed in the next verse with the next letter, until all twenty-two letters of the alphabet are represented. The effect is such that the experience of loss is total, stretching from *aleph* to *tav*, or A to Z.

The first lament, Lam 1, decries a city in ruin. A poet speaks in third person (1:1-11) as an onlooker who can scarcely believe what is seen. A vibrant, crown jewel of a city has fallen to the hand of her enemies, and no one is there to help or comfort her. Jerusalem, once proud and prosperous, has met with a total reversal of fortune, now humiliated among the nations. The reason lies with Jerusalem herself, as the lament acknowledges the sin that led to her downfall. The second half of the lament, 1:12-22, speaks in first person as the city bewails her plight. The suffering of the people is due to sin, which brings Yahweh's anger, which is expressed as divine judgment. With ten references to Yahweh, Lam 1 dives into the heart of Israel's struggle. Their present suffering comes at the hands of God. Although admittedly the result of their sin, the degree of sorrow ("Look and see if there is any sorrow like my sorrow" 1:12) is hard to fathom, and the contemplation of Yahweh as the enemy, though in the right, is as much a part of the agony as physical suffering. In the end, the groans of the people mingle with the plea that the human foes who have brought the destruction meet with the same fate.

The lament of chapter 2 graphically depicts a city fallen to the enemy. The dead lie in the streets, and anyone left alive faces starvation as babies suck on mothers' breasts without milk and mothers cannibalize their babies. A failure of leadership by king, priest, and prophet is lamented in the face of Yahweh's unrelenting anger. No doubt is expressed as to the cause of the destruction. "The LORD has done what he purposed" (2:17), the divine word fulfilled. A monotheistic view that interprets life based on the divine-human relationship attributes responsibility to people and action to God. Such belief leaves those tied to God, even when God has become the enemy, with nowhere else to turn but God. While 2:1-17 expresses the suffering brought on by Yahweh's anger, 2:18-19 calls for Zion to cry out to God. The pitiable appeal for God to look and consider the immensity of suffering is heard in 2:20-22.

The sixty-six verses of Lam 3, three times the length of the other four laments, is the heart of the Scroll. The voice of the lament is deeply personal, spoken as an individual sufferer's words—humiliated, mocked, abused, and abandoned. His suffering comes from the hand of God, a God to whom he has cried and not been heard (vv. 1-20). Yet, the sufferer chooses to hope (v. 21). Though "bereft of peace" (v. 17), the lamenter is alive, and to be alive is to be able to cry out to God. If there is hope, it rests with God, a God known also for steadfast love, faithfulness, and mercy (vv. 21-24). Fifteen verses are then given to the nature of God in whom the poet hopes. "The LORD is good to those who wait for him" (v. 25). God will not reject forever the ones presently being punished (v. 31). Central to hope is the understanding expressed in vv. 32-22: "Although he causes grief, he will have compassion according to the abundance of his steadfast love; for he does not willingly afflict or grieve anyone." Verses 40-47 are spoken as a community lament that calls on the people to return to Yahweh with the individual voice of the poet heard in vv. 48-51, pledging to cry continually until Yahweh once again looks with favor on the people. An individual lament closes the poem (vv. 52-66) in which the speaker asserts his innocence, expresses confidence in Yahweh to act on his behalf, and cries out for vindication against his human foes.

The poem of Lam 4 paints a horrific scene of Jerusalem under siege and the pitiable state of those who survived the city's fall. No one escaped the impact of destruction. Those who knew the privileges of life now know the worst life can bring. Like poem 2, graphic images are used to paint starvation, a slow death that finds women boiling their own children for food (v. 10). While the enemy attacked from without, the poem makes an inner attack on the nation's leadership—specifically, religious leadership whose sin is judged to be the real reason for the fall of the nation (v. 13). Like other calls for the enemy now to "get theirs," Lam 4 ends with the observation that the worst is over for Judah and warns the nation of Edom that a worse fate awaits it (vv. 21-22).

Lamentations 5 is a communal prayer for mercy. The fall of Judah to the Babylonians turned the tables, and a nation that was once on top finds itself experiencing life from the underside. Rape, torture, and forced labor speak to their powerless state. Opening with a plea for Yahweh to remember, look, and see their disgrace (5:1), the poem is forthright in its acknowledgement of the role of sin. They inherited the sin of their ancestors (v. 7), but fault does not stop there. "Woe to us, for we have sinned!" (v. 16) is directly linked to their present circumstances (vv. 17-18). A final appeal is made to Yahweh, who reigns forever, to restore the nation. Yet the appeal harbors doubt. Hope is put in the form of questions: Why have you forgotten? Why have you forsaken? (v. 20) The poet cries for restoration and renewal, a restoration to divine favor and renewal of life (v. 21). Yet the haunting words of the final verse, "unless you have utterly rejected us, and are angry with us beyond measure" (v. 22) reveal the true turmoil of the situation. Perhaps the unthinkable has happened, and this final cry will go unanswered.

The Festival of Ninth of Av

The Jewish observance of the Ninth of Av falls in mid-July to early August. On this date for centuries, Jews across the world exiled from the land of Israel would observe a full fast day, consuming neither food nor water. Their thoughts and tears were given to mourning the loss of Israel and Jerusalem, and their prayers would speak to the hope that one day they would return and the land would be restored. Though centered in the particular events of the destructions of the Temple, the Ninth of Av provided an established time for Jews through the centuries faced with their own disasters up to and including the Holocaust to identify with the moaning of their ancestors. The focal point of the evening observance of Ninth of Av is the reciting of the Scroll of Lamentations followed by medieval liturgical poems equally mournful in tone and theme.

Reflections

Whom are we to blame for pain and destruction? Following any disaster, there's always the pointing of fingers. After all, someone has to be responsible. In a no-cost-unless-recovery, sue-for-any-reason world, placing blame is outrageously profitable. There is a difference, however, between placing blame and accepting responsibility. Yet we've learned not to admit fault, so how can we talk about sin? Not only is sin-talk terribly old fashioned, but again, potentially libelous. The Scroll of Lamentations ties the sinful deeds of humanity to a judgment of death and destruction by God. Our theological sensibilities surely question a monotheistic view that regards such destruction as the wrath of God. The danger, however, is that in removing divine judgment from the equation; we remove the human factor as well. Blaming God is an easy way out. Understanding the role we play in death and destruction challenges us in the deepest part of our souls. Is this not the point where we need to cry out to God, asking for healing, restoration and renewal?

The establishment of the modern state of Israel in 1948 and the reunification of Jerusalem in 1967 has led to a change in the observance of Ninth of Av for many Jews today. Though traditional Jews remain committed to acts of mourning that both precede and occur on the Ninth of Av, for others the day has moved from a time of mourning to a time of remembering the full scale of Jewish history. For them, mourning and loss are only parts of the memories, which are joined with those that recall the restoration occurring in modern history. There is quiet celebration.

Celebrating Loss

There are moments in life that change us forever. A person who has worked hard in her or his job only to find the job taken away struggles with the loss of self-esteem. Lives change overnight when homes are destroyed by natural disasters, or unforeseen calamities threaten financial ruin. Death brings its own struggle. The loss of a parent breaks our hold on the past; the loss of a child, our tie to the future.

If individual disasters aren't enough to face, national and international disasters challenge us as well. We may not have known a single person in the Twin Towers on 9/11, but the loss on that day was felt by a nation. The 2004 Asian tsunami struck a half-world away, but we'll never forget the rage of the waters. We may not have family serving in the armed forces, but the news of each soldier's death surely stirs our hearts. In the face of such tragedy, there seems nothing to celebrate. When the pain is too great and the hurt too acute, the last thing we want to do is remember. Yet there is healing in communal lament that takes life's deepest hurts to God.

For ancient Israel, the loss of Temple, land, and king created a theological crisis of the gravest proportions. The Israelites considered the land to be their inheritance given to them by divine promise (Gen 12:1-3). The Davidic covenant spoke of an everlasting kingship (2 Sam 7:8-17), while Zion was the place where Yahweh's name dwells, a city protected under divine word: "The LORD of hosts will protect Jerusalem; he will protect and deliver it, he will spare and rescue it"

Reflections

It seems fair to say that people outside Judaism have little if any knowledge of the Ninth of Av. There is no mention of it in the biblical text, and while those reared on biblical stories and history will know of Solomon's Temple and perhaps its destruction, for many non-Jews the idea that there was a Second Temple Period, which ended with the Roman destruction in 70 C.E., will likely be new information. Though part of our shared stories, the loss of the Temple resonates within Judaism, yet not on any emotional level for Christianity. The tie is best made with portions of the Scroll of Lamentations that have become a part of the liturgy for Good Friday observances. Both the Ninth of Av and Good Friday deal with loss, indeed a loss that strikes at the heart of each religion. Anti-Semitism reached its height during the Holocaust. Some half a century later, the threat of genocide against other peoples and groups is a reality of life with religion as a secondary, if not primary, cause. How might the idea of "loss" serve as a catalyst for bonding divided people? Give thought in naming particular situations that have been changed through similar, if not equal, experiences of loss.

(Isa 31:5). The poems of Lamentations took national disasters with theological implications and placed them before God. If sin brings destruction from God, then repentance and crying out to God is the only hope for restoration. No matter how bleak the situation, if there is hope, it will come "to those who wait for him" (Lam 3:25).

Teaching Tips

1. Either as an individual or a group exercise, use an acrostic to compose a lament that gives expression to a particular instance of loss.
2. Throughout time, people have given expression to personal and communal loss through various forms of expression. Have class members give examples from literature, music, art, film, or other venues that in some way seek to deal with sorrow. Was religion part of the expression and if so, how?
3. Have students find the ten references to Yahweh (LORD) in Lam 1. Discuss what is being said about the nature of God in each reference. How do the ten references work together to paint a theological understanding of God? How does our understanding of God fit this model?
4. Lamentations 3 speaks of God's steadfast love (*khesedh*) and faithfulness. Have members read other OT passages that speak of the enduring love of God (Exod 34:6; Jer 33:11; Pss 100:5; 106:1; 107:1; 118:1-4; 136:1-26; Ezra 3:11). What is the significance of these words and how might they be incorporated in modern worship?

Sources

O'Connor, Kathleen M. "The Book of Lamentations" in *New Interpreter's Bible*, vol. 6 (Nashville: Abingdon Press, 2001) 1013-1072.

Session 4

Ecclesiastes

The book of Ecclesiastes is wisdom literature, taking its place among such books as Proverbs as well as the wisdom texts of Psalms and other OT passages. Wisdom writing is the most universal of all literature; it concerns itself with how one is to get along in life and is generally optimistic. Traditional wisdom stresses the good life that is the reward for those who work hard, follow the rules, and live in moderation. Ecclesiastes is skeptical of such attitudes, challenging conventional wisdom and offering a different worldview.

Sources

Clifford, Richard J. "Introduction to Wisdom Literature" in *New Interpreter's Bible*, vol. 5 (Nashville: Abingdon Press, 1997) 1-16.

The Scroll of Ecclesiastes

While most wisdom works focus on the meaning of life, Ecclesiastes reflects on how meaningless life is. There are two voices in the book: a narrator who speaks in the beginning and at the end of the book, and *Qoheleth*, the one whose observations and instructions are presented in the Scroll. Often translated as "Teacher" or "Preacher," the root word in Hebrew means "to assemble" and may imply a role in an "assembly." The word functions in the Scroll primarily as a proper name, which leaves us at a loss as to whom we actually hear. An attempt is made to tie the voice to Solomon (1:1), but no critical scholar would accept such authorship. Like the message of the book, the one who speaks it is enigmatic. Many questions are left unanswered. That's the way it should be. The Scroll of Ecclesiastes wrestles with what life is all about. The poet observes and, on the basis of the observation, instructs. Yet what is being taught is not simply to be heard but, rather, considered. Qoheleth's search for the key to life's meaning is presented as a lifelong quest. Our task cannot be an easy read.

The scroll opens with the declaration that all is *hebel*. The NRSV translates the word as "vanity." It's not just that we don't walk around saying "*hebel* of *hebels...hebel* of *hebels*, everything is *hebel*, that makes the meaning unclear to us. We also don't walk around saying, "Vanity of vanities! All is vanity." Since the word occurs some thirty times in the Scroll, we need desperately to get at its meaning. If we think of breath, mist, or vapor—something that passes quickly, is transient, or hard to hold onto—we'll be getting close. Basically Qoheleth looks at the world and, on the basis of human experience, concludes that nothing lasts or is of any real value. In fact it's all rather meaningless. Life basically is without purpose.

In looking for something to be of value, to have meaning, Qoheleth tried work (1:2-11), wisdom (1:2-18), and pleasure (2:1-11), but "all was vanity and a chasing after wind" (2:11). Comparing wisdom to folly, wisdom wins out, but in the end, both the wise and the fool die (2:12-16). For all of life's effort and toil, the end result is that the gain goes to someone else, a reality that leaves the searcher hating life (2:17-23). So what's to be done? Eat, drink, and find pleasure in the toil, for this "unhappy business that God has given to human beings" (1:13) is what we get and "to the one who pleases him God gives wisdom and knowledge and joy" (2:26)—such as it is!

Ecclesiastes 3:1-8 are poster words. They read well and without much thought; they are easily agreed to. There is truth in seeing life's opposites, or paradoxes, but such a view has history moving in circles without any purpose or goal—a scandalous thought for much of Old Testament theology that sees history as having a beginning and an end, all of which rests with God. For Qoheleth, human beings should simply take what comes their way and make the best of it (3:9-15).

For those who buy the Old Testament concept of justice—if you're good, you'll be blessed; if you're bad, you'll be punished—forget it! It's all a matter of chance. For Qoheleth's money, the dead are better off than the living, but not as well-off as the unborn (3:16-4:3). The value of human relationships is considered with some benefit noted, but in the end, "vanity and a chasing after wind" (4:4-16). And whatever you do, don't mess around with God, for we are directed to "fear God," the proper role of humanity in life (5:1-7).

Life teaches that injustice is tied to power (5:8); riches carry their own hardship, (5:10-12) and a person comes into this world with nothing and takes nothing out (5:13-17). The best course is to accept what God gives and forget about the rest (5:18-20). What look like blessings—wealth, children, long life—may in fact be meaningless. Not to experience life can be better than life's experiences. There's simply a lot we don't know and aren't going to know, and there's no use arguing about it (6:1-12)!

A series of proverbs calling for reflection on life (7:1–8:1) leaves us shaking our heads—sometimes in agreement, sometimes with an "I don't think so" nod. The best bet seems to be to err on the side of wisdom and live a life of moderation with nothing extreme, one way or another. After all, few men can be trusted, and no woman (v. 28)!

Wisdom is hard to come by (8:1). Keep a low profile around rulers (8:2-9); there's no real justice in life, and the ways of God can't be known (8:10-16). Death comes to all, the righteous and the wicked, but while there is life, there is hope. So enjoy life. Whatever life gives you, for whatever you toil, it's all you get, so go for it. Death lies ahead, and there is nothing awaiting you in the abode of the dead (9:1-10).

Ecclesiastes 9:13–10:20 characterizes wisdom and foolishness. A little wisdom can go a long way, but foolishness, even in small doses, negates wisdom's benefits (9:18-10:1). The worst is when foolishness finds its way into power (10:5-7, 16-20). Life is uncertain, and disaster may await (11:2); but something good might happen as well, and you don't want to miss out by failing to take a chance on life (11:3-6).

Life is good and should be enjoyed 11:7-12:8. Make the most of it when you are young, and never forget what lies ahead. Youth will give way to old age, life will give way to death, and all are answerable to God (11:9).

Study Bible

See Special Note in *NISB*, pp. 937-938

Reflections

1. With which parts of this series of proverbs do you resonate?
2. With which parts do you disagree?

An epilogue completes the work which summarizes the Teacher's life. Qoheleth taught what he learned. It adds a few comments about wise words and the problem with studying too much and out of the blue, concluding with an added orthodox statement to "Fear God, and keep his commandments; for that is the whole duty of everyone" (12:13).

The Festival of Booths (Tabernacles)

Judaism struggled over whether or not to include Ecclesiastes in the canon. In the end, the scroll was included and eventually found its home as the reading for the Feast of Booths. Booths, or in Hebrew, *Sukkot*, is a joyful autumn festival that lasts seven days and celebrates the end of the agricultural year when the wheat and grape harvests are complete (Deut 16:13). The festival celebrates more than harvest though, for Booths has been tied to the remembrance of the wilderness experience when Israel's ancestors dwelt in temporary shelters, or booths (Lev 23:43). A joyous celebration is thus anchored to historical memories of a time when daily existence depended on God. In the wilderness the people learned the lesson that the key to human existence is to fear God and obey the commandments. With such teachings, the reading of the Scroll of Ecclesiastes makes sense. On the Sabbath during *Sukkot*, Ecclesiastes speaks to the power of God and the meaning of existence for humankind.

Celebrating Life

If you stopped random people on the street and asked them to complete the phrase "Life is a ____," what might you hear? Certainly some statements would be printable, and others would not. Life is a roller-coaster ride with ups and downs, twists and turns that often catch us unaware. During graduate school days, my fellow student and husband learned to give what we called "what the hell" parties. In the face of hard work and a less-than-expected grade, a nasty phone call from a parishioner, or running out of money before running out of bills, we learned that the best thing we could do was celebrate. We've been doing this for more than thirty years now. We've had parties

Reflections

1. How do you complete the phrase. Life is a _____?
2. In what specific ways do you celebrate life?
3. What is the significance of gathering with friends for a party, no matter what the situation?

for close friends going through divorce and colleagues facing life-and-death medical procedures. We've thrown parties when someone got a job and when another person lost one. When hurricanes threaten our area, we break out the grills, and when the storm passes and the power is out, we invite everyone back for more.

Ecclesiastes can scare us with its pessimism, or spark us to seize the day. The Teacher got it right. Not one of us knows what tomorrow holds, and for all our knowledge, death remains a mystery. The very best we can say is that life and death belong to God. So "eat your bread with enjoyment, and drink your wine with a merry heart" (Eccl 9:7). Life is a gift. We must make it count. For as long as we have life, we have hope.

Teaching Tips

Select passages from Ecclesiastes and read them aloud. Have class members discuss their own experience on the basis of Qoheleth's observations of life.

Ecclesiastes paints a picture of life spinning in circles, a broken record that plays the same line over and over. Have participants find examples in music, art, literature, etc. that portray the skeptical side of life—a "spitting into the wind."

Sources

Towner, W. Sibley. "The Book of Ecclesiastes" in *New Interpreter's Bible*, vol. 5 (Nashville: Abingdon Press, 1997) 267-360.

Brown, William P. *Ecclesiastes*. Interpretation (Louisville: John Knox Press, 2000).

Session 5

Esther

An interesting connection between the scrolls is their struggle for acceptance as Scripture. Song of Songs was too racy and had to find acceptance through allegory. The skeptical theology of Ecclesiastes clashed with the positive outlook of traditional wisdom texts such as Proverbs. I recall my amazement when a former student from an Eastern European country told of a man's reburial because the burial text for his first funeral came from Ecclesiastes. Then there's Esther, and no text has struggled more. At least a fragment of every book of the Hebrew Bible was found among the Dead Sea Scrolls at Qumran, but not one letter from Esther. The absence of any mention of God in the Hebrew text as well as the lack of concern for Jewish dietary laws and customs led to a significant remake of the story in Greek with six additions that included mentioning the name of God fifty or more times. The reformer Martin Luther condemned the book of Esther, and for other reasons, a few centuries later, Hitler ordered copies of the book burned and the festival of Purim that the story of Esther establishes, banned.

Lectionary Loop

Sixteenth Sunday after Pentecost, Year B, Esther 7:1-6, 9-10; 9:20-22

Study Bible

See "Esther: The Greek Version Containing the Additional Chapters," *NISB* pp. 1401-1417.

The Scroll of Esther

The book of Esther begins and ends with a party. In fact, there are some ten parties or banquets mentioned in the text. The exaggeration of characters and events gives the story a comic-strip-like quality that leaves us with our mouths open, astounded by each day's turn of events and wondering what the next day will bring. The story centers on a young Jewish virgin, Esther, and her relative, Mordecai. They are among the Jews living under Persian domination in the capital city of Susa. The Persian king, Ahasuerus, is a partying man, and the story opens with a six-month-long party thrown for the upper crust of the land. A week-long party for the citizens of Susa follows the first, with the one rule being that guests are to drink to their hearts' content.

Queen Vashti hosts a party for women in another part of the palace. At some point amid male bravado, Ahasuerus summons Vashti to appear before his guests. Without explanation, Vashti simply says no. In the hands of the king's advisors, her refusal becomes cause for national concern, a law is passed that all wives must obey their husbands, and Vashti is banished from the palace. Of course, the king is left without a queen, and, in the interest of solving the problem, the advisors offer a solution that introduces Esther into the story. Together with the other virgins of the land, Esther begins a yearlong beautifying process in preparation for her night with the king. On the advice of Mordecai who has taken up a position at the palace gate, Esther hides her Jewish identity. She wins the favor of the virgins' handler, and then that of the king when her night of destiny arrives. Like Ruth's night on the threshing-room floor, the telling is discrete, yet moralists and feminists alike are forced to struggle with a heroine who sleeps her way to the crown. Indeed, the Greek version of the telling responds to such concern and has Esther despising her crown and living a life of self-loathing (Addition C / 14:15-16). In either case, Esther takes up life in the palace with Mordecai keeping watch close by, a position that proves fortuitous when he overhears an assasination plot against Ahasuerus and through Esther warns the king.

At this point, Haman enters the story, an arch villain to rival all others. He is a caricature of a person in power overcome with his own self-importance. Mordecai's refusal to bow to him leads Haman to seek a death sentence for all Jews. Under the threat of a pogrom, Mordecai takes steps to draw Queen Esther out of pampered palace life and into political action. At first oblivious to the situation and acting totally like the out to lunch female, Esther sends clothes to her uncle who has rent his clothes and covered himself with ashes, traditional signs of mourning. Informed of the looming disaster, Esther's response is equally disquieting when in response to the charge that she appeal to the king and plead for the salvation of her people, she reveals that a month has passed since she has seen Ahasuerus. While Esther and readers might pause to wonder why this is so, Mordecai forges ahead with his bad news/good news approach. Esther will not escape the fate of all Jews, but should she choose silence, help will come from elsewhere. Yet perhaps her destiny lies in this very moment (4:14).

Esther proclaims a fast, is welcomed when she appears before the king, invites him together with Haman to dinner, and during the course of the meal invites them both to dinner again the next night. Each appears as a silly man, giddy from the attention of the queen. The king, always given to excess, keeps offering Esther whatever her wish may be, up to half his kingdom. Haman, puffed up even more by his dinner experience, boasts to family and friends of his success. The only point of contention in his life remains Mordecai, and at the suggestion of his family, Haman prepares for Mordecai's demise. As chance would have it ("chance" being an operative motif in the story), Ahasuerus can't sleep that night and like many insomniacs addresses the situation with a boring read to lull him to sleep. Reminded of the foiled attempt on his life and realizing that nothing was done to recognize his benefactor, Ahasuerus, the most powerful man on earth who never has a thought of his own, decides to ask the next person he meets to describe for him a fitting reward. And—you guessed it—in a story where timing is everything, Haman walks into the room. Thinking the reward is for him, Haman outlines everything he would want and then finds himself tasked with bestowing the honor on the man he despises most, Mordecai. As quickly as he rises, Haman's descent occurs at lightning speed. Totally deflated by the public shaming he experiences in honoring his nemesis, Haman's report to his family and friends this time counters their earlier "you can do anything you want" advice and instead foreshadows his downfall.

Teaching Tips

Compare the Hebrew telling of the story of Esther with the Greek version. What do the Greek additions add to the story? Pay particular attention to the characters and the addition of religious language. How do the characters change? Is the effect positive or negative?

The Greek additions use the name of God over and over while the Hebrew does not. Does the name of God have to be mentioned for God to be present? Do you or do you not find God in the Hebrew version?

How do we hear religious language? Is religious language always acceptable, or are there times when what is left unsaid is more powerful than what is said?

The second dinner speeds events toward a quick resolution. Esther reveals Haman's plot against the Jews. The king's typical indecisiveness presents the occasion for saving face, accusing Haman of rape and ordering his death. Esther and Mordecai step into the vacuum left by Haman's demise, plotting the salvation of the Jews. A date set aside for the destruction of the Jews becomes a date when the Jews triumph over their enemies. Such a turn of events demands celebration, and the story ends with a party. The inauguration of the yearly Festival of Purim called for Jews in every generation to celebrate when sorrow turned to gladness and mourning into a holiday (9:22).

The Festival of Purim

In Jewish life, Purim is observed on 14 Adar, a date in late February or early March. Traditional Jews observe a day of fasting (the Fast of Esther) before Purim, recalling the fasting of Jews before Esther's appearance before the king. The *megillah* (scroll) of Esther is read on the evening of Purim and again in the morning. (Judaism begins a day at sunset, thus counting a day as evening and morning). Purim is a carnival atmosphere with special noisemakers used to drown out the name of Haman each time it is heard in the reading. Children dress in costume, similar to Halloween, and adults are allowed to drink "until [they] do not know (the difference between Haman and Mordecai)."

Legend has it that Haman wore a three-cornered hat, so *Hamantashen* (i.e. Haman's Hat or Pocket—small triangular cakes with fruit or poppy seed filling) are a specialty of Purim. Purim resembles many holidays around the world when people dress up in costume and let their hair down in disguise. Different from the festivals that have a decidedly religious bent, Purim nonetheless embodies a Jewish understanding of goodwill in the giving of small gifts to neighbors and friends and donations for those in need.

Celebrating Justice

Recalling again the words of Mic 6:8 ("What is good; and what does the LORD require of you but to do

---

Teaching Tips

Esther is not the only female savior in the Bible. Read the stories of Deborah and Jael in Judg 4–5 and the story of Judith in the Apocrypha. How do we hear these stories? Why is it important that we tell them?

Reflections

How each of us experiences life is tied to the issue of power. Does someone have power over us, or do we have power over others? How is power wielded? Does it work for good or harm, and how? Draw up a list of ten situations that define people as the powerful and the powerless. Is the situation just? If not, how might it be changed, and what would be the result for each group?

Reflections

Sadly, too many people around us and maybe among us are victims of abuse. We might be victims ourselves. For many known and unknown reasons, people who are victims of abuse—children of abusive parents, children bullied by other children, wives or husbands battered by spouses, elderly parents mistreated by their children—often remain silent in the face of the abuse. How does the story of Esther speak to such situations? Would "naming the enemy" help victims gain control of their situations? If so, how might the church encourage such action?

justice, and to love kindness, and to walk humbly with your God?") the Scroll of Esther challenges us to consider how justice is administered. There is no mention of God in the Hebrew telling, and there are no prayers. Whether the story is historical or not is debatable, but the plot rings true. We know that the world is made up of the powerful and the powerless and that life lived under the power of others is risky. We know from history if not experience that people of a different race, religion, or nationality can find themselves facing life or death based on the whim of those in authority. And we know that help can come from the most unexpected of places and in the most surprising ways. Still, when an entire people are condemned to death, a beauty queen is not the most obvious of saviors. Nor does throwing a dinner party seem a likely strategy for survival. One can make fun of Esther and ridicule her feminine ploys, but in the end her plan worked. It worked because real power comes in naming the enemy. That is a truth of the story and a key to understanding what it means to do justice. There are Hamans in this world who want to be bowed to, and there are people in high places without a thought of their own who allow unchecked power to flourish. Life itself can be at stake. Doing justice is confronting injustice and naming its cause. That is how the oppressed are freed, how sorrow is turned into gladness and mourning into a holiday.

Sources

Crawford, Sidnie White. "The Book of Esther" in *New Interpreter's Bible*, vol. 3 (Nashville: Abingdon Press, 1999) 855-941.

Queen-Sutherland, Kandy M. "Additions to Esther" in *Mercer Commentary on the Bible* (Macon, GA: Mercer University Press, 1995) 819-823.

_____ "Esther" in *Mercer Commentary on the Bible* (Macon, GA: Mercer University Press, 1995) 395-403.

Reflections

Compare all five *Megilloth* on the topic of love. What do they have to say, and what do they teach us? What overall significance do we find in the Scrolls, and how might we best incorporate their teachings in the life of the church?

A TIME TO LAUGH

A STUDY BY

DAVID ALBERT FARMER

David Albert Farmer is Visiting Professor of Preaching at Palmer Theological Seminary in Philadelphia and also teaches at Wilmington College in Delaware. He is the pastor of Silverside (American Baptist) Church in Wilmington, DE.

I. Introduction
   A. The Importance of Laughter
   B. Can We Laugh when We Read the Bible?

II. Session 1—"Page Obstetrics to the Geriatric Ward!"—Laughter at the Unexpected: Genesis 17:1-17; 18:1-15
   A. A Child of Laughter
   B. Abraham's Laughter
   C. Sarah's Laughter
   D. Laughter at the Unexpected

III. Session 2—Who Laughs Last?: Jesus' Love for the Absurd: Matthew 5:29; 7:3-5; 19:24
   A. Jesus' Love for the Absurd
   B. The Log in the Eye
   C. The Camel and the Needle's Eye

IV. Session 3—Piety and Pouting: 1 Kings 19:1-12
   A. Competition and Contest
   B. Elijah on the Run
   C. Elijah's Response

V. Session 4—Out of the Mouths of…Asses: Numbers 22:15-25
   A. Balak Requests a Curse
   B. Balaam Consults God
   C. God Sends Balaam to Balak
   D. Only the Ass Understands

VI. Session 5—The Danger of Boring Sermons: Acts 20:7-12
   A. The Shadow of Boredom
   B. A Crowded Room and a Long-winded Speaker
   C. Eutychus Falls to the Ground

Introduction

A Time to Laugh

The words of American poet, Ella Wheeler Wilcox:

Laugh and the world laughs with you,
Weep, and you weep alone.
For the sad old earth must borrow its mirth,
But has trouble enough of its own.
   (1883,public domain)

Beautiful and true. Adapted by Mrs. Patrick Campbell in correspondence to George Bernard Shaw:

Laugh and the world laughs with you,
Snore and you sleep alone.

The Importance of Laughter

I acknowledge and confess that I need laughter in my life. I love to laugh, and when I don't or can't I've learned that all is not well for me. The world situation has forced me not to want to laugh a lot lately, but I'm trying to do as much laughing as I can anyway. Will you laugh with me?

Someone has pointed out that children laugh an average of three hundred or more times a day while adults laugh an average of five times a day. We have a lot of catching up to do if we want to be happy and whole! Norman Cousins, who credits laughter with healing him of a very painful and life-threatening illness, described laughter as something like internal jogging because of how all the internal organs get worked out by a good belly laugh!

Among the health benefits of laughter are:

Sources

Dent, Alan, ed. *Bernard Shaw and Mrs. Patrick Campbell: Their Correspondence* (London: Gollancz, 1952) 32.

decreased blood pressure (after a rise), an immune system boost, and improved brain functioning. William Frye, a psychiatrist and professor emeritus at Stanford Medical School, claims to have demonstrated that one minute of laughter is equal to ten minutes on a rowing machine. Little bursts of laughter or giggles or smirks don't do it; we're talking belly laughs here. In fact, we're talking one hundred to two hundred deep laughs in order to get that all-important ten-minute cardio credit! If this is true, can you imagine what six minutes of laughter throughout the day would do for us?

The preacher in the book of Ecclesiastes says: "For everything there is a season...a time to weep, and a time to laugh; a time to mourn, and a time to dance" (Eccl 3:1a, 4). What is life without laughter? And what is faith without fun?

Jesus' beatitudes seem to follow right along with this part of the book of Ecclesiastes. Jesus said, "Blessed are you who weep now, for you will laugh" (Luke 6:21b). Laughter is a part of the best of life. Laughter is a part of what the ravages of life deprive us of and, consequently, what we hope for when we think of "better days," or life as it was intended to be lived.

Can We Laugh when We Read the Bible?

Our source of humor for this study will be—of all places—the Bible. Given the somberness that many of our traditions have pressed us to bring to all matters religious, especially to the reading of Scripture, the notion of laughing WITH the Bible makes more than a few people quite uncomfortable. It shouldn't be that way.

Conrad Hyers' points out in his book *And God Created Laughter: The Bible as Divine Comedy* that there's a good reason many of us have missed the humor of the Bible, even if we'd love to have noticed:

Anyone who has learned a foreign language will appreciate the problems involved. The subtleties of humor are usually the last elements of a language that students are able to grasp. The tendency is to read everything in a very literal, one-dimensional manner—as we tend to read the Bible. Furthermore, oral

Reflections

Ask your fellow learners to share times when they laughed in church—whether they should have or not!

Teaching Tips

Divide your study group into teams of three or four. Without giving an overview of the biblical passages that will be covered in this unit, ask each group to report back to the larger group one Bible story that they consider to be funny in some way.

humor cannot always be captured in a written account. How, for example, can one register in the words themselves whether the speaker was saying something tongue-in-cheek or smiling or laughing? Not a single wink makes its way to the printed page. (p. 4)

Somewhere along the way, probably growing originally out of fear of deities in polytheistic faiths, somberness has come to be pervasive in monotheistic religious practice, including the reading of Scripture. When most Christians read from the Bible, either silently or aloud, they do so with a solemn and serious tone.

Many of us generally think of God as angry and ill-tempered and, therefore, humorless. Jesus certainly did his best to help us see that none of those perceptions of God are accurate, but we have always only allowed Jesus to say to us what we think he said (because someone once told us) before we read his words afresh for ourselves.

My dear friends, in the spirit of hopefulness and abandon, we will open our hearts anew, and the joy of God in us and with us will give us the gift of laughter.

In the coming five sessions, we will jump around a bit in the Scriptures to some passages that I believe were intended be humorous for listeners and readers. Suspend any skepticism about the possibility of humor in the Bible, and laugh with me please for health and inspiration.

Sources

Hyers, Conrad. *And God Created Laughter: The Bible as Divine Comedy* (Atlanta: John Knox, 1987).

"Page Obstetrics to the Geriatric Ward!"—Laughter at the Unexpected

A Child of Laughter

There once was a baby—much-loved and long-anticipated—named Isaac, which in Hebrew means "laughter." How he got his name goes back to how hard his dad and mom laughed when, while waiting around for their AARP "50 Years of Membership" and "40 Years of Membership" cards, respectively, to arrive, God got word to them that they were going to have a baby—a child God had promised many years before when God told Abram he would be the father of a great nation (Gen. 12:1-3; 15:1-6). In their ancient time and place, a woman's worth was typically tied to her ability to bear children—especially male children. And Abram's wife, Sarai, couldn't conceive. In that day and age, it didn't occur to anyone that Abram, whose name meant "high father," might have been the infertile partner. It turned out that he wasn't, but it was sad Sarai's burden to bear.

The years passed and so had all the fertility treatments that anybody and everybody suggested to Sarai. She had gone to great lengths to secure an heir for Abram by giving him her servant Hagar, and Hagar bore a son named Ishmael. But Sarai was jealous of Hagar and Ishmael and sent them out into the desert alone to die (Gen 16:1-15). This part of the story certainly is not the least bit humorous and illustrates the lengths to which a couple desperate for children might go.

When all hope was gone that Sarai and Abram could ever have a child together—not to mention confidence in working parts—the most remarkable thing happened.

Lectionary Loop
Fourth Sunday after Pentecost, Year A, Genesis 18:1-15
Second Sunday in Lent, Year B, Genesis 17:1-7, 15-16

Teaching Tips

Discuss how difficult it must have been for Abram and Sarai to believe in God's promise that Abram would have his own heir. Ask participants to discuss the ways in which Abram and Sarai tried to remedy their childlessness (adoption of Eleazar; surrogate mother Hagar). Did these actions show a lack of faith or a desire to make the promise come true? Name other women in the Bible who were childless until God intervened to give them children (Rachel, Hannah, and Samson's mother [see session 4]). Eve also acknowledged that her child was given with God's help. What do you make of this motif in the Bible, that God is the giver of life?

God gave Abram advance notice. The old man heard that his new name would be "Abraham," which means "father of many." Mercy! That had a nice ring to it! By virtue of the fact that a name change was coming, Abram knew that some sort of uprooting event in his life was about to take place—even though he'd long ago handed over the efforts to change the world to younger generations.

Abraham's Laughter

OK, so Abram/Abraham is committed to this plan. The question is, how to get Sarai on board. Not surprisingly, the God of Genesis had already planned it out.

> God said to Abraham, "As for your wife, you shall not call her Sarai, but Sarah [princess] shall be her name. I will bless her, and moreover I will give you a son by her. I will bless her, and she shall give rise to nations; kings of peoples shall come from her." Then Abraham fell on his face and laughed. (Gen 17:15-17a)

If Abraham the Patriarch can laugh at something God says, then so can we! Laughter, after all, can be a kind of wonder.

Sarah's Laughter

God sent three messengers to break the big news to the elderly but lovely Sarah. As it turned out, she overheard them. While the three messengers were talking with Abraham outside the tent, Sarah was inside secretly trying to size up the unexpected visitors.

Abraham had laughed out loud. He was in stitches and didn't care who heard him laughing. But not Sarah. No. She wasn't supposed to hear the news the way she heard it, and she couldn't let company know that she'd been eavesdropping on their conversation with her husband. So, Sarah laughed, but she kept it to herself. She even denied having laughed when God asked her about it!

Laughter at the Unexpected

Frederick Buechner told the first contemporary and the funniest retelling of this story that I ever heard. He

Sources

For further discussion of Hagar's story, see Gafney, Wilda C.M. "The Book of Genesis" in *The Pastor's Bible Study*, vol. 3. Edited by David Albert Farmer (Nashville: Abingdon Press, 2006) 87-133.

Reflections

Could this aspect of our story be a lesson to those who think that retirement equates to being put out to pasture? God still has great plans for all the willing and the able. Discuss this statement with your fellow learners: "Only societies—and especially western ones—equate age with ineffectiveness." Discuss also the kind of humor usually poked at older people: what sorts of "old people" do we see on TV or in the movies? (Answers might include: crotchety old men, "grannies" who laugh at ribald stories, tottering, hard-of-hearing, and generally unattractive people). How much of our own cultural stereotypes do we read back into the biblical story?

speculates that Sarah and Abraham were "laughing at the idea of a baby's being born in the geriatric ward, and Medicare's picking up the tab."

Sarah had a rough row to hoe, no question about it! How many geriatric patients have you ever known who went into labor and needed the assistance of an obstetrician? Who ever had to make a trip to the mall to buy booties and support hose, Pampers and Depends, on the same run? She took it all in stride, though, and loved every minute of mothering Isaac—whose name, by the way, means "laughter!"

Reflections

When Abraham fell on his face and laughed, what sort of laughter do you imagine? Was it a full force belly laugh? A wide open, uninterrupted, can't-stop-yourself, uninhibited, roll on the floor laugh? Can you imagine that sort of laughter happening in the Bible? Discuss the reasons why Abraham is laughing. Ask the group to imagine different scenarios and reasons for Abraham's laughter.

Teaching Tips

Ask volunteers in the group to read the passage, taking emotional cues from the text and making sure the laughter sounds like laughter. How does this story inform our understanding of humor in the Bible?

Study Bible

See note in *NISB* on Gen 17:17-19 for a literary discussion on how Abraham's and Sarah's laughter stories were originally two separate accounts written by different writers.

Reflections

How do you imagine Sarah's laughter? Was it cynical? Joyful? Derisive? Fearful? Why might she have hidden her laughter? Why did she deny it? Why might she have been afraid to admit it?

Teaching Tips

Ask group volunteers to read this segment of the story aloud and experiment with various ways in which Sarah might have laughed and her response to being caught laughing. How does this story inform our understanding of humor in the Bible? Is it similar to or different than Abraham's story?

Sources

Beuchner, Frederick. *Telling the Truth: The Gospel as Tragedy, Comedy, and Fairy Tale* (New York: Harper & Row, 1977) 50.

_____ "Faith" in *Wishful Thinking: A Theological ABC* (New York: Harper & Row, 1973) 24-26.

Study Bible

See *NISB*, study notes, p. 35.

Who Laughs Last?: Jesus' Love for the Absurd

Jesus evidently enjoyed laughing at the absurd. In his own teaching, Jesus often used the absurd to help his listeners get the point he wanted to make. Especially within the context of some rather serious documents, the fact that we have evidence of Jesus being funny here and there gives us the hint that, by the standards of his native culture, he could be a riot.

The highly regarded Quaker philosopher, the late Elton Trueblood, wrote what I believe to be the most important book ever produced on the comic side of Jesus as presented in the four canonical Gospels. The book, originally published some forty years ago, is entitled, *The Humor of Christ: A Bold Challenge to the Traditional Stereotype of a Somber, Gloomy Christ*. Dr. Trueblood began his book with a kind of rationale:

> The widespread failure to recognize and to appreciate the humor of Christ is one of the most amazing aspects of the era named for him. Anyone who reads the Synoptic Gospels with a relative freedom from presuppositions might be expected to see that Christ laughed, and that he expected others to laugh, but our capacity to miss this aspect of his life is phenomenal. We are so sure that he was always deadly serious that we often twist his words in order to try to make them conform to our preconceived mold. A misguided piety has made us fear that acceptance of his obvious wit and humor would somehow be mildly blasphemous or sacrilegious. (p. 15)

Listen to this hilariously sarcastic admonition from Jesus:

If your right eye causes you to sin, tear it out and throw it away; it is better for you to lose one of your members than for your whole body to be thrown into Gehenna. (Matt 5:29, Inclusive Version)

Jesus' Love for the Absurd

The whole point of trying to understand what Jesus meant by this obviously not-to-be-taken-literally remark is to take into account his sense of humor and his love for the absurd. If we don't begin at that juncture, there is no way to get anything out what Jesus wanted to say here.

One of the hallmarks of Jesus' teachings was his rejection of literalistic interpretations of the ancient laws; he was, by his own admission, concerned with the spirit of the laws. Therefore, when he poked fun at these interpretations, he was not making fun of individual people, but of ways of thinking. For example, he believed that some of his fellow Jews, namely the Pharisees (and other religious leaders), typically missed the point of the ancient teachings because they wouldn't look past a literalistic, legalistic reading.

The Pharisees were the butt of many of Jesus' jokes. Jesus thought the Pharisees were so preoccupied with "how to look at what," that Jesus said—no doubt with a deadpan expression on his face—"If your eye causes you to commit a moral offense, the only option you have is to get rid of that 'sinful' eye!" Jesus found it laughingly ironic that the Pharisees were so involved in finding fault in others that they left themselves absolutely no time for self-examination.

The Log in the Eye

This brings us to the next teaching from Jesus on which I want us to reflect. Matthew's Jesus said:

Do not judge, so that you may not be judged. For with the judgment you make you will be judged, and the measure you give will be the measure you get. Why do you see the speck in your neighbor's eye, but do not notice the log in your own eye? Or how can you say to your neighbor, "Let me take the speck out of your eye," while the log is in your own eye? You hypocrite, first take the log out of your own eye, and then

Sources

Trueblood, Elton. *The Humor of Christ: A Bold Challenge to the Traditional Stereotype of a Somber, Gloomy Christ* (New York: Harper & Row, 1964).

Reflections

Some scholars have suggested that Jesus was or had been a Pharisee. If he were a Pharisee, how would that influence a reading of these Pharisees-as-the-butt-of-jokes passages?

Sources

Culbertson, Philip. "The Pharisaic Jesus and His Gospel Parables" in *The Christian Century* (January 23, 1985) 74-77.

Falk, Harvey. *Jesus the Pharisee: A New Look at the Jewishness of Jesus* (Eugene, OR: Wipf and Stock Publishers, 2003).

Maccoby, Hyam. *Jesus the Pharisee* (London: SCM Press, 2003).

you will see clearly to take the speck out of your neighbor's eye. (Matt 7:1-5)

It's a good and practical point Jesus stresses. The Pharisees, again the butt of this joke-with-a-point, were so completely absorbed in trying to prove their own goodness and their related self-proclaimed superiority that they had lost the ability to see how they might ever be at fault in any way.

The Pharisees were nitpickers. And in the comic corner of Jesus' mind, they looked like people with big logs stuck in their eyes, criticizing those whose eyes they thought had little bitty specks. As with much ironic humor, there is a painful truth in Jesus' biting image. Most of the people we know who are constantly critical of others have huge imperfections in their own lives to which they seem entirely blind.

The Camel and the Needle's Eye

Another humorous illustration Jesus used was this:

> Then Jesus said to his disciples, "Truly I tell you, it will be hard for a rich person to enter the kingdom of heaven. Again I tell you, it is easier for a camel to go through the eye of a needle than for someone who is rich to enter the kingdom of God" (Matt 19:24).

We all should know that God doesn't classify people according to any human-made system. God isn't thinking in terms of who is rich and who is poor, per se. God is thinking of who is suffering or in need and who can help them. Also, God cannot be God in someone's life if that person worships, i.e. makes central, someone or something else. One of those things is money.

Jesus was able to turn this into a ludicrous image. Just like a log in someone's eye, the spectacle of a camel going through the eye of a needle is absurd, and therefore, potentially humorous. The images bring a laugh and a spark of understanding to the truthful irony in Jesus' teaching.

Study Bible

See comment on Matt 7:1-6 for a modern, insightful critique of the Pharisaic attitude demonstrated. p. 1759.

Reflections

How does Jesus' use of irony and absurdity inform our understanding of humor in the Bible? How does humor help the hearer understand? Do you think Jesus' listeners laughed at these stories? Do you think they are funny?

Session 3

Piety and Pouting

1 Kings 19:1-12

I think the antithesis of laughter is pouting—the sound of silence with lips pursed and puckered, but not in preparation for a kiss. Pouting abounds in our culture where many people think they're "owed" so much from others, from life itself, and even from God.

Lectionary Loop
Third Sunday after Pentecost, Year C, 1 Kings 19:1-15a

Competition and Contest

The prophet Elijah is a famous example of pouting, but before we can get up close to see his puckered face, we have to be acquainted with another episode that had much to do with why, according to him, he had no choice but to pout. And we have to remind ourselves that Elijah lived in a world that was more polytheistic than monotheistic. Not only did many people worship and serve other gods, but also many of these gods had their own cultic followers. Wherever people gather in the name of a religion, there are religious professionals.

The religious professionals in question were Elijah and Elijah's main opponents, the prophets of Baal. The god Baal had many adherents and, thus, many priests to lead them. Many times, it seemed that Baal and his followers were ahead both in terms of the numbers of followers and in terms of people's devotion to him.

The word "Baal" itself means "owner" or "master." And in reference to a god, technically, it might have referred to several different deities. The god Baal in the background of this part of our story was most likely the "great Baal" of Canaan. If so, he was the son of El, the high god of Canaan, and the cultic activity

245

around the worship of Baal wasn't one smidgeon less elaborate than the finest Hebrew worship of their Yahweh God.

The competition between the followers of Yahweh (the God of Israel) and Baal (one of the gods of the Canaanites) was stiff indeed. And the household situation of the ruler of the Jews at that time, Ahab, made the competition all the more intense. Ahab was a monotheist; at least he had been a follower of Yahweh, a kinsman of the greatest of all the prophets, Elijah. However, his wife Jezebel followed Baal. To help keep her group in the lead, she was more than willing to have a few Hebrew religious professionals (prophets) killed off from time to time. Her husband simply acted like he knew nothing at all about it.

The best way to see who's stronger is to have some kind of contest, right? The Olympics, a school-yard fistfight, a verbal put-down match at a denominational meeting—you name it. When we have to prove who's stronger, there has to be a contest of some sort.

"My god is tougher than your god," the Yahwists and the Baal-worshipers would say to each other. One day, though, some of the followers of Baal openly and repeatedly challenged the followers of Yahweh with a taunt. A contest was set: whose god would send fire from the sky to burn a sacrifice? The odds were steep: it would be four hundred fifty to one. There would be four hundred fifty Baalite prophets against Elijah, who would represent Yahweh, the God of Israel.

The contest ensued, and though the followers of Baal called on their god from morning to noon, not a spark came from the heavens. But when Elijah called upon Yahweh, everything was consumed with fire, even the stones on the altar (see the story in 1 Kgs 18:20-40).

Elijah on the Run

In part because he was the winner and had the support of the crowds who observed this great feat, and in part because so many of his colleagues had been killed off by Queen Jezebel, Elijah, man of God that he was, ordered that the four hundred fifty losing prophets of Baal be slaughtered. And they were. No one was going to oppose Elijah that day because his God could bring

> ## Reflections
> Discuss religious competition in the world today. What are its consequences? Can you find any humor in the way religious professionals and religious groups promote their views?

fire right out of the sky—no one, that is, except the evil queen!

Jezebel wanted Elijah dead for what he'd done to the prophets she'd helped to educate by financially supporting them while they were in the Baalite divinity schools! The only fit response for Elijah was death, so she sent her personal messenger to Elijah with a royal promise. It went something like this: "So may the gods do to me, and more also, if I do not make your life like the life of one of [our prophets] by this time tomorrow" (1 Kgs 19:2).

Elijah went from local hero to a fugitive, of sorts. Jezebel sent her Baalite soldiers on a mission to hunt and slaughter him as he had ordered her beloved prophets killed. Elijah was frightened, and justifiably so.

He walked a whole day's journey all alone into the dreaded wilderness, thinking that he'd be hardest to find there. Exhausted at the end of that journey, he sat down under one of the few trees he'd seen and told God that the ministry was too rough a profession for him, that he wanted to die instead of going on. In that frame of mind, he fell asleep there. When God's angel, or messenger, awakened him, there was a cake of bread at his head and a big jug of water.

Elijah ate and drank and went back to sleep—symptomatic, perhaps, of episodic depression. Again the angel awakened him, this time telling him to eat some more of the bread and drink some more of the water in preparation for the remainder of his journey.

That next leg was a humdinger. Elijah walked for forty days and found his way to Mount Horeb, which was called the Mount of God. Somewhere on that big mountain, Elijah found a cave, went inside, and fell asleep.

When he was awakened from that sleep, it was not by the "angel" of the Lord, but by the "word" of the Lord, presumably the direct presence of God. Elijah awakened pouting, thus our story of pouting and piety. God asked him, "Why in the world are you in here?"

Elijah's Response

Elijah's whiny response is perhaps the poutiest part of the Hebrew Scriptures. Listen to his words again and remember it: "I have been very zealous for the LORD, the God of hosts; for the Israelites have forsaken your covenant, thrown down your altars, and killed your prophets with the sword. I alone am left, and they are seeking my life, to take it away" (1 Kgs 19:10).

Elijah was pouting, big time. His prophetic lip was pooched out as far as it could go—and in the face of God, no less! When God called Elijah out of that Horeb cave, one of the most spiritually moving scenes in all of Scripture ensued. God directed him:

> "Go out and stand on the mountain before the LORD, for the LORD is about to pass by." Now there was a great wind, so strong that it was splitting mountains and breaking rocks in pieces before the LORD, but the LORD was not in the wind; and after the wind an earthquake, but the LORD was not in the earthquake; and after the earthquake a fire, but the LORD was not in the fire; and after the fire a sound of sheer silence. (1 Kgs 19:11-12)

God was in the silence, not in the fanfare.

Teaching Tips

Ask for theatrically-inclined group members to pantomime or otherwise act out what Elijah was doing and how he looked as he realized that God was and had been near him all along—in the silence.

Teaching Tips

Even though Elijah's life was in danger, his response to God's question, "Why are you here?" is humorous if we read it as a pouting response. Ask group members to recall also the story of Jonah, who pouted because God let his shady plant die while at the same time resented that all of Nineveh was saved. Do you find humor in these stories? Discuss ways in which these pouting prophets remind group members of themselves.

Study Bible

See comments on 1 Kgs 19:11-12 (p. 515) for a brief reflection on how this event in Elijah's life introduced something new about God into the theology of ancient Israel.

Out of the Mouths of...Asses

Balaam took some kind of turn in his life that caused those who knew him and knew about him to hate him. For that reason, a sinister cloud covers his whole life. The storytellers, the hearers, and eventually the writers view him with disdain even when the earlier parts of his story are told. This same thing goes on in the Christian Scriptures with Judas, the one from Jesus' inner circle who betrayed Jesus of Nazareth into the hands of Rome. No one remembers, or cares to, that Jesus—a very fine judge of character—chose Judas to be one of his closest advisors. Judas started out as a good guy. So did Balaam.

In fact, Balaam's piety is exemplary in the story we have of him. As the Hebrew people made their way out of Egypt in search of their so-called "Promised Land," they came into the region of Moab. Moab became fearful of the possibility of invasion. The Moabite king, Balak, called on a soothsayer by the name of Balaam to pronounce a curse on the Hebrews. Somehow it was known that Balaam had special powers of pronouncement. The word was that whomever Balaam cursed experienced the full brunt of that curse. And in contrast, when Balaam pronounced a blessing upon someone, she or he became unmistakably blessed.

Balak Requests a Curse

King Balak sent his emissaries, with payment in hand, to make a request to Balaam. The request was: put a curse on the Hebrews. From all indications, Balaam wasn't a Hebrew. He seems to have been a monotheist.

> ### Reflections
> What do you know about the power of blessing and curse in ancient cultures? How does this situation speak to our world situation today? In what ways do modern groups of people attempt to curse each other in self-protection or as an act of aggression? How can groups of people bless each other?

Now if you didn't already think poorly of Balaam, as did our writer or writers, and this part of the story was all you knew, you'd think Balaam was a fine man of faith, generally speaking. In Balaam's mind, at least, he did what he did because God called him to do it and because God empowered him to bless or to curse.

Balaam received Balak's representatives and heard their request. As was his custom, he made no promises to them. Instead, he said, "I will pray about it, and I will do only what God tells me to do; I will say to you and to any others only what God tells me to say." He wasn't a pay-now-preach-later prophet type. He was more like one of those lawyers on television who doesn't get paid for your catastrophe unless you do.

Balaam Consults God

Balaam, true to his word, consulted with God on whether or not to curse the Hebrews. The interchange between Balaam and God reveals how the people thought God communicates with the particularly pious. But did you notice that Balaam's God didn't know all or much that was going on?

- The God in this story had to come to Balaam to find out what was going on.
- This God didn't know who Balaam's visitors were and had no idea what they wanted with Balaam.
- Balaam's God had to talk things over with Balaam, in a sense, before making a ruling about what to do regarding a polytheistic king's request to curse the people whom some called "God's chosen."

Balaam invited his guests to spend the night, and said that the next day he would share with them what he'd heard from God. In a word, God's response was no.

Thus, Balaam went to his guests and gave them news they did not want to hear: God said, "Don't curse the Hebrews." Even if the Hebrews were going to mess with the Moabites, who were minding their own business in a land that had been theirs for generations, Balaam could not do what Balak requested.

But King Balak wouldn't take no for an answer. In response to what he heard, he sent more money and "bigger guns." Balaam consulted with God again, but this time God said, "No, and go!" Balaam could travel with them to see Balak in person, but there was to be no cursing of the Hebrews.

God Sends Balaam to Balak

We might wonder why Balaam went to visit with the king only to tell him what his cabinet members could have told him just as well. Why did God send Balaam to see Balak in person? God was willing to work with a man whose particular gift, soothsaying, was not on the "A" list of preferred professions in the minds of most monotheists of that day. Though Balaam was considered useful, somehow, he had done nothing other than what God told him to do. This is a very important part of the story as it next unfolds. Balaam is about to get in big trouble, and only his ass saves him. (That's a line you've most likely never heard in church before!)

As Balaam traveled with Balak's would-be bullies, and the small troupe got separated from each other, leaving Balaam and his two servants by themselves. God commanded Balaam to retreat immediately, but in a way that Balaam—who hasn't made a single move so far without God's direction—cannot see or understand. God is potentially angry enough at Balaam to have him killed for crossing some invisible line in the sand.

Only the Ass Understands

The most interesting (and humorous!) part of the story, though, is that only the ass understands what's going on, and only the ass is bright enough to figure out how to avert disaster for its master. The donkey sees the armed angel of God just waiting for the unsuspecting Balaam to cross a line he doesn't even know exists. Balaam can't see the angel. There is an element of humor in the midst of the tension, since a humble and abused beast of burden is the only one who sees things as they really are. In the midst of decidedly unfunny animal cruelty, the donkey shows us who the real ass is. Balaam's ass speaks. After a third unjust beating, the ass explodes in defense of itself. This is

> ### Reflections
> What do you make of God's evident change of heart? How can Balaam be held responsible for what he doesn't even know about? What does this story tell us about Balaam's relationship with God?

the only time in the Hebrew Bible where an animal speaks other than when the serpent in the Garden of Eden lures Adam and Eve into the most consequential eating *faux pas* in recorded mythology.

The donkey yells out, "What is wrong with you?!? Whom do you think you're hitting here?"

Balaam, who was supposedly a man attuned to God, responds with far less dignity than his donkey, "I'm hitting you because you're making a fool of me. You run me off the pathway. People will think I can't steer. You brush up against the wall and scratch the blood out of my foot! You lay down for a nap—with me still on your back—when I'm trying to get to the king of Moab in a timely manner. My servants are laughing themselves silly at my expense!"

The donkey said, "You've been riding me all your life! Has anything like this EVER happened before?"

Balaam had to admit that it hadn't.

The donkey continued its diatribe, "Then might it not occur to you that instead of beating me, you should try to figure out what's going on?"

At that moment, God opened Balaam's eyes. He suddenly saw the armed angel of death ready to take him out. He wanted to know what in the world was going on. He offered to turn back at once. And, after all of that, the angel of death, who would have killed Balaam had it not been for the ass said, "No, go with the men, but don't promise to curse Israel." This response is confusing: Isn't that what Balaam already was doing? Why this near-deadly intrusion?

I don't think we can find a particularly satisfactory explanation to these questions. The story may be flawed and/or fragmented as we have it. Instead of sorting through the mess of a story, we might do well to listen to the only one in the story who had a clue: the faithful and brave donkey. The donkey is the one who:

- saw the danger that threatened Balaam and bore his wrath for doing what was necessary to save him,
- didn't flinch or run away from what eventually scared Balaam out of his wits,

• eventually demanded justice from Balaam and, in the process, wouldn't let the truth slide.

This story is a reminder that as attuned as we may imagine ourselves to be with God, we are not immune from misunderstanding and being blind to the actual dangers. At times we have been certain that God was leading us in a particular direction but have found ourselves instead on a path of destruction. And sometimes, an absolutely unexpected source of wisdom pulls us from that path.

Reflections

Describe which character in this story shows the most righteousness. Describe a time when you were sure you were doing what God planned for you, only to find out that someone you always overlooked or underrated was the one who knew better. What does this story teach us about knowing God's will? What are some unlikely sources of revelation on our path today? Are you afraid of being made a fool, or can you listen to the talking donkeys in your life?

Session 5   Acts 20:7-12

The Danger of Boring Sermons

This is the story of Eutychus, whose name went down in history because of his personal experience with the near-fatality of a boring sermon. The preacher of the most pivotal sermon in the life of young Eutychus was none other than the early church's greatest missionary, the apostle Paul. How ironic, as you will see a little later, that the name *Eutychus* means "lucky"!

The Shadow of Boredom

I'm not sure Paul ever had any self-reflective moments about how interesting he was as a preacher. He certainly lived in a time and place during which excellence in rhetorical skills was one of the most highly valued of all professional capabilities. To say the least, hearers had high expectations of anyone who dared to speak to a gathered group. But there are those speakers, preachers among them, who believe that if their message is significant enough, they don't have to worry about being interesting to those who hear them. That, as we shall see, can be a deadly misconception.

Preachers run the danger of committing two cardinal sins. One is falling into doctrinal faltering, the extreme of which is the propagation of heresy (in someone's or some hierarchy's view). The other is being boring. I think that heresy may be easier for a congregation to forgive! A hearer can rethink or self-correct, mentally speaking, an error in thought or reasoning on the part of the preacher if that hearer is one who thinks enough to care about what was said. But once someone you trust, or want to trust, leads you into the valley of the shadow of boredom, you may never forget or forgive.

The longest sermon ever preached in one setting lasted thirty-seven hours. Remember that the next time your pastor goes over five minutes! Before 2001, as best I've been able to verify details, the Guinness World Record for any type of public speaking event was twenty-seven hours. It was topped on June 29-30, 2001 by the Reverend Chris Sterry, a diligent Anglican vicar in Whalley, Lancashire, who set out to beat the world record in order to raise money needed to keep his parish independent and not subject to the rulings of the state church. He shot for a thirty-six-hour sermon and made it to thirty-seven hours! Sterry began preaching on a Friday morning at 6:30 and finished on Saturday evening at 7:30. He announced in advance that his text would be the Old Testament. That's it. He also announced that hecklers would be welcome. The sermon may or may not have been boring at points, but there is no record of anyone sitting through the whole thing!

A Crowded Room and a Long-winded Speaker

Eutychus' encounter with Paul's preaching took place in Troas. And, the writers who pulled together both the Gospel of Luke and the book of Acts tell us that the night before Paul was to leave Troas he was conversing with some people who had gathered to meet him and learn from him. The conversation became a sermon when enough people were in place. As Paul preached on, it got dark, and several lamps had to be lighted. The sermon went on until midnight.

From all indications, the room was very crowded. Some were on mats, some were standing, some were on benches, and at least one person (Eutychus) sat on a windowsill. We all know people who are most engaging and who, in a relaxed environment, can keep our attention and keep us engaged for hours. While we could attribute Eutychus' accident to the lateness of the hour, I think we more properly have to say that, as the evening wore on and on, Paul's sermon got boring. The key event is reported to us in the book of Acts:

A young man named Eutychus ["Lucky," remember?], who was sitting in the window, began to sink off into a deep sleep while Paul talked still longer. Overcome by sleep, he fell to the ground three floors below and was picked up dead. (Acts 20:9)

Anybody watching Eutychus closely enough would have known that he was nodding off while perched in a precarious position. But no one noticed. Not a single person in a whole room full of people. How could this be? One of two things must have been happening:

1. The people were so enthralled with Paul's scintillating sermonizing that not a single person would have taken riveted eyes off of Paul. That could have been the case, but—well—there is another option as well.

2. Nearly everyone was nodding off. (Recall that Paul couldn't see very well, so he had no idea nodders were dozing off; he may have thought they were nodding in agreement with his wee-hours wisdom!) The reason no one saw Eutychus teetering on the windowsill is because they were all about gone, too. They'd long since stopped hoping Paul would just shut up. They had checked out mentally, which was a shortcut to a nap. This is what I think happened.

Eutychus Falls to the Ground

When people down on the street heard the thud, they ran to Eutychus and thought he was dead. That the young man was hurt rather seriously is, of course, not funny in the least.

The citizens began to cry and scream for help. Someone picked up the body that they thought had lost its life. Paul was brought down to help in some way. It was the least he could do for having bored the poor guy to sleep and probable death. Paul looked at Eutychus and announced that he wasn't dead and would be fine.

Some people see this story as death-to-life narrative, but there is no evidence for that at all. Paul just looked at him and had enough experience to know he

Teaching Tips

Sermons can be deadly. Here's proof, and you have your own stories too! Ask participants to recall times when they thought a sermon or speech would never end and what they did to endure it. Discuss why the story of Eutychus falling asleep and falling out the window is humorous. Would it have been humorous if it had not had a happy ending?

wasn't dead—regardless of what those who first came to the body in the darkness thought.

Frankly, Paul wasn't altogether happy that his sermon had been interrupted, and he encouraged people to go back upstairs with him so that he could finish. Some few did, and he ate with them and talked on till dawn; others said, "No way in Hades."

Study Bible

See the *NISB's* brief commentary on Acts 20:7-12 for an alternate interpretation of "Lucky" Eutychus.

Teaching Tips

Have class members make the excuses they'd have made if, after the boring sermon and the accident, Paul had asked them to go back upstairs with him for more sermon!

Reflections

How does this story inform our understanding of humor in the Bible?

SOURCES

Sources

The Gospel of John

Bettenson, Henry, ed. *Documents of the Christian Church*. 2nd ed. (Oxford: Oxford University Press, 1963).

Cotter, Wendy. *Miracles in Greco-Roman Antiquity* (London: Routledge, 1999).

Culpepper, R. Alan. *The Gospel and Letters of John*. Interpreting Biblical Texts (Nashville: Abingdon, 1999).

Dent, Alan, ed. *Bernard Shaw and Mrs. Patrick Campbell: Their Correspondence* (London: Gollancz, 1952) 32.

Ellison, Ralph. *Invisible Man* (New York: The New American Library, 1952).

Hendricks, Obery. *Living Water* (San Francisco: HarperSanFrancisco, 2003).

Koester, Craig R. "'The Savior of the Lord' (John 4:42)," *Journal of Biblical Literature* 109/4 (Winter 1990) 665-680.

Mitchell, Stephen, ed. *The Enlightened Heart: An Anthology of Sacred Poetry* (New York: HarperPerennial, 1989).

Newheart, Michael. *Word and Soul: A Psychological, Literary, and Cultural Reading of the Fourth Gospel* (Collegeville, MN: The Liturgical Press, 2001).

_____ "shok & awe, shuk & jive" in *DC Poets Against the War: An Anthology*. 2nd ed. Edited by Sarah Browning, Michelle Elliot, and Danny Rose (Washington, D.C.: R.D. Baker and Argonne House Press, 2004) 85-86.

Samuel, Bill. "Friends (Quakers) and Women," at Quakerinfo.com. http://www.quakerinfo.com/quakwomn.shtml.

United Methodist Hymnal: Book of United Methodist Worship (Nashville: The United Methodist Publishing House, 1989).

The Book of Exodus

Brueggemann, Walter. "The Book of Exodus: Introduction, Commentary, and Reflections" in *New Interpreter's Bible*, vol. 1 (Nashville: Abingdon, 1994) 675-981.

Childs, Brevard. *The Book of Exodus: A Critical, Theological Commentary*. Old Testament Library (Louisville: Westminster, 1974).

Fretheim, Terence E. Exodus. Interpretation (Louisville: John Knox, 1991).

McDaniel, Thomas. "The Ten Commandments" in *The Pastor's Bible Study*, vol. 2. Edited by David Albert Farmer (Nashville: Abingdon Press, 2005) 157-221.

Meyers, Carol. *Exodus*. New Cambridge Bible Commentary (Cambridge: Cambridge University Press, 2005).

Pixley, George V. *On Exodus: A Liberation Perspective*. Translated by Robert R. Barr. (New York: Maryknoll, 1987).

Sugirtharjah, R.S., ed. *Voices from the Margin: Interpreting the Bible in the Third World*, New ed. (Maryknoll: Orbis, 1995) 213–85.

Williams, Delores. *Sisters in the Wilderness: the Challenge of Womanist God-talk* (Maryknoll: Orbis, 1993).

Great Texts for a Healthy Spirituality

Anonymous. *The Cloud of Unknowing*. Edited by James Walsh, S.J. (New York: Paulist Press, 1981).

Augustine. *The Confessions of St. Augustine*. Translated by John K. Ryan (Garden City, N.Y.: Doubleday Image Books, 1960).

Baillie, John. *Christian Devotion*. (New York: Charles Scribner's Sons, 1962) 41.

Brother Lawrence, *The Practice of the Presence of God*. Translated by E.M. Blaiklock. (Nashville: Thomas Nelson Publishers, 1981).

Bonhoeffer, Dietrich. *Letters and Papers from Prison* (New York: Macmillan Co., 1972).

De Chardin, Teilhard. The Divine Milieu (London: Collins, 1960).

De Cussade, Jean-Pierre. *The Sacrament of the Present Moment*. Translated by Kitty Muggeridge (San Francisco: Harper & Row, Publishers, 1966).

Duquoc, Christian and Casiano Floristan, eds. *Where Is God? A Cry of Human Distress* (London: SCM Press Ltd, 1992).

Galbraith, John Kenneth. Economics and the *Public Purpose* (New York: New American Library, 1988).

Goodall, Jane. *Reason for Hope: A Spiritual Journey* (New York: Time Warner Co., 1999).

Heschel, Abraham Joshua. *Man Is Not Alone* (New York: Farrar, Straus & Giroux, Inc., 1951).

Hill, Christopher. *Society and Puritanism in Pre-Revolutionary England*. 2nd ed. (New York: Schocken Books, 1967).

Jones, Rufus. *The Double Search* (Philadelphia: C.J. Winston Co., 1906).

Kelly, Thomas R. *A Testament of Devotion* (New York: Harper & Row, Publishers, 1941).

Merton, Thomas. *Thoughts in Solitude* (Garden City, N.Y.: Doubleday Image Books, 1958).

Pascal, Blaise. *Pensées*. Translated by John Warrington (New York: E.P. Dutton & Co Inc, 1960).

Roszak, Theodore. *Where the Wasteland Ends: Politics and Transcendence in Postindustrial Society* (Berkeley, CA: Celestial Arts, 1990).

Steere, Douglas. *On Listening to Another* (New York: Harper, 1955).

Wiesel, Elie. *All Rivers Run to the Sea: Memoirs* (New York: Schocken Books, 1995).

Texts of Courage, Failure, and New Hope

The Association for Clinical Pastoral Education. http://www.acpe.edu

Henderson, Randi and Richard Marek, eds. *Here Is My Hope: A Book of Healing and Prayer: Inspirational Stories from the Johns Hopkins Hospital* (New York, Doubleday, 2001).

Kushner, Harold S. *When Bad Things Happen to Good People* (New York: Avon, 1983).

Suchocki, Marjorie Hewitt. *The Fall to Violence: Original Sin in Relational Theology* (New York: Continuum, 1995).

A Party Called Faith

Anderson, Gary A. "Introduction to Israelite Religion" in *New Interpreter's Bible*, vol. 1 (Nashville: Abingdon Press, 1994) 272-83.

Baab, O.J. "Widow" in *Interpreter's Dictionary of the Bible*, vol 4 (Nashville: Abingdon Press, 1962) 842-43.

Berlin, Adele. *Lamentations*. The Old Testament Library (Louisville: Westminster John Knox Press, 2002).

Brown, William P. *Ecclesiastes*. Interpretation (Louisville: John Knox Press, 2000).

Clifford, Richard J. "Introduction to Wisdom Literature" in *New Interpreter's Bible*, vol. 5 (Nashville: Abingdon Press, 1997) 1-16.

Crawford, Sidnie White. "The Book of Esther" in *New Interpreter's Bible*, vol. 3 (Nashville: Abingdon Press, 1999) 855-941.

Dosick, Wayne. *Living Judaism: The Complete Guide to Jewish Belief, Tradition & Practice* (San Francisco: HarperSanFrancisco, 1995).

Exum, J. Cheryl. *Song of Songs*. The Old Testament Library (Louisville: Westminster John Knox Press, 2005).

McCown, C.C. "Gate" in *Interpreter's Dictionary of the Bible*, vol. 2 (Nashville: Abingdon Press, 1962) 355.

Nielsen, Kirsten. *Ruth* The Old Testament Library (Louisville: Westminster John Knox Press, 1997).

O'Connor, Kathleen M. "The Book of Lamentations" in *New Interpreter's Bible*, vol. 6 (Nashville: Abingdon Press, 2001) 1013-1072.

Farmer, Kathleen A. Robertson. "The Book of Ruth" in *New Interpreter's Bible*, vol. 2 (Nashville: Abingdon Press, 1998) 891-946.

Towner, W. Sibley. "The Book of Ecclesiastes" *in New Interpreter's Bible*, vol. 5 (Nashville: Abingdon Press, 1997) 267-360.

Queen-Sutherland, Kandy M. "Additions to Esther" in *Mercer Commentary on the Bible* (Macon, GA: Mercer University Press, 1995) 819-823.

_____ "Esther" in *Mercer Commentary on the Bible* (Macon, GA: Mercer University Press, 1995) 395-403.

Rylaarsdam, J.C., "Feasts and Fasts" in *Interpreter's Dictionary of the Bible*, vol. 2 (Nashville: Abingdon Press, 1976) 260-64.

Webb, Barry G. Five Festal Garments: *Christian Reflections on The Song of Songs, Ruth, Lamentations, Ecclesiastes and Esther* (Downers Grove, IL: InterVarsity Press, 2000).

Weems, Renita J. "The Song of Songs" *in New Interpreter's Bible*, vol. 5 (Nashville: Abingdon Press, 1997) 363-434.

A Time to Laugh

Beuchner, Frederick. *Telling the Truth: The Gospel as Tragedy, Comedy, and Fairy Tale* (New York: Harper & Row, 1977).

_____ "Faith" in *Wishful Thinking: A Theological ABC* (New York: Harper & Row, 1973) 24-26.

Culbertson, Philip. "The Pharisaic Jesus and His Gospel Parables" in *The Christian Century* (January 23, 1985) 74-77.

Falk, Harvey. *Jesus the Pharisee: A New Look at the Jewishness of Jesus* (Eugene, OR: Wipf and Stock Publishers, 2003).

Gafney, Wilda C.M. "The Book of Genesis" in *The Pastor's Bible Study*, vol. 3. Edited by David Albert Farmer (Nashville: Abingdon Press, 2006) 87-133.

Hyers, Conrad. *And God Created Laughter: The Bible as Divine Comedy* (Atlanta: John Knox, 1987).

Maccoby, Hyam. *Jesus the Pharisee* (London: SCM Press, 2003).

Trueblood, Elton. *The Humor of Christ: A Bold Challenge to the Traditional Stereotype of a Somber, Gloomy Christ* (New York: Harper & Row, 1964).

LECTIONARY

Lectionary

Year A

SCRIPTURE INDEX

Scripture Index

HOW TO USE
THE COMPACT DISK

How to Use the Compact Disk

The compact disk located in the back of *The Pastor's Bible Study: Volume Four* may be used to supplement and enhance the study experience. The disk includes:

- The full text of *The Pastor's Bible Study: Volume Four* in Adobe Reader® (.pdf) format

- PowerPoint® presentations containing outlines for each study within the volume, in both PowerPoint® Presentation (.ppt) and PowerPoint® Show (.pps) format

- Study outlines and reflection questions in rich text file (.rtf) format that may be edited, printed, and given to group participants.

To access any of this material, insert the compact disk into the CD-ROM drive of your computer and browse to the item(s) you wish to select using your PC Windows Explorer, or your Macintosh Browser.

Using the Adobe Reader® Book

To use the Adobe Reader® book containing the full text of *The Pastor's Bible Study: Volume Four*, you must have Adobe Reader® software installed on your computer. If you wish to install this free software, download it from the web at www.adobe.com/products/acrobat/.

Note: Technical support for installation of the Adobe Reader is available at www.adobe.com.

Once Adobe Reader® is installed on your computer, browse to the file named **PastorsBibleStudyV4.pdf** on the disk and double click on it to open it. After opening the *PastorsBibleStudyV4.pdf*, you may search any keyword or phrase in *The Pastor's Bible Study: Volume Four*.

Another useful feature of the Adobe Reader® file is the addition of links to other resources on the supplemental disk. These links are at the beginning of each of the six studies. Clicking on a link will open the selected resource on your computer in its default program. Just be sure that *The Pastor's Bible Study: Volume Four* compact disk is in your CD-ROM drive.

Viewing PowerPoint® Presentations

There are twelve PowerPoint® files on the disk, two for each of the six studies. These two PowerPoint® files contain presentations of study outlines. All PowerPoint® files are in a folder named **PowerPoint**. To view the PowerPoint® files that accompany *The Pastor's Bible Study: Volume Four*, you must have Microsoft PowerPoint® software or PowerPoint® Viewer installed on your computer.

.PPT files: The .ppt files are files associated with the full version of Microsoft PowerPoint®. If you have the full version of PowerPoint® software installed on your computer, you may double click on the .ppt files to open them in PowerPoint® and customize your study presentations.

Note: The Microsoft PowerPoint® program is not included on The Pastor's Bible Study: Volume Four *disk. Technical support for PowerPoint® is available at www.microsoft.com.*

.PPS files: The .pps files are "stand alone" files that may be viewed using the PowerPoint® Viewer, which is installed on most computers. If you wish to install this free software, download it from Microsoft at http://www.microsoft.com/downloads/details.aspx?FamilyID=048dc840-14el-467d-8dca-19d2a8fd7485&DisplayLang=en or visit www.microsoft.com and search on the key words "Power Point Viewer".

In most cases, using the .pps files will be the best choice for presenting the outlines to study participants. To begin the presentation:

- Place the disk in your computer's CD-ROM drive.
- Click on the link found on the appropriate study outline in Adobe Reader® to start the presentation. (Or, you may open the .pps file by browsing to it on the disk and double-clicking it.)
- Click anywhere on the slide, or use the page down button, to move through the presentation.

Note: If you click past a point in the outline and wish to go back, use the backspace or page up button on your computer's keyboard.

Using Study Outlines

Study outlines for all six sections are in a folder named **Study_Outlines**. Double-click on an outline to open the rich text format (.rtf) file in your computer's default word processing program. You may then customize your study experience by making changes to the outline. You may also access these files by clicking on the links provided in the Adobe Reader® Book.

Note: At the end of each session outline, participant assignments for the upcoming sessions are noted, including Scripture reading assignments and New Interpreter's Study Bible *references. Providing the outlines to participants will enhance their study experience.*

Using Reflection Questions

Reflection questions for all six studies are in a folder named **Reflection_Questions**. Double-click on an outline to open the rich text format (.rtf) file in your computer's default word processing program. You may then customize your study experience by making changes to the reflection questions. You may also access these files by clicking on the links provided in the Adobe Reader® Book.

Contacting Technical Support

To contact one of our Technical Support Representatives, call: **1-615-749-6777, Monday through Friday, 8:00 a.m. to 5:00 p.m.**, Central time.